Apart from Freud

Notes for a Rational Psychoanalysis

By Jonathan Cohen

Publication date: August 2001

ISBN: 0-87286-378-6 262pp

Trade paperback original $18.95

Psychology/Psychiatry/Philosophy

For further information please contact:
Stacey Lewis, publicist
stacey@citylights.com
415 362 1901
Nancy Peters, staff editor

CITY LIGHTS BOOKS
261 Columbus Avenue
San Francisco, CA 94133
ph 415 362 1901
fax 415 362 4921
www.citylights.com

APART FROM FREUD

Notes for a Rational Psychoanalysis

JONATHAN COHEN

City Lights Books
San Francisco

10 9 8 7 6 5 4 3 2 1

Cover: Amy Trachtenberg
Cover type: Robin Raschke
Book design: Nancy J. Peters
Typography: Harvest Graphics

Library of Congress Cataloging-in-Publication Data

Cohen, Jonathan.
Apart from Freud : notes for a rational psychoanalysis / by Jonathan Cohen.
p. cm.
Includes bibliographical references and index.
ISBN 0-87286-378-6
1. Psychoanalysis. 2. Psychotherapy. I. Title.
RC480.C5685 2001
616.89'17—dc21 00-065639
CIP

CITY LIGHTS BOOKS are edited by Lawrence Ferlinghetti and Nancy J. Peters and published at the City Lights Bookstore, 261 Columbus Avenue, San Francisco CA 94133.
Visit our web site: www.citylights.com

To my beloved wife Rikki Ducornet
and children Joshua and Adrienne Cohen
from whom I have learned the most, of what is important.

TABLE OF CONTENTS

PREFACE

Freudianism has been among the most influential theories of the twentieth century and is still the basic framework of psychoanalysis, despite the enormous proliferation of other schools and sects. Its impact on the social sciences has led to a widespread acceptance of its ideas as true. But a growing number of people from various disciplines have come to recognize Freudianism's enormous limitations—for example, its emotivism, its limited cultural-temporal provenance, its biologistic justification of patriarchy, and, in general, its derivation from and allegiance to the philosophy of liberal individualism, with all *that* theory's attendant problems—and are attempting to resituate Freud in the larger firmament of ideas. This larger firmament is the realm of ideas about *values* as they inform our choices and actions as moral and political beings. The dissatisfaction with Freudianism is part of a larger critique of present-day social science and philosophy, which critique strives to bring values within the compass of science.

Apart from Freud is a contribution within the critical tradition of Freud studies that aims at a different psychoanalysis altogether, based on thinking rather than emotional logic and using non-symptom-based criteria. By virtue of being able to communicate meaningfully with the broader intellectual world, this psychoanalysis informs us about creative and destructive interactions between individuals and society in a wide variety of social and political contexts, not just families.

The book arose out of a combination of clinical necessity and intellectual curiosity. As a practicing analyst, I was frustrated with the current state of affairs—notably the fact that, as presently constituted in its many variations, psychoanalysis generally fails in its basic task of curing neurosis. In fact, the very concept of cure has become something of an embarrassment, leading analysts to endlessly equivocate on the subject. After years of my own experience and of observing the work of others, I realized that psychoanalytic treatment tended to produce neither moral individuals, sexually liberated individuals, nor people capable of deep or critical thought, but rather people with modified or perfected neuroses. I came to believe that Freudianism is a remarkably bad theory, dangerous to patients in treatment and harmful to society as a whole. It increasingly struck me as both unnecessary and wrong that a psychology that purports to grapple deeply with the modern psychic condition should avoid, as assiduously as Freudianism does, consideration of central moral, political, and economic dilemmas. I searched psychoanalytic curricula in vain for serious treatment of these problems. And I could not accept the typical self-serving psychoanalytic justification of these clinical and intellectual failures, originating with Freud, that attributes them to an innately asocial and "wild" human nature, rather than to the limitations of the theories themselves.

The key to understanding these difficulties lies in frankly recognizing the enormous circularity of Freudian theory, which leaves it beyond the reach of rational criticism and, given its particular suppositions, a reactionary defender of the cultural status quo. This problem has never been adequately recognized or addressed, and has thus been carried over into virtually all post-Freudian versions of psychoanalysis. Freud is a persuasive writer and rhetorician and it is not difficult to be taken by the broad sweep of his ideas and their apparent daring, without bothering to look closely at the array of background assumptions upon which they are based—not to mention the dubious proposition that psychoanalysis is a "medical" procedure in which proper patients participate compliantly, as though being anesthetized or operated upon. When I began (around 1980, after a tour of duty as a military psychiatrist, and on starting full-time psychoanalytic practice) systematically inquiring into the clinical failures and into the background assumptions, I discovered that they were intimately interconnected. Psychoanalysis fails typically because of Freudian constraints on thinking and behaving. Conversely, psychoanalytic success typically depends on the analyst's "breaking the rules" by using "unorthodox" techniques, a fact that I discovered in my practice and that I and my colleague (Kinston & Cohen, 1986, 353-355) also found documented in the psychoanalytic literature, but without recognition of its radical significance.

I thus found myself in the peculiar and unpopular position of trying to describe how a psychoanalysis would look and function if it were stripped of its indefensible Freudian assumptions. This naturally involved the conundrum, which colleagues were quick to point out, of the logic or right of considering such a treatment and set of ideas "psychoanalysis."

This seeming paradox is actually a trivial terminological problem, easily dealt with, but one that involves a curious fact of intellectual history, amply demonstrated in this book. Freud both founded psychoanalysis and, over the course of a long career, subverted one of its most important tenets—that unconscious beliefs *especially* need critical examination because they are among the most powerful of human motivations—by providing a specious set of arguments to justify the uses of authority, in the raising of children and the governance of society, to shape a *particular* kind of personality. I thus came to recognize that a serious problem in Freud scholarship was the natural but questionable equation of psychoanalysis with Freudianism, whereas a better strategy is to regard Freudianism as a *special case* of psychoanalysis, applicable to a particular kind of child rearing and view of self and society. I believe that this different critical strategy represents one of the book's important contributions.

With this realization, I began to inquire into the often unrecognized assumptions or *background knowledge* of psychoanalysis, in biology, neurology, anthropology, linguistics, and social- and moral philosophy—going to the sources of the ideas that strongly informed Freud's ideas of sexuality, repression, neurosis, and unconscious mental functioning in general. This inquiry leads to a picture of Freud as a remarkably conservative, if not reactionary, thinker when it comes to social and political matters. For example, and contrary to his too easily accepted self-characterization as indifferent to philosophy, much less economics, it turns out that his theories of repression and character formation are strongly determined by his acceptance of thinkers like Hume, Smith, Malthus, and Spencer, the theorists of the "liberal" free-market state.

The results of these inquiries, along with the changes I began to make in my own clinical practice, enabled me to demystify what has become an excessively arcane and inaccessible field in ways that, I hope, readers will find intellectually exciting and clinically illuminating. The demystification—the recognition, for example, that the obscure Freudian concept of *hypercathexis* means no more than the uncritical acceptance of received ideas, as embodied in language—sets the stage for transforming psychoanalysis into something more like applied philosophical discourse, with the aim of clarifying dogmatic (unconscious) ideas of self and testing out better ideas, as opposed to a privileged medical procedure. This is what I call a "thinking cure"—a method based on shared critical thinking about what it signifies to be unconscious of one's moral nature, one's personal history, and one's political world.

Several months into psychoanalysis, a patient, a professor of humanities who had for years struggled with severe neurosis, been labeled manic-depressive, and been treated (unsuccessfully) with various drugs, recalled a tragic childhood experience. His customary view of himself (as cowardly and sexually awkward and defective, despite his imposing appearance) had been shaken by having stood up aggressively to a wife-beating bully. When I suggested that perhaps his capacity for moral and physical courage was being awakened by the work we were doing together, he told me the following story: In his sixth year, and clearly in response to a very threatening family situation in which his mother infantilized him, making him into an imaginary invalid, he had suffered several nights in a row from a vivid, frightening nightmares in which his room was bathed in yellow-orange light. He cried out for his father to turn out the lights. His father's response to this conflicted symbolic appeal for "illumination" was to threaten to lock him up as crazy if he did not cease his pestering. The dreams ceased, to be followed by ten years of family madness, before he was sent off to boarding school. When I suggested to my patient that the recent "uncharacteristic" experience of standing up to tyranny had awakened, for purposes of critical reexamination, this old childhood trauma, in which his father decisively proved to him that there would be no sanity whatever in the family, he said that he had always thought of this experience in "psychoanalytic" terms, as an Oedipal repudiation by the father, jealous of his "special" relationship with the mother. The Oedipal "interpretation," substantially mirroring the abusive parent-child situation, interfered with his ability to think critically about these formative relationships.

This man's example demonstrates one of the main themes of this book: Freudianism, by constraining psychoanalytic thinking along the lines of "Oedipal" logic, dims the light that we are capable of generating, even as children, in the darkest and maddest of rooms. The changes my patients have made in their lives, many of which are extraordinary by usual psychoanalytic standards, attest to people's creative and transformative capacities, when encouraged to think critically about the authoritarian structures of ideas and language that they have unwittingly incorporated into their personalities. Psychoanalysis should not be a normalizing, leveling process but a process of radical growth, freeing people to think for themselves and participate constructively in the world of activity and ideas—and therefore transgressive of traditions, however hallowed, that subvert individual freedom and moral responsibility. The idea of psychoanalysis in this sense transcends the walls of the consulting room and becomes coextensive with liberatory child rearing, education, and governance.

Here, then, is my modest contribution to a difficult but important field, which I offer with gratitude to the numerous patients who have, over the years, trusted me to work closely with them, to the analytic and other thinkers who have preceded me, to Iain Boal and Murray Wax, who offered useful observations about the manuscript, and to my wonderful and rigorous City Lights editors—Nancy J. Peters and James Brook—who have had the confidence to bring this book to publication.

INTRODUCTION

> But when it [belief of any sort] has come to be an hereditary creed, and to be received passively, not actively . . . there is a progressive tendency to forget all of the belief except the formularies, or to give it a dull and torpid assent, as if accepting it on trust dispensed with the necessity of realizing it in consciousness, or testing it by personal experience, until it almost ceases to connect itself at all with the inner life of the human being.
>
> —J. S. Mill, *On Liberty* (1859)

> When psychoanalysis becomes an institution, when it is applied to so-called "normal subjects," it utterly ceases to be a conception that can be justified or discussed on the basis of cases; it no longer cures, it persuades; it shapes for itself subjects who conform to its own interpretations of man. It has its converts and perhaps its rebels; it can no longer convince. Beyond the true and the false, it is a myth, and Freudianism thus degraded is no longer an interpretation, but a variant of the Oedipus myth.
>
> —C. Levi-Strauss, *Structural Anthropology* (1963)

Freud achieved the remarkable feat of establishing, virtually single-handedly, a novel intellectual tradition, which remains the reigning tradition of clinical psychology and psychotherapeutic psychiatry. It is based on two ideas, neither of them original but which Freud combined, elaborated theoretically, and made the basis of a practical system of psychological analysis and treatment. The first is that the child is father to the man—that early experience crucially shapes our personalities and our views of ourselves and the world. The second is that this shaping of experience manifests largely in strongly held beliefs of which the person is more or less unaware (unconscious). Freud elaborated these ideas at length to account for the psychological development of individuals and society. He proposed a method of treatment to cure neurosis, based on an interpersonal, dialogic process in which unconscious personal beliefs are articulated and discussed so as to foster perspective on those beliefs and enable personality change—the famous "talking cure." He discovered that in the course of this process neurotic symptoms, which symbolically express unconscious beliefs and tendencies, often disappeared.[1]

With respect to his specific theories Freudianism has been regarded much as its author intended: as a naturalistic, biologically based account of these personality-shaping processes. In proposing explanatory theories and interpretations Freud sought to emphasize inevitable and unvarying conflicts between instinctual sexual and aggressive urges and the demands of civilized life.

However, in closely reading Freud with a view to correlating the general with the specific theories, and in turn with the clinical phenomena to which they are applied, one discovers that the specific theories are extremely problematic. His explanations are based on unsupportable biological, anthropological, and historical assumptions. His theory of moral development, including the Oedipus complex and the superego, turns out to be a conventional utilitarian morality based on adherence to social rules. And the social theories upon which Freud relied, to justify those rules, turn out to be those developed in the seventeenth and eighteenth centuries to rationalize the dominant social order of liberal market society and patriarchy. Freud's unacknowledged indebtedness to certain of the social philosophers of classic liberalism may well have contributed to the rapidity with which his specific theories were accepted—they are in fact an outgrowth of this centuries-long philosophical tradition. The specific textual and historical analysis of his work, which justifies these sweeping assertions, constitutes much of the present book.

I am not the first to make such assertions. My claim to the reader's attention rests on the possibility of showing a way beyond the long-standing polemic that reigns in psychoanalytic criticism. Its most vigorous critics, inflamed by analysts' tendency to dismiss them, argue that the psychoanalytic tradition is and always has been intellectually bankrupt; while equally vigorous defenders assert its essential intellectual viability and seek to stigmatize critics as "Freud bashers." Serious dialogue is hard to sustain in such an atmosphere. This book is a critical investigation from within the tradition, by one educated in and practicing it, that seeks to show the specific ways in which Freudian theories have in fact limited and undermined psychoanalysis's potentialities—by which I mean the potentialities inherent in the two general theories. That perspective enables me to develop an approach to satisfy the

[1] In this book I assume a certain general familiarity witb Freudian ideas, mindful of the fact that many people know these ideas second or third hand. For readers who want a more direct introduction, there are a number of good overviews and encyclopedic dictionaries. Among Freud's works, the most accessible are the *Introductory Lectures* (1915-16; 1916-17) and the *Outline of Psychoanalysis* (1940). The former has been reprinted in many editions as *A General Introduction to Psychoanalysis* (1924). Calvin Hall's *A Primer of Freudian Psychology* (1954) provides a compact overview. There are a number of classic textbooks that provide a deeper introduction: Fenichel (1945), Nunberg (1955), and Nagera (1969-70). Finally, there is the wonderful conceptual glossary of Laplanche and Pontalis (1973).

requirements of a rational psychoanalysis, one based on ideas rather than language and emotion, which in its practical application I call a "thinking cure."

In large part, unresolved questions in the debates about psychoanalysis stem from the confusion of epistemological matters with clinical ones. Clinical questions, starting with definitions of mental health and illness, are subjective and hard to judge, being largely a function of prevailing cultural attitudes (a good example of which is the current psychiatric attitude toward depression, regarded implausibly as a disease and attacked with medication, rather than being seen as a natural and necessary response to life). Yet clinical phenomena, as interpreted by the Freudian or other psychoanalytic systems, have been given weight out of proportion to their evidentiary value. As a profession, psychoanalysis is primarily a clinical discipline conducted within the framework of strongly hierarchical training institutions representing various "schools." The discussion of cases is largely confined to practitioners interested in effectiveness as defined by their schools and in career advancement. Important epistemological questions, which cannot be decided on clinical grounds, have therefore gone begging for adequate critical discussion.

Partly as a result of these complicated one-hundred-year-old social dynamics, psychoanalysis's credentials as a system of knowledge are very much in doubt, while the center of gravity of the debate has slowly shifted. Freud's claim that it is a science, or even a rational form of inquiry, has been largely abandoned except for skirmishes at the margin. Most practicing analysts no longer concern themselves with these debates but in fact stake their claim to validity on its hermeneutic or narrative value. Taking a page from postmodern and structuralist approaches to language and literature, they argue that the comprehensibility of a clinical narrative is all-important, one that reveals something essential about the potentialities of experience and mind. They point to the clinical benefit of rendering personal narratives more understandable through interpretation of unconscious ideas and fantasies, using a variety of analytic idioms. Increasingly, therefore, psychoanalysis has been seen not even as a single clinical tradition but as a loosely connected set of schools, each dominated by a different idiom of interpretation based on specific theories more or less derived from the Freudian. This alone makes critical thinking difficult, for arguments can always be attacked for leaving out the latest effort to correct and modify the original theory. And psychoanalysts are notorious for simultaneously clinging to the word of Freud while contradictorily agreeing that he was mistaken in many of his assumptions, theories, and applications.

In other words, this is a difficult and tricky intellectual terrain to navigate. One manifestation that the careful reader of psychoanalysis will surely notice is that debates have a fragmentary quality. They tend to revolve, often with great heat, around some component concept like instinct, repression, sexuality, gender differences, transference, boundaries, optimal interpretations, analytic neutrality, or myriad other "technical" details of treatment but hardly ever with the core set of ideas upon which psychoanalysis is founded, which is the Freudian. While Freud is almost universally revered within the field as a wide-ranging and pioneering thinker, the full range of his thinking is hardly ever taken into account when debating a component concept, so that the most interesting arguments are left out. For instance, the cross-correlations between, say, anthropological and clinical evidence, or neurological and linguistic evidence, or clinical and social-philosophical thinking, upon which Freud depended heavily, are seldom thought about, much less critically debated. The result is that, to borrow Mill's (1859, 38-39) passionate language, Freudian ideas are, even among the cognoscenti, "received passively, not actively," and given "dull and torpid assent." Like the political and moral ideas Mill was concerned about in the England of his day, they are on the way to becoming dead dogmas, passionately defended as long as no one threatens to bring them to life through critical examination.

This phenomenon, extraordinary in a field that takes itself so seriously, struck me with great force when, as a young analyst, I first tried to sort out some confusing issues. Thinking about repression, which is as close to a fundamental concept as there is in psychoanalysis, I discovered that hardly anyone in the field seemed to care that its theory was full of contradictions and that the fascinating and troublesome problem of the origins of repression (in technical terms, the relation between primal and secondary repression, which bothered Freud) was for the most part swept under the carpet.

For all these reasons—the centrality of Freud's ideas to psychoanalysis, the dogmatism with which those ideas are held, the fragmentary and polemical quality of debate, and the lack of a good critical overview of his work from within the tradition—I chose to consider in this book only Freud's contribution. This is partly to provide such an overview. I defer to a later work an examination of neo-Freudian schools—Jungian and Adlerian psychoanalysis, Kleinianism and object relations, self psychology, intersubjectivity theories, and Lacanianism. This is also a strategic choice based on my belief that the divergences between these derivative theories and the parent theory are not nearly as significant as they are made to appear. My overall purposes can best be achieved by laying the groundwork of a thorough critique of the parent theory unconfounded by later modifications. This being said, I realize that the significance of post-Freudian modifications is not self-evident and will require a thorough treatment later.

Apart from the intellectual coherence or incoherence of Freudian ideas, there is the matter of clinical value. Psychoanalysts, beginning with Freud, are fond of citing the clinical value of their work as an ultimate justification for their theories and beliefs. Critics of the various schools of psychoanalysis, however, are justly skeptical of claims of clinical benefit. They note how ephemeral individual clinical results can be when examined closely or over time. They observe correctly that few if any of Freud's treatments were successful. These critics note how impossible it has been for analysts themselves to agree on criteria of cure. At a conceptual level they are skeptical of postmodern approaches to mind, doubting that significant new understandings of mental life can be gained by pondering the variety of individual narratives. They insist on a procedure that at least approximates scientific thinking, with theories that can be tested by evidence. Adducing, furthermore, an ethical argument, they cite the all too common experience in which dubious or patently evil processes of indoctrination are experienced as subjectively helpful, as in brainwashing and propaganda. And they note the abundant similarities between psychoanalysis and such practices.

In this book I address the problems of psychoanalysis by assessing Freudianism from a perspective that has not been used before, at least in the way I use it: moral character and the human moral system. By this I mean those aspects of mind that involve conscious and unconscious judgments of the moral qualities of experience—good and bad, right and wrong, helpful and harmful, creative and destructive. This perspective corresponds to psychoanalysis's main theoretical and practical concerns and provides, I believe, sufficient breadth and depth to deal with the serious problems that beset the field.

Such an assessment needs not just a shift in emphasis, but a restructuring of much of the conceptual framework of psychoanalytic and psychiatric thinking. The extent of the restructuring might be glimpsed from recognizing that an adequate analysis of conscious and unconscious moral judgment requires taking into account innate knowledge in a broad sense—by which I mean, for example, such inborn reactions or responses as the expectation of being treated in a life-sustaining way by people in one's immediate environment—as well as the traditional emphasis on childhood experience. This leads to a discontent with an Oedipal interpretation of moral development, with its very peculiar and constricted assumptions about what is innate ("id" impulses, for the most part) versus experiential. It makes more sense to think of moral aspects of personality as comprising a moral system in the mind in the same way that, in physical medicine, we organize elements into entities like circulatory and nervous systems, paying as much attention to innate elements as to experiential influences.

From this perspective I inquire of Freudianism whether it asks coherent questions about the human moral system and provides reasonable answers to those questions. Many key questions bearing on the truth and value of psychoanalysis's claims can be coherently framed in terms of competing visions of this system—whether (as Freud believed) it is a set of rules acquired through education and socialization, whose evolutionary purpose is the "taming" of natural instincts that would otherwise make civilized existence impossible, or whether (as I believe) it is a system rooted in innate human propensities and knowledge that, like language, develops when given necessary stimulation and support from the social environment. I arrived at this belief by way of two intersecting paths, both of which radically challenge Freudianism. Freudianism takes for granted the truth value of a set of rules for moral character, which I call Oedipal rules. But clinically, to help a person cure rather than remodel his or her neurosis requires that person to not only recognize the anachronistic ("transference") quality of particular urges and actions, but to critically question the moral system according to which any urge or action is judged, consciously or unconsciously. In other words, the automaticity of cure upon analyzing the patient's transferences is a Freudian myth that breaks down clinically precisely because it requires acceptance of the very rule-based moral system and derivative concept of moral character which is problematic in neurosis. And to critically question one's moral system a kind of philosophical inquiry must be made to intersect with the psychological. A society to which Freud's id concept applies is one that has completely succumbed to rules and mechanistic explanations in place of a genuine morality—in which, in other words, the normative character is neurotic. Therefore, it is important for analyst and analysand to inquire how, when, and why one has, as an individual and a member of a cultural community, come to accept such a set of rules. Although in this book I neither propose a comprehensive answer to this question nor a fully satisfactory alternative, I am convinced that the patient's active questioning of his or her moral self is a crucial requirement of cure. Successful treatment, in other words, requires the patient to become something of a psychoanalyst and something of a philosopher.

In exploring these intersections between psychology and philosophy I am obliged to deal with problems in anthropology, sociology, linguistics, history, and political and social philosophy. This is necessary for two main reasons. First, Freud was a wide-ranging observer and thinker who drew many of his key arguments from fields other than psychology and medicine. His work cannot be assessed in depth without tracing his ideas back to their sources in the problems that fascinated him and from which he sought answers to psychopathology and the dilemmas of human existence. Second, social science has now furnished critical tests of the Freudian theory of incest taboo, long considered impossible. This new evidence has allowed us to reexamine his theory and that of his main rival, Edward Westermarck.[2] For this reason I devote much of Chapter 2 to a review of these theories and to the recent work in anthropology and human sociobiology that appears to be resolving the Freud-Westermarck debate in favor of Westermarck.

---

[2] To anticipate Chapter 2, the Finnish sociologist, anthropologist, and moral philosopher Edward Westermarck (1862–1939) put forward in his 1891 *History of Human Marriage* a Darwinian theory of incest aversion that was first widely appreciated and then eclipsed by Freud's. In recent years it has returned to prominence as the more plausible theory.

I am compelled to agree with Freud's critics that his theory, as it stands, is indefensible, because it is determined by perspectives that make it a reactionary defender of the status quo. At the same time, the two general propositions underlying psychoanalysis appear to warrant belief. I suggest an explanation of this seeming paradox. Freudianism actually stakes out an artificially boundaried form of inquiry within the larger domain of psychoanalysis, that of the two general theories (i.e., the importance of childhood influence and of unconscious beliefs). But it does so without awareness or acknowledgment. Both the artificiality of the boundaries and the lack of awareness depend on the way that Freud subverts meaning in a number of key areas that are objects of traditional philosophical inquiry but from which Freud seeks to stand apart, often by creating new, idiosyncratic definitions or by smuggling purely utilitarian definitions into quasi-biological theories. For example, as is made clear in the late summary work, *Civilization and Its Discontents,* the aim of human existence, which in classical philosophy was thought of as the realization of a human *telos* or aim, which includes innate knowledge and experiential factors such as social roles, is taken to be nothing but "happiness," equated with the pursuit of pleasure while accommodating to moral rules. Pleasure is further reduced to the discharge of id impulses, and ultimately equated with neuronal discharge. In such a system, as Freud makes explicit, moral concepts like justice mean no more than what the powerful in any era determine they shall mean. And in Freud's middle phase, when he was attempting to integrate linguistic reasoning into his theory of consciousness, the abstruse quasi-neurological concept of "hypercathexis" means no more than the acceptance of received ideas. Freud repeatedly subverts meaning in this way with respect to mind-body problems, to problems of innate versus experiential knowledge, and to problems of language, social and political philosophy, and history. One of the incidental virtues of this book is, I believe, the demystification of Freudian language by deconstructing arcane neologisms like "cathexis" and "hypercathexis" into terms and concepts of ordinary psychological and philosophical discourse.

What I describe in detail as the interconnected artificial boundaries of Freudianism center on Freud's uncritical acceptance of a system of ideas and values that may be termed "Oedipal" because its leading expression is his theory of the Oedipus complex. Freudian psychoanalysis makes sense if one assumes the necessity and validity of this system, but not otherwise. My analysis of Freudianism offers suggestions as to how it might be transformed from a special-case to a general psychological theory.

Freud's subversions of meaning entail ways of thinking in which authority-based beliefs crowd out a more open process in which theories are tested against experience, including the empirical data of fields that constitute background knowledge for psychoanalysis—biology, neurology, anthropology, sociology, economics, linguistics. In examining controversies in these background fields I sometimes characterize Freudian thinking as irrational, as opposed to rational or scientific. I do not strive to give a precise definition to these terms, both because I question whether such definition is possible at this stage in our understanding of knowledge and because their contextual meaning is best illuminated by examining the intellectual history. In other words, this is an ordinary intellectual judgment—rationality as the freedom of reasoning from the influence of the desires—rather than one based on technical criteria derived from a particular philosophy of science (although I have been inspired by the debates between some great philosophers of science, to whom I occasionally refer).[3]

My practical standards of rationality differ in different circumstances. When examining chains of argument the emphasis is typically on logical coherence and intellectual consistency and sometimes, in areas of history and social philosophy, on values. In areas where evidence permits the weighing of alternative theories, notably in the anthropology and biology of incest aversion, the emphasis is on how well Freudianism stands up to these empirical tests. But the overriding emphasis throughout, whether or not explicitly stated, is on values in action—i.e., on the impact of Freudian ideas, as translated into clinical theory and methods, on the patients who are the objects and intended beneficiaries of these theories.

I feel it important to acknowledge my gratitude to the pioneering work of Freud, in part because this indebtedness may not always be evident from the harsh criticism I level at him, leading some readers to confuse me with critics of the "psychoanalysis-bashing" variety (Masson, the later Crews, Swales, and others), who consider psychoanalysis an unmitigated catastrophe and evil.[4]

[3] My approach is close to the philosopher Harry Jaffa (1952, 12), who, in his classic work on the nexus between Aristotelian and Thomistic ethics, wrote: "The question, then, of fundamental concern is whether . . . there is a basis for such judgments [of value] that is not arbitrary. . . . If, that is to say, the canons of the exact sciences supply the criteria of what is or is not to be considered 'scientific,' then it may be that both the degree of assurance possible and that required for satisfactory value judgments will always fall far short of what would be in an exact sense scientific. But for the very reason of that low order of requirement there may be no need for such a science, any more than the carpenter needs the geometer's knowledge of angles in order to do his work. In the same way we may say that a science of value judgments involves different criteria from any of the exact sciences."

[4] Although much of the commentary of these critics (for a good sample, see Crews 1995; 1998) cannot be faulted, I believe they make a fundamental mistake in equating Freudianism with psychoanalysis—an understandable mistake but one that is no more justified than equating economics with Smith and Ricardo, or anthropology with Frazer. The "fathers" of the modern social sciences bear the burden, not altogether their fault, of having armies of blind followers for whom the father's theories are a new conventional wisdom and who are thus saved the considerable trouble of thinking for themselves. This creates the impression of a hegemonic movement. But truth is not determined by a popularity contest, and critics should not be deceived into thinking that the popularity of certain ideas closes a field. Freud's theories need to be rigorously criticized, but he should not be held accountable for the sheepish behavior of his followers. One would never dream of equating physics with Aristotle, but this is because the process of critical thinking institutionalized in science makes testing and replacement of theories a normative and somewhat orderly process. We are still very far from that in the social sciences.

My criticism is leveled at the specific ideas Freud developed to elaborate what I call the "general theories," with the implication throughout that that basis not only remains a vital core to be differently elaborated, but would have lacked much specific content without him. It is work done on the general theories under the banner of Freudianism that allows us in retrospect to see what is drastically wrong with it, how seriously inadequate it is to express the potentials inherent in the general theories.

Much of Freud's intellectual history can be understood in terms of struggles to salvage a coherent theory out of the repeated clinical and intellectual failures of his ideas. Both kinds of failure stemmed from the growing alienation of his psychoanalysis from social and political reality. Almost invariably the method of salvage is to refashion the theory in a more authoritarian and socially reactionary way, often obscured by scientific-sounding rhetoric. This tendency is conspicuous in his late social-philosophical works.

To his enduring credit, Freud discovered a widespread pattern of experience, often quite unconscious, in which sexual repression is accompanied by internalization of a cultural moral code. This discovery, of the unconscious pervasiveness of puritan morality, is important. However, Freud's explanations of the phenomenon, which he labeled the Oedipus complex, are extremely questionable. For, as many social thinkers have recognized, puritanism is the morality of patriarchy and of liberal-capitalist society (the latter connection was famously made by Max Weber, 1904). It is a form of morality that is in many ways oppressive, especially to women and children, and regressively destructive of inquiry into the biological and social nature of human beings. Key questions about psychoanalysis's value as a therapeutic procedure center on whether it should promote adaptation to this cultural norm and its underlying assumptions and values, or enable people to think critically about it. These questions are of course largely evaluative but associated with classical philosophical and epistemological ones that are open to much more rigorous discussion than they have received.

This book is an argument for a "rational" psychoanalysis, by which I mean no more than an elaboration of the general theories in ways that can stand up to criticism and to empirical tests. To those who would argue that it is vain to strive for a rational understanding of the irrational, I reply that the opposite is true. All phenomena are irrational until they are understood, and this is no less true of atoms or weather than of the human unconscious. I am in this sense a "methodological monist," to use Chomsky's term (1996, 35). Furthermore, it is only by striving for a rational psychoanalysis that one can challenge Freudianism on its own terms. Its great appeal, after all, is that in contrast to religious forms of enlightenment, it is based on understandings rooted in the biological and social sciences that can be debated and modified.

With regard to clinical applications, the concept of rationality should be understood as referring to the process by which analyst and patient think critically about complex imaginative analytic material and about their own interaction. Such an approach to psychoanalysis will not diminish its idiosyncratic richness or complexity. And if the result of this paring down of psychoanalysis so it can be defended in the ways I describe is to make us realize how little we genuinely know about the mind and about psychopathology, we might find courage in the thoughts of Oliver Wendell Holmes, who said that if the bulk of the pharmacopoeia of his day were to be thrown into the sea it would be so much the better for patients and the worse for fishes.

The book begins by suggesting, in Chapter 1, "The Basic Neurotic Reaction," that a useful way of framing the central problem of psychopathology is in terms of unconscious and fixed convictions of a largely moral nature (typically, judgments of badness and defectiveness) rather than the traditional and superficial method of categorization by symptoms (anxiety, depression, phobias, hallucinations, etc.). Neurotics who seek treatment are people who have come to an awareness, often intuitive, that they are dominated by such convictions, about which they cannot think clearly. This clinical introduction leads to Chapter 2, "The Freudian View of the Human Moral System." There I introduce the idea that Freudianism's horizons are limited by what I call "artificial perspectives," which confine observation and thinking along dogmatic lines. As part of my discussion of the Oedipus complex in this chapter I provide a long but important digression into the Freud-Westermarck debate about incest aversion and recent evidence bearing on it.

In Chapter 3, "Extending Westermarck," I show how his hypothesis invites a fertile way of thinking about biological and cultural psychosexual development. I speculate here about what is innate versus experiential in human personality and how innate tendencies would likely register in a being capable of reflective and symbolic thought.

In Chapter 4, "From Inquiry to Orthodoxy," I discuss Freud's early theory of two major instincts— self-preservation and libido. I argue that in this instance as in others, Freud's initial intuition was correct but was overridden by his commitment to certain socially conservative philosophical principles. Chapter 5, "The Ego Psychology Solution," is devoted to the crisis caused by the clash between Freud's philosophical commitments and his self-preservation model, which was actually supported by clinical evidence to which he turned a blind eye. His resolution of this crisis in the form of "ego psychology" required that he subvert the meaning of creative versus mimetic thought, and this had repercussions on his neurological, linguistic, and social-philosophical ideas. In particular, I demonstrate his strong but unacknowledged indebtedness to Hume's psychology and social philosophy and to what I regard in general as the "irrationalist" side of British empirical-utilitarian philosophy.

Chapter 6, "Freud's Emotivist Fallacy," augments the "artificial perspectives" argument, showing the weakness of the emotivist perspective that becomes increasingly prominent in Freudian theory.[5] In Chapter 7, "The Trauma Solution," and Chapter 8, "The Ultimate Solution," I pick up the thread of Freud's attempt to construct a coherent theory from the perceived failure of his dualistic instinct theory. Chronologically, this coincided with the First World War and its aftermath. His response reflected the ambivalence of his social thinking. While making important observations on psychic traumatization, Freud came to interpret the war as supporting a new unified view of instinct, which became the cornerstone of his final theoretical statement. In this theory human beings are portrayed as innately incestuous and murderous, these "instincts" representing the full complement of relevant genetic endowment. Because this sexual-aggressive impulsivity is now unbalanced by any instinctual tendency toward social preservation or morality, people require to be socialized into the ways of arbitrary power. This is the conclusion that informs his late works of social philosophy, which I discuss in Chapter 9, "Freudianism Post-1920." I regard this conclusion as the failed culmination of an intellectual program driven by an ideological commitment that ironically comes to mirror and justify the mental attitude of the neurotic.

In the opening section of Chapter 10, "A Thinking Cure," I discuss the important question as to whether psychoanalysis, shaped so powerfully by Freudian ideas, is correctable. Here I hark back to the important distinction made early in the book between the general theories of unconscious influence and the specific Freudian theories, seen now as subverting the potential to create a rational and humanistic psychoanalysis. I argue that such a correction is possible. In the balance of this chapter, I provide some clinical illustrations of psychoanalyses conducted as combined psychological and philosophical inquiry; that is, as critical inquiry into the grounds of a person's unconscious convictions about his or her self and the world. Such an approach can, I believe, truly reverse the core neurotic tendency to dogmatically and unconsciously accept the results of early socialization. The final chapter provides a glimpse of a systematic alternative to Freudian psychoanalysis.

---

[5] Emotivism or emotive theory refers to the philosophical view that ethical and value judgements are not reports, assertions, or propositions, but rather expressions of feelings or attitudes.

1

THE BASIC NEUROTIC REACTION

A person is a subject that is responsible for his actions.
—Immanuel Kant, *The Metaphysics of Morals*, 1797

He was alone, abandoned, lost, hopeless, cold. Cold especially—a deep interior cold nothing could change. Although the basis of his unhappiness, this glacial deadness, he would cling to it always, because it was the love of his being, he had built the being around it.
—Paul Bowles, *The Sheltering Sky*, 1949

The Subject Matter of Psychoanalysis

What is neurosis?

In developing his special theories, Freud assumed that neurosis is a functional disturbance of personality resulting from an inevitable conflict between appetitive biological instincts and the demands of civilized life. In turn, this reflects a broader assumption that such conflict defines the way in which human societies emerge and evolve and by which individuals are acculturated into them.

These assumptions have an intuitive appeal, for they correspond to the way many people experience things. But as first principles they are simplistic, eliminating at the outset any ideas of human nature that go beyond force and necessity.

An obvious contender for a more complex view, one that informs various developmental perspectives in psychoanalysis, is the idea that neurosis is a form of immaturity. Immaturity is incomplete psychosocial development, assuming that the aim of development in any society is mature and healthy functioning. The appeal of this idea as a first principle would seem to be spoiled at the outset by the problem of cultural relativity, since standards of maturity and sanity always reflect a specific culture's conceptions of human nature and moral character. Such conceptions change, and not in any linear or predictable way, even within a tradition. Ideals from one culture and era are regarded with incomprehension or horror by another. For example, the ancient Greek ideal of manhood included slave ownership, infanticide, and the natural inferiority of women—customs and habits regarded by modern Western society as barbaric. On the other hand, the notion of organizing civil society around "the free market" would be seen as bizarre by the ancient Greeks. But a developmental first principle is reasonable if we include a certain perspective. This is the perspective that becomes possible in a culture that has achieved a degree of sophistication, sometimes called the "birth of philosophy," in which *critical reflection* becomes a value, alongside conformity to tradition.

Kant (1784, 286), for example, defined enlightenment as "man's release from his self-incurred tutelage. Tutelage is man's inability to make use of his understanding without direction from another." Anticipating a main problem of modern society, he writes: "If I have a book which understands for me, a pastor who has a conscience for me, a physician who decides my diet, and so forth, I need not trouble myself. I need not think, if I can only pay—others will readily undertake the irksome work for me."

Kant's warning reverberates in the words of contemporary thinkers who warn us of the insufficiency of critical reflection in the modern era. Paul Feyerabend's approach to the philosophy of science and his attempt to find common ground between science, philosophy, and the arts has critical thinking at its core: "The first idea, that of *criticism,* is found in almost all civilizations. It plays an important role in philosophies such as Buddhism and Mysticism, it is the cornerstone of late nineteenth-century science and philosophy of science, and it has been applied to the theatre by Diderot and Brecht" (1981, ix). And the economist John Galbraith (1971, 401) concludes his analysis of the modern industrial state and its increasingly affluent citizenry with a warning about the deterioration of liberty in societies where priorities are allowed to be determined by an uncritical acceptance of the arguments of industry: "The danger to liberty lies in the subordination of belief to the needs of the industrial system. . . . If we continue to believe that the goals of the industrial system—the expansion of output, the companion increase in consumption, technological advance, the public images that sustain it—are coordinate with life, then all our lives will be in the service of these goals. . . . All other goals will be made to seem precious, unimportant or antisocial."

Such thinkers warn us that the *possibility* of critical reflection, even in advantaged cultural contexts, is no guarantee of its exercise. To return to a psychoanalytic theme, such reflection must be added to the definition of psychic immaturity if we are to make sound use of a developmental principle.

In societies in which the material and political conditions of life permit and encourage critical reflection, the mature and moral individual, in addition to being highly functional within the culture, can also question established views. Such questioning may lead the person to enter into conflict with his or her own tradition(s) and/or to seek understanding and betterment in light of previous or foreign traditions. The great appeal of the historical and transcultural social sciences—history, sociology, anthropology, archaeology, linguistics, political science, and literary and art criticism—lies in this capacity for critical questioning of one's cultural norms. If we keep this added perspective in mind, cultural relativism need not invalidate the idea that neurosis is a form of immaturity, now understood to mean a kind of philosophical or critical immaturity—of not being sufficiently responsible for one's beliefs and actions, to borrow Kant's concept.

Freud was a questioning individual. One of his personal strengths and enduring accomplishments was to recognize in himself, his patients, and his culture a pattern of psychosexual immaturity that he labeled the Oedipus complex—a constellation of anger, fear, and obeisance to and rebellion against patriarchal authority. It is not at all clear from his work, however, that this complex is any more widespread in neurotics than in the population at large. Neither does his work demonstrate clearly what the relations are between the Oedipus complex and neurosis. For the argument can and has been plausibly made that it is those people who are especially disturbed by this cultural norm, and seek to transcend rather than accommodate to it, who are particularly prone to psychic difficulty, an unsurprising result given the level of neuroticism (i.e., unconsciousness and conflict about determining beliefs) in our culture. Freud is to be credited with recognizing the prevalence of the Oedipus complex and faulted for not asking the questions most in need of asking: How is it that so many of us are caught up in it? What does it tell us about the organization of our world and the raising of our children? To the extent that it is destructive, what can we do to repair the damage?

In Freudianism neurosis is the generic term for a set of mental dysfunctions (anxious, phobic, hysterical, obsessive, and depressive neuroses) that stem from pathologies of repression, considered the root "defense mechanism"—mental operations by which expressions of instinctual urges are rendered unconscious so as to protect the civilized self from disruption. Pathologies of repression result, in turn, from suboptimal internalization of Oedipal attitudes and beliefs, with consequent exaggerated conflict over instinctual impulses that should be smoothly repressed. Psychosis represents a more serious failure to internalize Oedipal standards, as manifest by more drastic defenses such as "splitting of the ego" and "denial of reality," while so-called character disorders such as borderline personality represent intermediate formations. In this categorization, relative excess or insufficiency of repression generates specific conflicts, mechanisms, and symptoms.

As may be evident from the above paragraph, these definitions and formulations are circular to a high degree. Pathological repression results from faulty internalization of Oedipal beliefs, leading to exaggerated fear of instinct, which leads to pathological repression and faulty internalization. As I became increasingly skeptical of this circular Freudian theory and wary of its distorting effects on therapy, I sought to see things in a fresh light. Since the central problem of neurosis, stated in a noncircular way, is the uncritical acceptance of an Oedipal belief system, I began to look to what patients believed about themselves and the world, as indicated by their explicit ideas and what one could reasonably infer about unconscious beliefs from their overt expressions, attitudes, and behavior. It appears to me now that the circular Freudian way of seeing and thinking has made it difficult for analysts to appreciate some fairly obvious facts about the people who seek their help. Foremost among them is that these people typically express a psychological reaction that is simultaneously a moral reaction: namely a deep conviction of badness and defect. By "deep" I do not mean anything more mysterious than this: a conviction so strong as to be completely believed, admitting no exceptions, and (for the most part) unconscious. I consider this the "basic neurotic reaction." It is common to the variety of reactions Freud studied but the very structure of Freudian thought tends to render it invisible.

The following vignettes about patients in psychoanalysis, along with some broad inferences about their basic problems, represent typical neurotic patterns.

Clinical Presentations

1. The Engineer

A not uncommon clinical pattern is one in which the patient criticizes the real abuses and deficiencies of his or her early life but, lacking confidence in the criticism, fails to make use of it in a constructive way . Rather, the damaging influences are invested with the force of law so that the patient remains enslaved to them. Such was the case with a professional engineer who sought analytic help with lifelong problems centering on psychic and sexual impotence.

This small, intense, middle-aged man, if thoughtful about his life, is bitter, irritable, and easily upset.[6] He holds strong social views of a libertarian, free-market-capitalist, and social Darwinist sort. His father was a banker, outwardly mild-mannered, who preached a policy of accommodation to his

[6]For the sake of simplicity I will present all clinical material in the present tense.

shrewish and cruel wife, a woman who consistently tormented and insulted the children. In her view the girls were stupid and lazy and my patient was babyish and worthless, "not worth the powder to blow you up." As a boy he was shy, insecure, polite, religious, and guiltily enraged without knowing it. His favorite hobby was building larger and larger bombs, which he finally abandoned when he realized he was gaining the expertise to really do harm. In his twenties he began recognizing how constricted his personality was. It dawned on him that his mother's hatred, combined with his father's pseudointellectual passivity, had damaged him severely, as it clearly had his three sisters. Ever since then he has borne a smoldering resentment, aggravated by failures to live up to his ambitions to be a loving and creative man.

His problems center on a deep lack of conviction about his independent perceptions, thinking, and judgment. Just as in early adolescence his doubts about the existence of God and the hypocritical Catholicism in which he was raised were paralyzed by fear that he might go to hell, he could not stop experiencing his early life as having, in some ultimately authoritative way, determined the fundamentals of his existence once and for all. Thus he would argue, as his mother had done, that he must be "intrinsically flawed." Not only can his anger not be trusted as a legitimate signal of threat to the self, but he is angry at people and things that are objectively positive and helpful. All this lends an air of peculiarity to his intellectual life. Despite being an intelligent man seeking enlightenment, he has never truly admired any intellectual figure. He tends to be impatient and dismissive of intellectual or philosophical inquiry as being paltry and inadequate, and serious reading makes him anxious. In effect he "trashes" all valuable human activity while envying those who engage in it.

A reasonable low-level inference in this case is that in contrast to his insecurity about his *own* thinking, he is profoundly convinced of the correctness of his *parents'* judgments about him. Unable to effectively oppose his socialization, and like a man under a spell, he has spent his life proving his parents correct.

I began to pursue this inference by drawing attention to the sham quality of the criticism of his upbringing, for although he expressed outrage at the damage he had suffered, he clearly was ashamed, guilty, confused, and self-deceiving. This made sense to him, and his dreams began to reveal some of the associated conflicts and issues.

Freud appreciated that dreams have special significance, but he interpreted them tendentiously to confirm the presence of Oedipal wishes and feelings rather than in light of myriad other and more interesting functions, including detection of problems, framing of questions, and seeking of new solutions. This man's dreams from early in analysis show those functions. For example, in response to first becoming aware of the shallowness of his critical faculties, this patient dreamed *he was operating a large trash-compacting machine outside a hospital. He looked inside and noticed a small black dog at the bottom, walking on its hind legs, human-fashion, and carrying in its front paws a human infant. Horrified, he realized that the dog was an experimental animal being discarded. Reaching for the emergency shutoff, he stopped the machine and descended into it to rescue the dog and the baby. There he discovered the body of a woman, covered by trash, damaged but alive. His horror increased when he realized that human experimentation might also be taking place. He brought the woman to the surface. In the hospital, he found himself attempting to arrange for hospitalization for the unfortunate victim, who had meanwhile multiplied into four people. He was arguing with the head nurse, who turned out to be his oldest sister. She insisted that she could not take them, as she had to save room for her paying patients. He thought of offering his credit card, even though there was little money in the account. But as this scene went on, he began to doubt his passion, thinking that perhaps, after all, these people were not the unfortunate victims he had perceived but rather undesirable "dregs of humanity" who might as well be abandoned. This thinking was reinforced by seeing one of them, a black woman, stealing a candy bar from a vending machine.*

In this imaginative and highly symbolic dream my patient portrays a variety of conflicting judgments about past and present life circumstances. He is acting decisively to stop the trashing machine (his indiscriminate anger and dismissal), at least until he can examine and judge his victims. But the examination produces confusing results, reflecting his profound ambivalence. Either the victims are horribly and unfairly abused, or they are subhuman dregs of humanity who deserve no better. One might interpret that through my confrontation of him I had aroused compassion and curiosity, while at the same time becoming vulnerable to his trashing, for it is hard to avoid "transference" themes of hope mixed with skepticism in the references to hospitals and medical experimentation. Will he be helped or merely cruelly experimented on by psychoanalysis? The dream raises the dilemmas of his life and solves them, for the moment, by returning to a familiar cynicism that attributes to whole classes of human beings the same congenital inferiority his mother attributed to him.

2. The Psychiatrist

Freud not only accepted the common judgment of his day that homosexuality, one of the "perversions," is pathological but he saw it as an inferior form of pathology. Neuroses, in his view, represent the "negative" of perversions, in that neurotics repress Oedipal fantasies whereas perverts enact them (1905, 165). This dubious theory stigmatizes homosexuals as lacking the strength of Oedipal law, a clear bit of Freudian egocentrism that confuses neurosis with issues of sexual choice. In fact, homosexuals who happen to be neurotic display no less repression than heterosexuals, as indicated by the following case.

This young psychiatrist entered psychoanalysis because he was deeply uncertain whether his homosexuality was natural for him or a distortion of his true nature. As a boy he had been fond of girls but he became fearful of them in adolescence and turned to homosexuality. Now, years later, homosexuality is losing its appeal, as he realizes that he is no more prepared to fall in love with a man than with a woman. Yet he feels trapped. A major practical problem lies in his desire to eventually marry and have children. He wants to know whether that is a realistic hope.

His homosexuality involves a certain gender confusion and unconscious fear and hatred of his mother—a homophobic Christian Scientist—and protest against the reactionary belief systems of his childhood. His mother had actually been a primitively patriarchal figure who sought to indoctrinate him into beliefs that God the Father *prohibits possession of one's own body.* This man's dominant memory of his early years is of his mother praying over him, seeking to get him to confess evil thoughts, while he writhed in pain from severe migraine headaches. His father, a wealthy entrepreneur, sought to have his three children emulate his philosophy that money is freedom, an idea my patient found corrupt and abhorrent but persuasive. Canny and secretive, the father was clearly also frightened by sexuality and deferred to his mad wife while superficially bossing her around—a perfect illustration of the corrosive effect of sexual repression on marriage. My patient grew up, in short, in a school for sexual repression, hypocritical religiosity, and narrow capitalist ideology. Homosexuality became a way of "shoving it down the throat" of both of his sexually immature and reactionary, but fearsome, parents.

This man is intelligent, handsome, and sophisticated, but highly irritable. Believing in love, commitment, personal and intellectual integrity, and the responsible care of patients, he is distressed when he cannot measure up to his ideals. But he is also very conflicted about being too much of an individual. He thinks of himself, and in many ways is, overly fastidious and demanding; but he is also profoundly insecure. Rather like the engineer of the previous example, it is a major awakening for him to discover how deeply worthless he considers himself to be. This is manifest, for example, in pervasive fears that if he dares to go against trends in his profession with which he disagrees he would be brought up on charges, and in profound cynicism about the possibility of any enlightened intellectual or political change. While valuing reason, he never expects to be treated reasonably.

A justified inference in this man's case is that he holds a deep conviction, in spite of his mature judgment, that as his mother believed and his father implied there is something innately bad about his mind and his body. In this view, his male lovers represent more lenient authorities who grant permission for him to exchange ideas and have some pleasure, which is always, eventually, accompanied by guilt.

When he comes to recognize that he actually fears his body, in unconscious compliance with his parents' moralistic teachings, he is able to begin to question this attitude with real determination—accompanied, naturally, by a great deal of confusion, conflict, regret, and anger.

Among other things, he seeks to engage his parents in honest dialogue about family affairs, both personal and financial, only to be confronted by new versions of moralistic claptrap or self-serving evasion. The effective action that would free him from their unwarranted influence, and therefore from having to use sex as a weapon in the covert battle against them, is to radically diminish their status, and that of their peculiar values, in his mind. This becomes an important task that occupies our analytic work for a number of years.

As he develops increasing confidence in thinking for himself and his relation to authority changes, so do his views of himself as a passionate and sexual man. Originally convinced that his homosexuality was a direct expression of hatred and mistrust of women, he comes to realize that a sexually fulfilling love relationship with a man or woman represents a condition impermissibly positive within his traditional belief system. He becomes increasingly open to the possibility of falling in love with a person of either sex.

3. The Physician

The basic neurotic reaction may be strongly present in people who are "well adjusted" from an external point of view and relatively asymptomatic, challenging usual schemes of diagnosis. It stands to reason, however, that people convinced of their defectiveness might be humble, resigned, stoic, highly responsible, and seemingly quite mature. But, as the woman I will now discuss came to realize, such humility and maturity without benefit of critical awareness permits little creative growth.

This woman, a physician, entered psychoanalysis because she could not deeply and passionately engage with people, although she was passionate about skiing and the outdoors, her dogs, art, music, and travel. It was the stark contrast between these passions and the bloodlessness of her engagement with others that made her seek treatment.

She was the only child of a socially and intellectually advantaged couple. Both parents had overcome difficulties to achieve advanced education, but neither was able to construct a sane family life. Her father, a prominent psychoanalyst, was depressed and secretly alcoholic throughout his life. He hid behind paternal authority and academic position, consistently misunderstanding his daughter's expressions of unhappiness and later undermining her efforts to comprehend what was wrong in the family. Her mother, a withdrawn intellectual, became more so during my patient's childhood, eventually retreating into a drugged state for many years, which the father managed to ignore while my patient was given over to the care of a succession of maids.

During medical school she had an analysis that failed to seriously engage her. Although drawn to psychiatry, she was frightened by it and pursued another specialty. She married a colleague, a very bright man, but after a passionate courtship their marriage became distant and asexual. She is dismayed to realize that she unconsciously reenacts her parents' dismal relationship, despite all her efforts to escape their influence.

Psychoanalysis, and psychiatry even less, pays too little attention to people like this, whose pathology is of an overcompliant inhibitory sort, with little overt anxiety, depression, or usual symptoms. While an active and busy woman, she is profoundly inhibited intellectually, morally, and sexually. She feels that she cannot understand and judge things of a political, historical, or social nature because they are too complicated and confusing, despite her good intellect and intuitions. A lifelong subtle form of dyslexia has contributed to these problems and to her tendency to think more in visual images than verbally. As a result of her inhibitions she tends to be cynical about aspects of life that seem beyond her ken, feeling she cannot adequately explore them so as to develop a point of view. In her social relations she has friendships but no loves. While she has been passionately in love and considers sex a "potency" deeply missed, she adapts all too easily without it. The pallor of her existence, she slowly came to recognize, is an extension of her childhood, which was a schooling in obedience to irrational authority, guilt, and diminished expectations.

Early in the therapy she found an image for the isolated, wan quality of her personality. Recalling a television commercial from her youth, she described an invisible "Gardol shield" that not only separated her from what is good and desirable in life but rendered critical thinking and judging alien. She recognized that she had as a child and adolescent substantially given up on the human world in resignation and confusion, withdrawing into vivid, eventful dreams. But learning about life from her dreams is difficult because a different form of shield operates. Dreaming is like "going to the movies" and seeing exotic stories that have little to do with her actual self. However suggestive her dreams, for me to attribute symbolic and *especially moral significance* to them is to attribute qualities to her that are barely credible. Much of her progress in analysis comes from an increasing capacity to reflect and think critically about aspects of life that she registers through creative dreaming.

Early in treatment all her dreams had a persecutory element, reflecting an underlying conviction of malevolence. Typically, she was being hunted down to be killed or turned into a zombie. In the dream context this was often a response to possessing forbidden knowledge. Clearly, self-knowledge was morally dangerous. Other dreams, of abysses and black holes, portrayed terror of emptiness and death. These dreams assume an important function when they become linked with experience of the analysis. We are able to see, for example, that she uses them as moral and intellectual ballast, to represent and restore a negative reality when something especially good or illuminating happens between us. As she is able to get her mind around the reality of her basic neurotic reaction—her unconscious conviction that she *must not know or think*—a sense of hopefulness develops along with a capacity for moral judgment. She realizes that, like the Harlow monkeys[7] who have no choice but to attach themselves to pathetic wire-mesh imitations of parents, she has mentally attached to, identified with, and become the spokeswoman for her inadequate parents. Her hopefulness and sadness involve the recognition that her basic perceptions of right and wrong, good and bad, generally mistrusted, have always been better than her parents'. She is in fact capable of positive attachment to a person who makes moral and intellectual sense. As she begins to awaken she starts to paint, in part to objectify her visual and dream images, describe them, and work with them. Slowly, she also begins to awaken sexually.

Later in the analysis our relationship, now quite important, becomes a strong focus. She dreams of being lost or my being unrecognizably changed whenever there is a major break in the work, such as for vacations. Her ambivalence toward me as a catalyst of change is palpable. In one dream, for example, *she is sailing down a tropical river. She approaches an interesting-looking settlement on the bank and considers stopping. But there is a complicated dock (read "doc") with turns and channels that must be negotiated. In the course of attempting to dock, her boat somehow breaks apart, and she finds herself floating in the water, holding on to flotsam.* The dream, she recognizes, mirrors her concerns that analysis is somehow too complex for her—or that it is paradoxically too effective at breaking apart familiar assumptions, leaving her unable to fashion a coherent life for herself.

Currently in our work, dreams easily expand into dialogues concerning her actual life, and she learns from them. She dreams, for example, that *she is visiting friends. As she leaves their house, she encounters a bewildering collection of cars parked on their lawn and searches for hers. She finds one that looks like it, but she isn't sure. Her key works the lock, so she assumes the car is hers. Then she notices another, with the trunk open and loud rock music blaring from the back. That one is hers, she realizes.* She recognizes without difficulty some of the transparent symbolism and uses the dream as a jumping-off point for important speculations. For example, she has been struggling for some time with a decision about leaving her hus-

[7] This refers to classic studies of the effects of maternal deprivation in primates. Harlow (Harlow & Mears, 1979) demonstrated that infant monkeys deprived of real mothering would attach strongly to "surrogates" constructed of wire mesh or cloth, but suffer severe damage in the form of heightened fearfulness and timidity, depression, etc.

band. Has she exhausted possibilities with him, given things a fair chance? Will there be other men? Clearly, the dream has something to do with singularity and plurality. The idea that her key might fit in more than one lock, or her lock receive more than one key, has obvious sexual and gender significance, which now is more than an interesting intellectual idea. She now misses the potency of passionate sex, of which she thinks herself capable and doubts she will ever achieve with her husband. The open trunk and the blaring music have interesting connections. She has always been self-conscious about her body, for she thinks she has too big a behind. This is a persisting manifestation of her irrational self-negativity. In the dream the behind of the car, however, emanates loud rock music, which is one of her great enjoyments. Interestingly, her associations are to the politically radical lyrics of a song she had long known only by melody. Thus the dream refers in important ways to "putting words to music," including applying radical political ideas to personal situations like her marriage, for her husband bullies her like her father did. Such ideas are becoming real and viable tools in her understanding of the world.

Argument

These cases illustrate some of the complex ways in which mental symptoms and personality problems express the person's basic neurotic reaction, his or her unconscious and automatic conviction of defect and lack of justification for making the most basic of critical intellectual and moral judgments. Clinical psychoanalytic discourse is demystified when these irrational convictions are identified and straightforwardly talked about.

Evidence of Oedipus complexes existed in every case and was used at times to clarify specific anxieties and symptoms. That knowledge is significant, however, only as a vehicle for framing important questions about beliefs and attitudes. Psychoanalysts who follow Freud tend to think that Oedipal interpretations illuminate a deep structure of the mind. But they are in fact superficial, only clarifying for patients what they basically already know, and they beg the important questions. The engineer, for example, knew very well that he was inordinately conflicted in his reactions to the arbitrary, condemnatory authority of his parents and that some of his symptoms reflected fantasies of bodily or sexual harm. It is solipsistic and of questionable if any benefit to "interpret" such patients' repressed anger and the like in terms of Oedipal dynamics. In the engineer's case, such ideas had (in a prior therapy) led him on a vain quest for (as he put it) "the root cause" of such feelings, and failing to find it only confirmed his conviction of defect.

At best, in very healthy people, emotions are sensitive partial indicators of complex mental processes taking place within us or between us and others. But in neurosis emotions typically mislead the person about basic problems of good and bad, right and wrong, safety and danger. Thus, the phobic person fears trivial dangers, the obsessive anguishes over minor or nonexistent faults, and the paranoid person dreads harm from people who mean well toward him. Since Oedipal theory is based on a neurotic type of cultural myth, attempts to reduce this emotional and moral confusion through reference to that theory merely provide the patient with a mythic vocabulary rather than generate understanding. Oedipal "interpretations" provide a false sense that something is being understood while, in fact, perpetuating the basic neurotic reaction.

Typically, what patients fail to recognize is that they share with many people socialized in the ways of our culture, and with parents all too willing to misuse their authority, deeply ambivalent attitudes and values and therefore repressed urges and potentials of all sorts, which need to be critically examined in relation to dominant but largely unconscious belief systems. The truly interesting problems are those created by the dawning awareness of being trapped in an Oedipal belief system that consistently generates self-destructive conclusions by distorting perceptions, undermining judgment, and making it difficult to act effectively against those influences that were and are damaging.

The Oedipus complex is largely a system for making historical and evaluative judgments. It is this very basis for judging that becomes open to question in people who arrive at a point of neurotic crisis. To fail to exploit this opening sufficiently is to fail to develop the potentialities of the general theories of psychoanalysis.

The problems for psychotherapy created by conflicted adherence to an Oedipal belief system do not stem from instinctually based "resistances," as Freud believed. Rather, they are *intrinsic to the system itself,* arising from patients' understandable inclination to experience tentative moves in the direction of freedom from this system as undeserved and disturbing. If one is convinced of one's innate defectiveness, as the belief system dictates, being encouraged to consider alternatives as rational possibilities is not only intellectually problematic but disturbing. Such help is likely to be perceived as naive and indulgent or as simply an attempt to substitute one dogma for another. This is probably the largest single obstacle to psychoanalytic understanding. The engineer, for example, remained certain for several years of his analysis that he was "intrinsically flawed." The psychiatrist believed that his critical judgments of his family and the values they represented were the mark of an inferior and excessively sensitive soul. And the doctor remained convinced for many years that anyone else in her growing-up circumstances would have handled things better and that I was giving far too much credit to her capacity to think and judge.

Freudianism, built on an emotivist and utilitarian concept of moral character, cannot help such people solve the problems of deepest concern. For the most important things to take up with them concern the basis of their judging: their unconscious commitment to Oedipal ideas. A psychoanalysis that adheres to these ideas can produce only modified, or more efficient, versions of an Oedipus complex. That is why so many analyses prove interminable. And that is the main clinical reason for insisting that psychoanalysis be based on a very different view of the human moral system.

2

THE FREUDIAN VIEW OF THE HUMAN MORAL SYSTEM

The world is primarily a moral order.
—Robert Pirsig, *Lila: An Inquiry into Morals* (1991)

The Human Moral System

If we value psychoanalysis's general theories and purposes—to understand unconscious belief systems at a personal level as a way of relieving mental suffering—we should ask whether Freudian ideas are rational expressions of those theories and purposes. In other words, do they provide a method, compatible with the general theories, for investigating the specifics of mental life in ways characteristic of the natural sciences, so as to be able to communicate with other disciplines that use a similar approach? A good statement of the position of "methodological monism" implied by this question is given by Chomsky (1996, 35-36, italics in original):

> Mental phenomena (events, entities, etc.) can be studied naturalistically, like chemical, optical, or other phenomena. We construct explanatory theories as best we can, taking as *real* whatever is postulated in the best theories we can devise (because there is no other relevant notion of "real"), seeking unification with studies of other aspects of the world—the one and only world—while recognizing that it might take many paths. And that it might even be unattainable, either because there is no unified account, or there is one but it lies beyond our cognitive reach.

Consider the phenomenon of human moral judgment. One of Freudianism's claims to serious attention is made by moral philosophers (e.g., Lear, 1990; Sherman, 1995; Wallwork, 1991) who regard it as a positive contribution in this important area by valorizing unconscious emotion and thought in a uniquely rational way. Other significant moral traditions (Hinduism or

Christianity, for example) value unconscious moral judgment but seek mystical rather than rational enlightenment. It is its natural-scientific approach to unconscious and subjective experience that gives psychoanalysis its special appeal.

Yet any fair-minded assessment of the Freudian theory of morality—its instinct theory, for example, or its theories of repression and superego formation—must conclude, with Whitehead (1954, 28-30), that they are, at best, "half-truths" with doubtful empirical support. As a longtime practitioner of and skeptical inquirer into psychoanalysis, I find it hard to fault Whitehead's assessment: "The ideas of Freud were popularized by people who only imperfectly understood them, who were incapable of the great effort required to grasp them in their relationship to larger truths, and who therefore assigned them a prominence out of all proportion to their true importance." (28) This book will amply verify that assessment.

Certainly, as Whitehead implies, one must be wary in faulting a complex and persuasive body of thought for its imperfections without making the effort to show in which ways it fails and exploring possibilities of correcting it either from within or outside its own traditions. After all, systems of half-truths—that is, attempts at rational explanation mixed with irrational beliefs—have often been precursors to more reliable systems. Once a discipline develops a coherent set of ideas and a reliable way of testing them, as has happened in some of the sciences, irrational beliefs tend to drop away with continued investigation.

I approach the moral aspects of personality as interrelated processes, some biologically derived, some purely cultural, that develop and function together as a *moral system,* analogous to a linguistic or cognitive system of mind, in the sense of Chomskyan linguistics.[8] By "moral aspects" I mean simply what people have intuitively recognized (as embodied in the subject matter of moral philosophy) as pertaining to the *quality* of experience, aspects of mental life that are interesting, rewarding, growth-promoting, life-enhancing, for the individual and for the society of which he or she is a part—what Greek philosophy referred to collectively as *arete,* generally translated as "excellence" or "virtue."

The concept of a human moral system with important biological elements (but which develops through interaction with the social environment) will seem strange to those accustomed to the Freudian way of thinking, which, for the most part, portrays morality as formed through a complex social-learning process imposed on and suppressing a human nature that is

[8] Chomsky,beginning in the 1950s, revived and extended the old concept of universal or "generative" grammar and reinvigorated the study of linguistics as a branch of cognitive biology—demonstrating that the universality of complex language is the product of a special human instinct. Human language represents an instance where complexity in the mind is not necessarily caused by learning, but exists prior to learning.

intrinsically asocial and amoral. My choice of this concept is based on a different approach to knowledge and experience. Deriving from traditions of inquiry apart from psychoanalysis and its philosophical progenitors, including Aristotelian moral philosophy with its appeal to reason as the guiding force in the development of our innate capacities, this approach provides a means to integrate observations from other fields, to challenge incoherencies in the Freudian system, and to offer correctives.

For example, the study of human and animal sexuality (which I discuss later in this chapter) leads to the conclusion that human beings, in common with virtually all social animals,[9] have as part of their genetic makeup not an incestuous but an anti-incestuous sexual instinct. This finding, along with many other lines of evidence and reasoning, renders Freud's assumptions and conclusions about human sexuality wrong, and his framework of ideas about the nexus between sexuality and morality suspect.

Hypotheses generated from this approach to the moral system will be shown to have a coherence that Freudian hypotheses lack and to communicate more intelligibly with other fields. They are also clinically significant. The basic neurotic reaction is one in which critical judgment of painful and damaging life circumstances is interfered with, so that rather than acting constructively, people behave in ways that hurt themselves and others, repeating damaging patterns from the past. Capacities to reflect, judge, and plan, which are present in rudimentary fashion early in life and which normally should guide action in the direction of maturity and be sources of strength and satisfaction, instead give rise to anxiety and guilt. Much of this typical pathological experience can be treated straightforwardly, if adequately conceptualized.

The Freudian Approach to Morality

Freudianism operates with a model of the human moral system, centered on the concept of the superego, that is fundamentally a social-learning theory. In this theory the moral system is designed to restrain biologically based motives that are selfish and asocial. Specifically, it is an entity made up of compromises between what people innately desire and conditions imposed by civilized existence. In Freudianism the moral system cannot in principle be repressed. It is primary entities (instincts) and their close derivatives (wishes and fantasies) that are repressed (i.e., rendered "unconscious," their expression and effectiveness as motives interfered with) in *forming* the moral system. Once formed, the moral system takes over from society and becomes the agent of repression in the individual.

[9] The naked mole-rat (see note 21 to this chapter) is one of the rare exceptions, which in this case does not disprove the biological rule.

The concept of superego (Freud, 1914b, 92-98; 1923, chapter 3) concretizes, in the idea of a discrete mental structure, the Freudian notion that equates moral agency (i.e., the source of conscience and guilt) with internalized social prohibitions, originally coming from parents:

> [T]he super-ego is described as the heir of the Oedipus complex in that it is constituted through the internalization of parental prohibitions and demands. . . . [T]he *formation* of the super-ego is a corollary of the decline of the Oedipus complex: when the child stops trying to satisfy his Oedipal wishes, which have become prohibited, he transforms his cathexis of his parents into an identification with them—he internalises the prohibition. (Laplanche & Pontalis, 1973, 436, italics in original)

In this view sexual and aggressive instincts limit what can be expected of moral development. The central problem of neurosis is seen as repression that is *relatively* excessive, that is, more than people can comfortably bear; while in psychosis and certain personality disorders repression is insufficient. Only social relearning of a proper degree of repression (in clinical psychoanalysis, for example) can experientially change this equilibrium.

It should be apparent that the truth of the Oedipal theory of morality cannot be decided on the basis of clinical work done *according to the theory.* If theory defines reality, no distinction is possible between the two, and there can be no empirical test of the theory, no way to criticize it on the basis of evidence. If humans by definition have Oedipus complexes which determine their moral systems, no non-Oedipal moral systems will be discovered.[10]

However, we can decide whether, using Freudian theories, questions about significant phenomena can be coherently formulated. We may start by noting that Freud's theory of neurosis has two roots, anthropological and clinical. Both are problematic.

The anthropological root, presented in *Totem and Taboo* (Freud, 1913), employs an analogy Freud drew between neurotic symptoms and the mental lives of "primitive" peoples, and is predicated on the assumption, widespread in his day, that our human ancestors were sexually promiscuous and incestuous. The guiding idea of this theory is that human society developed to contain and transform our primitive incestuous instincts so as to inhibit inbreeding and promote nuclear families and structured social interaction.

[10] Oedipal theory does generate a prediction, but one that requires anthropological evidence for empirical testing—thus my emphasis on the importance of *background knowledge* in psychoanalysis. This prediction states, in effect, that failure to develop an Oedipus complex (as a result of socialization in an aberrant subculture, for example) will produce people with subhuman mentalities, in the sense of lacking internal control. See the section further on in this chapter concerning the Freud-Westermarck debate for a discussion of this prediction and the considerable anthropological evidence now bearing on it.

The clinical root is the retrospective inference from clinical analyses that "the earliest sexual excitations of youthful human beings are invariably of an incestuous character" (Freud, 1913, 123-124) and that it is the necessary repression of such impulses in childhood that creates the vulnerability to neurosis in later life.

Combining the two views, Freudianism sees repression as a reprise in the individual of primal civilizing conflicts leading to the development of a microcosm of social evolution within the individual, in the form of the Oedipus complex. The clinical and the anthropological theories function as homologues, sharing the common assumption that the moral system is a highly unstable product of cultural evolution that needs to be reinforced in each generation through socialization by the exercise of authority.

This assumption pervades all aspects of Freudianism, even seemingly unexceptionable precepts. Consider its clinical goals, "to love and to work" (attributed to Freud by Erikson, 1950, 265), with its wonderfully epigrammatic simplicity. A moment's reflection shows that such a formula is deceptively empty of meaning precisely because it assumes moral significations that cannot legitimately be assumed. Love and work have been invoked throughout history to excuse the most heinous transgressions against freedom and justice, not to mention their routine use as instruments of social control. Historically, love of country, crown, or God has routinely justified genocide, as witness the Spanish Conquest, the North American Indian genocide, and slavery. Such corruptions of meaning abound no less in our modern, Orwellian world: invocations of the work ethic ("Arbeit macht frei") greeted inmates to Auschwitz; "national security" or patriotic ardor justified ethnic or political "cleansing" in Russia, China, Bosnia, Cambodia, and Kosovo; and lest we think our democratic state immune, our supposed self-love (our "national interests") excuses or supports terror and mass killing in Guatemala, El Salvador, Chile, Burma, Iraq, and Indonesia, to mention only some of the recent objects of our policies.[11] Such perversions occur routinely in our social and political world when the specification and application of concepts like freedom and democracy, or love and work, are dictated by authority rather than critically examined; when they are received passively rather than actively, given "dull and torpid assent."

[11] In the United States, the tradition of political dissent from wars of imperial conquest has emphasized this point. It was perhaps stated by no one better than Mark Twain, a passionate anti-imperialist (but not a pacifist) who was horrified by the subversion of republican values in the United States' brutal and deceitful takeover of the Philippines (1898-1902), which initiated its career as a "world power." Here is a typical quote from his satiric "War Prayer" (1923; see also Twain, 1992): "[F]or our sakes who adore Thee, Lord, blast their hopes, blight their lives, protract their bitter pilgrimage, make heavy their steps, water their way with their tears, stain the white snow with the blood of their wounded feet! We ask it, in the spirit of love, of Him Who is the Source of Love, and Who is the ever-faithful refuge and friends of all that are sore beset and seek His aid with humble and contrite hearts. Amen."

Love and work are not simple virtues, and perhaps not virtues at all, in families and societies where love is exploited and where available work supports values that enslave people. The significance of Freud's epigram depends completely on unstated considerations, and such considerations are for the most part absent from Freudian theory. These reflections indicate what is occulted in Freudianism. Hidden assumptions about the nature of the moral system, the role of socialization, and the values of modern society create artificial perspectives that confine thinking in predictable ways.

The Artificial Perspectives of Freudianism

Freudianism's hidden assumptions can be analyzed according to their leading rhetorical characteristics: instinctivist, Oedipalist, historicist, and essentialist. They share certain ideologies and certain readings and misreadings of biology, anthropology, linguistics, social philosophy, and history that recur throughout the work and form the bulk of its background knowledge.

Instinctivism

Freud's formulations of the origins of neurosis in the personal life of the individual, a mainstay of his theory throughout its many revisions, are an uneasy marriage between a view of cultural sex morality as hypocritical and destructive and the idea that arbitrary social control of sexual impulses is natural and necessary. As far as individual development is concerned, this union takes the form of an ontogenetic hypothesis to the effect that the sexual development of the individual results inevitably in the formation of an "Oedipus complex" of sexual desire toward the parent and siblings of the opposite sex, in conflict with demands, transmitted through parental and societal prohibitions, to repress such desires.

The childhood Oedipus complex is the crucible for adult personality and moral character, for depending on the relative success with which the child "resolves" this complex, he or she will suffer from an excess of repression, the precondition for later neurosis, or be relatively healthy—in short, have a neurotic or a normal "superego."

Fundamental to Freud's view of moral development is his particular conception of the sexual instinct in humans. A conflict between what would appear to be incompatible views of cultural sex morality (as hypocritical and destructive on one hand, natural and necessary on the other) is resolved by a type of reductionistic thinking that attributes simplistic qualities to sexual (and later to aggressive) instincts. The attribution serves to justify a strict social construction of cultural forms and moral dispositions, with a strong tendency to favor authoritarianism in both. The problem is not with with the concept of instinct itself, but with the way that Freud reduces the complex concept of instinct to mere impulsion. I term this "instinctivism," and consider it the first and foremost artificial perspective in Freudianism. How does this thinking develop in the course of his work?

Early on, Freud's perception that psychic repression mirrors society's hypocritical intolerance of sexuality is clear and strong. A passionately worded statement expressed the position, in fact, that contemporary critics of sexual morality like von Ehrenfels (1903, 1907) did not go far enough in condemning cultural hypocrisy. Freud (1908, 204) used clinical observations persuasively to show that among the worst and most pervasive effects of such hypocrisy was the "spread of modern nervous illness":

> It is one of the obvious social injustices that the standard of civilization should demand from everyone the same conduct of sexual life—conduct which can be followed without any difficulty by some people, thanks to their organization, but which imposes the heaviest psychical sacrifices on others. (192)

He paints a bleak picture:

> Fear of the consequences of sexual intercourse first brings the married couple's physical affection to an end; and then, as a remoter result, it usually puts a stop as well to the mental sympathy between them, which should have been the successor to their original passionate love. The spiritual disillusionment and bodily deprivation to which most marriages are thus doomed put both partners back in the state they were in before their marriage, except for being the poorer by the loss of an illusion. (194-195)

Women are especially damaged by the harsh and hypocritical demands put upon them, but for both men and women, "the preparation for marriage frustrates the aims of marriage itself" (198). And the toll on overall maturity, including intellectual and ethical maturity, is extraordinary, again especially for women:

> Their upbringing forbids their concerning themselves intellectually with sexual problems . . . and frightens them by condemning such curiosity as unwomanly and a sign of a sinful disposition. In this way they are scared away from *any* form of thinking, and knowledge loses its value for them. The prohibition of thought extends beyond the sexual field, partly through unavoidable association, partly automatically, like the prohibition of thought about religion among men, or the prohibition of thought about loyalty among faithful subjects. (198-199, italics in original)

And as a final condemnation of hypocrisy, "The 'double' sexual morality . . . is the plainest admission that society itself does not believe in the possibility of enforcing the precepts which it itself has laid down" (195).

For the individual child, sexual repression stems from compliance with parents who unreasonably restrict his or her sexuality, producing a fearfully distorted picture in the child's mind that can persist into adulthood. This is a straightforward extension of his social argument. When it comes to accounting for the *psychological* mechanisms and consequences of this socially caused repression, however, Freud's thinking becomes circular, revealing unconscious prejudices at odds with the social critic.

The historical-causal sequence that Freud believes is paradigmatic for neurosis—the child prohibited from touching his or her genitals—is described succinctly in *Totem and Taboo* (1913, 29, italics in original):

> The clinical history of a typical case of "touching phobia" is as follows. Right at the beginning, in very early childhood, the patient shows a strong *desire* to touch, the aim of which is of a far more specialized [i.e., more erotic] kind that one would have been inclined to expect. This desire is promptly met by an *external* prohibition against carrying out that particular kind of touching. The prohibition is accepted, since it finds support from powerful *internal* forces, and proves stronger than the instinct which is seeking to express itself in the touching. In consequence, however, of the child's primitive psychical constitution, the prohibition does not succeed in *abolishing* the instinct. Its only result is to *repress* the instinct (the desire to touch) and banish it into the unconscious. Both the prohibition and the instinct persist: the instinct because it has only been repressed and not abolished, and the prohibition because, if it ceased, the instinct would force its way through into consciousness and into actual operation. A situation is created which remains undealt with—a psychical fixation—and everything else follows from the continuing conflict between the prohibition and the instinct.

In this passage "internal" is specified (29, n2) to mean: "That is, from the child's loving relation to the author of the prohibition."

Note that this formulation is circular as regards space (inner-outer), time (before-after), and causality (cause-effect). The word "internal," especially combined with "force," is intended to conjure up an innate intrapsychic process, yet clearly refers to something *taken in* from the outside. It involves to a relationship, and thus to social and intersubjective experience upon which the child's loving attitude is predicated. In this relationship the child is *being forced* to promptly give up his or her sexual activity. This fact leaves it unclear whether a prior noncoercive relationship is to be assumed, as the precondition of the child's later acceptance of prohibition, or whether coercion is a condition of loving and being loved.

This use of language and mode of reasoning, so characteristic of Freud, intentionally (albeit probably unconsciously) blurs the distinction between what is innate and what is socially required or tolerated. As we know, such distinctions are not easy to make, and there is good reason to believe that much complex instinctual behavior requires environmental input of a specific kind at specific periods of development in order to manifest properly (in the next section I will discuss this property of instinct in detail in relation to sexuality).

Since Freud's example stands for the entire set of prohibitions and constrictions on the child's natural behavior and inquisitiveness, enforced more or less arbitrarily within the family (and by extension, for other natural behavior prohibited by society), it begs questions of definition and valuation. Are such prohibitions reasonable or unreasonable, necessary or unnecessary? Are they, and their acceptance by the child, indeed expressions of "love," or of power and control? In many moral traditions, including our own Judeo-Christian tradition, the power of parental authority (derived from divine authority) and the obedience of children are often regarded as expressions of love. But few, I think, would argue that either is a strong or unambiguous expression. Slaveowners were indulgent of their slaves' well-being and prided themselves on their slaves' obedience. When slavery ceased being morally acceptable (i.e., divinely authorized), however, the argument that either was an expression of love ceased being intellectually persuasive.

Freud's psychological (as opposed to sociological) formulation of neurosis, therefore, begs large and important questions of the necessity of authoritarian socialization in parent-child relations, assuming rather than demonstrating it. To not beg this question is to require that we take into account our cultural preconceptions about children and child rearing, which in turn reflect conceptions about being and becoming mature individuals. Under what conditions does a relationship based on authority and control, whether of parent to child or ruler to ruled, come to be perceived as love? What is the psychology, in other words, of obedience? We certainly know from common experience, as Freud did, that in many coercive or abusive situations affecting children and adults, perceptions of being loved are inversely proportional to the genuineness of love and care shown.

In the development of his psychology Freud consistently blurs the distinction between innate dispositions and socially caused experience, thus making the category of "inner" experience and the very concept of instinct profoundly ambiguous.

The result is that his theory of individual neurosis is a hypothetical and largely fantastic schematization of what is in reality a complex interplay of memory and interpretation of and reactions to parental and social attitudes and prohibitions. At the same time, it fails to deal with the central problem of neurosis, the person's excessively uncritical and therefore unconscious acceptance of destructive experience and its effects. Freud's schema corresponds metaphorically and in some cases literally to the experience of some patients, who have been raised under conditions of arbitrary sexual and other prohibitions and deprivations: "I have transgressed, and the beneficent authority against whom I have transgressed justly punishes me and informs me of my badness." But it is simplistic and misleading in the extreme, doing violence to basic concepts of instinct, morality, and judgment, to infer as Freud does that what is being illustrated in these speculations is some law of nature.

By turning social repression into something biologically ordained, Freud distorts the meaning of ordinary concepts in ways that are significant clinically. Consider, for example, the concept of freedom, as in "free association," a hallmark of his clinical procedure. By imposing on the patient the obligation to speak without reservation to an analyst under no such obligation, the Freudian procedure runs the risk of being, and often is, a training in authoritarian social learning, not in freedom and equality. To be a social and clinical reality, freedom must be actualized in relationships and institutions that are equal, democratic, and skeptical of arrogated authority—a very difficult thing to achieve. Obviously, psychoanalysis ought to strive for such relatedness. However, in the world of Freudian morality, the patient's withholding of himself or herself in the one-sided psychoanalytic situation prescribed by the "basic rule" of free association is described as "resistance." In instinctivist logic the patient is assumed to be resisting some instinctual "force" that needs to be overcome, rather than the arbitrariness of the analyst's judgments, of which one ought to be skeptical. Learned debates take place in psychoanalysis about whether the treatment of "resistance" is compromised by modifying so-called "neutrality," Freudianism's Orwellian term for the analyst's arrogated privilege of maintaining an unequal, authoritarian position.

The history of psychoanalysis has been characterized by efforts, hesitant and controversial as they may be, to compensate for these problems by introducing elementary concepts of social framework (the so-called object-relations theories) and reciprocity (concepts of countertransference). There is a need for scholars to systematically inquire into these efforts, but they are likely to succeed only to the extent that they examine instinct and social learning from a rigorous perspective.

Oedipalism

Freud's theory that the Oedipus complex is a basic constituent of human personality, a structure in the mind evolved over eons to control incestuous sexuality, inhibit inbreeding, and preserve the nuclear family is one of the defining theories of psychoanalysis, yet it is one of its most problematic. As pointed out by Popper (1962, 37-38) and others, it has been extremely unclear whether there could be any clinical observation that would demonstrate a person without an Oedipus complex, that is, disprove the theory. The philosopher Sidney Hook (1959) sympathetically explored with leading psychoanalysts the prospect of clinically testing Oedipal theory. His account (212-219) of the tremendous difficulties encountered by the analysts in describing "what kind of evidence they were prepared to accept which would lead them to declare in any specific case that a child did not have an Oedipus complex," is revealing. One analyst predicted that such a child would act like an idiot. Another became genuinely perplexed. A third went into a rage, calling Hook a misogynist and troublemaker.

At a cultural level the problems are equally severe. Freud applied his instinctivist approach, with its combination of biological reductionism and cultural conservatism, to grand problems of society and history: How did we as a culture-producing species get to be the way we are? His intellectually ambitious effort to establish the Oedipus complex as the cause not just of neurosis but of civilized morality and culture is impressive in its scope and erudition. His writings in anthropology and social philosophy are the work of a first-rate mind, restlessly concerned to assimilate existing knowledge and address age-old questions about the human condition. Yet the perspective produced by this instinctivism-writ-large, which I will call Oedipalism, is seriously and in many respects dangerously flawed.

Freud's theory is an example of a family-socialization theory, represented in its modern social-psychological version by the work of Parsons (1958, 334), who believes that the incest taboo "insures that new families of procreation will be set up by persons socialized in two distinct families of orientation." The main methodological problem of this theory has consisted in the fact that, to the extent that nuclear family structure and incest prohibitions are universal, there is no way to test the covariance of one with the other (Aberle et al., 1963).

Fortunately, two fascinating "experiments of nature" offer convincing evidence regarding incest aversion, one of the great problems of anthropology and sociology.

Incest Aversion and the Freud-Westermarck Debate

The intellectual strategy underlying Freud's Oedipalist perspective is best illustrated in the historical-anthropological speculations of *Totem and Taboo.* In this small book, one of Freud's favorites (Strachey, 1953, xi), he addresses the anthropological problems of totemism, exogamy, and incest aversion by interpreting the causal sequences he perceives in neurosis as a recapitulation of the cultural evolution of the human species. Through a "collective mind" approach to cultural evolution, he seeks to add a historical dimension to his explanation of neurosis, as the price human beings pay for civilized existence. Individuals become neurotic because they are striving to fulfill ancient cultural demands necessary to safeguard the nuclear family, and thus society, against unbridled sexual competition. These inevitably require the repression anew, in each generation, of individual sexual motives.

Totem and Taboo deals primarily with the phenomenon of incest aversion, which Freud regards, virtually by definition, as a cultural prohibition of universal provenance, seen in its starkest and most extreme form in a "horror of incest" among the people he takes to be the "most backward and miserable of savages" (1), the Australian aborigines. Noting that incest prohibitions in this culture are organized according to a complex system of classificatory kinship which, in keeping with a popular theory of the day, he takes as "a survival from the days of group marriage" (7), he concludes (7-8, italics in original) that "totemic exogamy, the prohibition of sexual intercourse between members of the same clan, appears to have been the appropriate means for preventing group incest; it thus became established and persisted long after its raison d'être had ceased." He notes that the aboriginal system of marriage classes extends far beyond the totemic groups (i.e., the group-marriage residues) in a "bewildering complexity" (8), and concludes that this must reflect the extremity of their horror of incest, which has led them to proliferate prohibitions in order to control and avoid it. He (9) infers from this that "they are probably liable to a greater temptation to it [incest] and for that reason stand in need of fuller protection." One notes, of course, the strong parallel to the reasoning he uses in developing his psychology of individual neurosis.

Carrying this parallel further by taking incest prohibitions as an example of the general class of cultural prohibitions or taboos, he extends his formula to the general class: That which is most strongly prohibited must be that which is most strongly, but unconsciously, desired. He now makes a phylogenetic leap from the cultural present to the distant past, and back again:

> Taboos, we must suppose, are prohibitions of primaeval antiquity which were at some time externally imposed upon a generation of primitive man; they must, that is to say, no doubt have been impressed on them violently by the previous generation. *These prohibitions must have concerned activities towards which there was a strong inclination.* They must then have persisted from generation to generation, perhaps merely as a result of tradition transmitted through parental and social authority. Possibly, however, in later generations they may have become "organized" as an inherited psychical endowment. Who can decide whether such things as "innate ideas" exist, or whether in the present instance they have operated, either alone or in conjunction with education, to bring about the

permanent fixing of taboos? *But one thing would certainly follow from the persistence of the taboo, namely that the original desire to do the prohibited thing must also still persist among the tribes concerned.* (31, my italics)

Here we see quite clearly the symmetry between Freud's psychologies of neurosis and of cultural prohibition, a symmetry based on *analogy* between the latter and what he takes to be the paradigmatic history and pattern of neurosis: the child's desire to touch his or her genitals—external prohibition—acceptance of the prohibition out of "love" for the prohibitor—repression of the desire, with resulting conflict and ambivalence (29). He bolsters this argument with many illustrations, taken mostly from Frazer's *Golden Bough,* indicating ambivalent attitudes associated with various cultural practices in the treatment of enemies, of rulers, and of the dead (chapter 2) and with practices involving animistic and magical thinking (chapter 3). Since Freud's psychology of neurosis depends on an implausible notion of instinct and on a confusion of cause with effect, internal motives with external pressures, and obedience with love, it would seem likely that the extension of this paradigm to cultural prohibitions and practices would, to say the least, suffer from the same basic fault.

Indeed, when Freud returns to his main theme of incest aversion as the "root of exogamy" and totemism (122), in order to debate the man who poses the greatest challenge to culturalist views, these logical faults proliferate. This man, the Finnish sociologist and moral philosopher Edward Westermarck, had startled the world of cultural anthropology and functional sociology by putting forward, in his 1891 (and multiple later editions) *History of Human Marriage,* a Darwinian theory of incest aversion, involving a complex developmental instinct that evolved through natural selection.

Westermarck was the first evolutionary anthropologist. Contrary to Freud, who was mainly interested in evolutionary theory for what it could tell us about paternal authority, he was primarily interested in how the evolution of families and social organization reflect the increasing importance of paternal care of the young, an interest that informed his larger project on the development of morality. In light of evolutionary thinking and what was then known about primate social organization and preliterate cultures, Westermarck considered it unlikely that early man engaged in promiscuous sexual intercourse, that classificatory kinship systems were a residue of earlier group marriage practices, or that aversion to incest could be adequately explained by law, custom, or tradition. Rather, he speculated, the instinctual aversion to incest and inbreeding (which would be harmful to the species) found in lower animals has probably evolved into a complex human behavioral instinct:

The home is kept pure from incestuous defilement neither by laws, nor by customs, nor by education, but by an *instinct* which under normal circumstances makes sexual love between the nearest kin a psychical impossibility. (1891, 319; italics in original)[12]

As to the proximate mechanism, he speculates

> that there is an innate aversion to sexual intercourse between persons living very closely together from early youth, and that, as such persons are in most cases related, this feeling displays itself chiefly as a horror of intercourse between near kin. (320)

The biological cause of this aversive instinct is the detrimental effect of inbreeding, which is independent of man's *awareness* of the effect, a late development. Summarizing what was then known (not very much) about the effects of inbreeding in plants, animals, and humans, Westermarck concludes:

> I cannot but believe that consanguineous marriages, in some way or other, are more or less detrimental to the species. And here, I think, we may find a quite sufficient explanation of the horror of incest; not because man at an early stage recognized the injurious influence of close intermarriage, but because the law of natural selection must inevitably have operated. (352)

Westermarck's hypothesis has turned out to be remarkably good, and impressive evidence has accumulated in recent years to support it. This theory and Freud's argument against it have framed the "Freud-Westermarck debate," a debate that has generated some of the most productive social science of recent times.

Freud puts forward two objections. For one thing, he cannot believe that an instinct could possess the degree of complexity Westermarck attributed to it. In keeping with his view of instinct as a simple biological urge and his corresponding assumption that the psychological expression of such an instinct would be fairly direct, he considered Westermarck's instinct impossibly sophisticated. Ignoring the fact that a behavioral instinct mechanism would be expected to respond to a complex stimulus like childhood familiarity, not a legal category like kinship (which categorization, not blood relation, commonly controls incest rules), he (1913, 123) argues that:

[12] In the fifth edition of his book Westermarck dropped the words "instinct" and "instinctual" in favor of the term "innate aversion," in order (as he explained in a later article [1934, 40]) to avoid useless controversy about the term. The term has again become quite controversial, and some thinkers have favored dropping it, tainted as it has been by outmoded notions of biological determinism. I consider this an unsatisfactory terminological avoidance of important conceptual problems. The distinction between "innate" and "instinctual" is one without real difference, and the use of concepts like "biological disposition" simply begs important questions rather than solving them. In this chapter and throughout this book, I will use the word "instinct" where I mean innate, genetically programmed behavioral disposition. Hopefully, any ambiguity surrounding the term will be clarified by context and usage.

> A biological instinct of the kind suggested would scarcely have gone so far astray in its psychological expression that, instead of applying to blood-relatives (intercourse with whom might be injurious to reproduction), it affected persons who were totally innocuous in this respect, merely because they shared a common home.[13]

Secondly, he finds unexceptionable Frazer's objection, that if Westermarck were correct prohibitions would be unnecessary, so much so that he (1913, 123; citing Frazer, 1910, 97) quotes him at length:

> It is not easy to see why any deep human instinct should need to be reinforced by law. There is no law commanding men to eat and drink or forbidding them to put their hands in the fire.... The law only forbids men to do what their instincts incline them to do; what nature itself prohibits and punishes, it would be superfluous for the law to prohibit and punish. Accordingly, we may always safely assume that crimes forbidden by law are crimes which many men have a natural propensity to commit.... Instead of assuming, therefore, from the legal prohibition of incest that there is a natural aversion to incest, we ought rather to assume that there is a natural instinct in favour of it, and that if the law represses it, as it represses other natural instincts, it does so because civilized men have come to the conclusion that the satisfaction of these natural instincts is detrimental to the general interests of society.

Considering these two arguments decisive, Freud (123) concludes that "the view which explains the horror of incest as an innate instinct must be abandoned."

Rejecting Westermarck's biogenetic Darwinian explanation, Freud's choice is to develop a "historical" (125) explanation of incest aversion, which he does in the final sections of *Totem and Taboo,* under the rubric of a "return of totemism" in childhood. This is a suprapersonal extension of his concept of the "return of the repressed" in individual neurosis; what "returns" to inform the modern child's attitudes toward self and others, and sometimes to produce neurosis, is in the nature of a racial complex of memory, conflicted feeling, urge toward totemism, and counter-urge. Here again he (126-132) notes an analogy between totemlike experiences in childhood (notably, animal phobias with their associated ambivalent attitudes toward fathers) and the experience of totemism in primitive cultures. He proposes, however, that this analogy is more than analogy, is in fact a behavioral homology reflecting the same mental structure. That is, present-day clinical phenomena reflect an organized

[13] This is a version of what the philosopher Bernard Williams later called the "representation problem." The argument of Frazer's that Freud endorses in the succeeding text paragraph is an attempt to solve what I call the "necessity problem." I will discuss both problems further on.

mental structure that is continuous (largely by cultural transmission, but perhaps also by biogenetic inheritance) with a structure of great antiquity.

It is of the greatest significance that Freud's theory is an argument by homology, in contrast to his earlier arguments (e.g., that primeval man must have experienced more severe incestuous temptation) based on analogies between cultural taboos and obsessional neurosis. It underscores the importance of the anthropological theory of incest aversion for his entire psychoanalytic project. For in going from argument by analogy to argument by homology, Freud is going from description to an attempt at explanation. Although he would later (1915 letter to Ferenczi, quoted in Grubrich-Simitis, 1987, 80; see also Grubrich-Simitis, 1988) characterize his anthropological speculations as "phylogenetic fantasy," it should be clear that his idea of neurosis representing a "return of totemism" and other phylogenetic models represents a serious causal theory. In this regard, it is important to note that the proposed mechanisms of transmission or continuity are ambiguous. Although Freud's strong rejection of Westermarck's hypothesis, coupled with his predominant theory of cultural transmission, creates the impression of a stark contrast between opposite theories (which I believe is substantially the case), it is also true that Freud acknowledges at various points in *Totem and Taboo* and elsewhere the possibility that biogenetic inheritance plays a role. We will need to consider the significance of this acknowledgment. Modern Freudians for the most part divorce themselves from the problematic biology and serious philosophical issues entailed in these arguments, seeing the universality of the Oedipus complex as based rather on "the species-specific constants of the early human experience (the care and early libidinal attachment between the caretaker, mother, infant, etc.)" (Suarez-Orozco, 1988, 269).

Freud's argument is in the nature of an historical reconstruction of the emergence of human consciousness, complete with father-guilt and unconscious ambivalence, out of the hominid "primal horde" social organization proposed by Darwin. In this reconstruction the adolescent males of the horde, excluded from power and sexual privileges by the dominant patriarch, banded together at some point in the primeval past and rose in rebellion against the patriarch, killing and probably devouring him, usurping his power and his women, that is, their group mothers and sisters. The consequent remorse over their deed led them to mistrust each other to the extent that they could not enjoy their spoils. As a means of survival, they partially relinquished their ill-gotten gains, transformed their relationship into one of friendship, and sought symbolic atonement by resurrecting the slain father. This took the form of totemic beings (typically animals) representing spiritual ancestors toward whom they maintained an ambivalent attitude, worshiping and seeking permission from them but periodically reenacting the primal murder, slaughtering and eating them. The totemic organization of society that is thus established is the primal source of religion, kingship, and later the patriarchal state. As Fox (1980, 79-80) points out, this reconstruction, which has been amply criticized, even by Freud himself, does not necessarily imply a single discrete event but multiple events, or a pattern of behavior, developing at a certain stage in human evolution.

Critique of Freud's Theory

Freud's theory of the incest taboo is described by anthropologists and sociologists as a "family theory," that is, of societal prohibitions designed to safeguard the nuclear family against unbridled sexual competition. It is a member of a larger set of theories that he based on a social-construction interpretation of incest aversion and other cultural regulations. It is plausible, though not very probable, that universal cultural regulations could arise strictly through voluntary action and their effects be transmitted by cultural tradition. The greater probability of a biogenetic theory is based on the logical presumption that cultural invariants strongly imply genetic determinants, whereas strict cultural determinism ought to be associated with wide variability (Ruse, 1981-1982, 123).

This being said, one must recognize that Freud's is not a strict social-construction theory and can be read as implying or being compatible with a biogenetic theory. There are passages in *Totem and Taboo* and elsewhere that support the idea that he realized a strict social-construction theory was implausible and envisioned rather a coevolution of a biogenetic tendency (which depends for its "activation" on specific input from the social environment, as described in his scheme of Oedipal development within the family) and cultural norms corresponding to or derived from it. For example, immediately following his presentation in *Totem and Taboo* (31) of what would appear to be a pure social-construction theory of taboo transmission ("perhaps merely as a result of tradition transmitted through parental and social authority"), he raises the possibility that "in later generations they may have become 'organized' as an inherited psychical endowment." And in the final section of the book he deals more extensively with the problems of a purely sociological view:

> Social psychology shows very little interest, on the whole, in the manner in which the required continuity in the mental life of successive generations is established. A part of the problem seems to be met by the inheritance of psychical *dispositions* which, however, need to be given some sort of impetus in the life of the individual before they can be roused into actual operation. (158, my italics)

Similarly, in the earlier *Three Essays on the Theory of Sexuality* (1905c, 177-178) he writes: "One gets an impression . . . that the construction of these dams [against sexuality] is a product of education, and no doubt education has much to do with it. But in reality this development is organically determined and fixed by heredity . . . ." And in a footnote added to the 1915 edition of that work (225n3) he states that the incest taboo "has no doubt already become established in many persons by organic inheritance."

In this reading, as anthropologists like Fox (1980) and Spain (1987, 1988) have noted, the contrast between the Westermarck and Freud theories of incest aversion is not as great as would appear, or as both authors made them appear.

I find it difficult to believe, however, as so many commentators do (e.g., Wallace, 1983, 192-193), that Freud's "vacillation" with regard to biogenetic versus cultural transmission reflects a real openness to ideas rather than his characteristic ambivalence toward established convention and authority. In his theorizing about incest aversion, Freud's acknowledgment of biogenesis does very little to change the center of gravity of his argument, which says that every generation must learn, through obedience to irrational patriarchal authority, to create the Oedipus complex anew. Biogenesis for him functions like "general intelligence" in the arguments mounted against Chomskyan cognitive theory (see articles in Piattelli-Palmarini, 1980). It equips and predisposes individuals in each generation to rediscover the need for patriarchal authority and the Oedipus complex, the specifics of which are provided by family and society.

Thus, although I acknowledge a certain theoretical convergence between Freud and Westermarck, I believe it is superficial and not a basis for reconciling the two thinkers in a significant way, as attempted by Fox (1972, 1980) and, later, Spain (1987, 1988). Fox, one of the foremost modern anthropological researchers into kinship and incest, observes that in cases where the development of normal incest aversion fails through unnecessarily strict sexual prohibitions in childhood (the typical situation in the Victorian Vienna into which Freud was acculturated), incest aversion is nonetheless guaranteed through more draconian means like neurotic anxiety and guilt. He argues that incestuous fantasies and neurotic guilt could be interpreted as biogenetic in origin, a subspecies of a more straightforward developmental progression in the "normal" Westermarckian case. This is supported by (1972, 1980) an elegant (but seriously flawed; see, e.g., Parker, 1976, 295-298) theory of human evolution from primates.

In other words, the expression of the anti-incest instinct is in Fox's view complicated by the fact that child-rearing norms in our society have involved such poor understanding of natural development (for example, overconcern about childhood sexuality) that we have actually made our tasks as parents more complicated, producing consequences that are unintended and even opposite from what we intend, for example, unnecessary blocks in the path of psychosexual maturity. What Fox calls the "Freud effect" (1980, 50) is an example of such unintended consequences as a result of improper understanding: "Cultures which essay to prevent incest between siblings often manage to promote precisely the feelings they aim to inhibit" (19).[14] Why that understanding justifies Fox's special pleading on behalf of Freud is hard to understand. The aim of a clinical psychology like psychoanalysis is to understand mental reality and promote psychological health. It is curious that, for Fox, Freud's endorsement and justification of an incorrect and neurotogenic understanding of psychosexual development does not diminish his belief that those understandings are compatible with Westermarck's, which carry radically different implications for clinical psychoanalysis.

Fox's efforts to rescue Freud, in other words, miss the main intellectual and practical points of the controversy, certainly as far as psychoanalysis is concerned. If cultural incest aversion is built upon a precultural, phylogenetic base and requires sexual freedom and intimacy with siblings in early childhood for its "activation," in the manner of other complex behavioral instincts, then prohibitions against the very conditions required for the normal unfolding of the instinct are not only biologically unnecessary but counterproductive and pathogenic—a fact with enormous implications for the science and ethics of child rearing, education, social policy, and psychotherapy. Such prohibitions may be justified by traditional conceptions of childhood and parenting but not by an understanding of human nature, or by logic or morality. That cultural misunderstandings and unintended social and psychological consequences are normative is an important phenomenon to be *understood,* not mimicked in psychological and sociological systems.

Thus, the differences between the Freudian and Westermarckian approaches to incest aversion and to moral development generally remain profound, underscoring the need to think critically about them.

Brief History of the Freud-Westermarck Debate

Freud's theory of incest aversion was not, as he represented it, a radical departure from received opinion but rather a version of the dominant social-constructionist theory of the time, to which most anthropologists and sociologists subscribed well into this century. It is only in recent decades that the conflict between starkly opposed points of view, represented on one side by Freud and a great weight of authoritative opinion and on the other side by Westermarck, came to be of great interest for social science scholars, in part because of the availability of empirical evidence to resolve it, in part because of

[14] Popper (1962, 93 & n11, italics in original; see also 1957, 65) formulated as a principle of an autonomous sociology this "law of unintended consequences": "institutions and traditions . . . even those which arise as the result of conscious and intentional human actions are, as a rule, *the indirect, the unintended and often the unwanted byproducts of such actions.*"

a shift away from the dominant functional-culturalist paradigm. The incest taboo was and is widely regarded as one of the great problems of anthropology and sociology. Freud's view of incest aversion is central to his psychoanalytic system, determining how fantasy life is to be interpreted and treatment conducted. Thus, the critical attention that has come to be focused on theories of incest aversion combine questions about the coherence of the Freudian system with broader questions about human nature as reflected in anthropological, sociological, and psychological data. New findings and knowledge in these traditional fields have in recent decades fertilized the new fields of evolutionary biology, population genetics, and human sociobiology, which have inclined toward a Westermarckian solution of the incest problem. Given the rarity of natural experiments that can furnish critical tests of theories, the Freud-Westermarck debate constitutes one of the great chapters of contemporary social science, with enormous import for a rational theory of psychoanalysis.

Like many social science debates, this one was not altogether original with Freud and Westermarck, for both points of view have long histories. For this intellectual history I am indebted to Arthur Wolf's (1995) important monograph *Sexual Attraction and Childhood Association,* from which I draw freely in what follows. Wolf (6) notes that the basic intuition behind Westermarck's aversion hypothesis was "in the air" in the 1880s, with a number of German and English anthropologists referring to it. While Westermarck clearly deserves the credit for articulating it as a serious scientific hypothesis, its roots lie in ancient but always controversial intuitions about the natural source of moral ideas, just as the opposite theory, embraced by Freud, represents an even more ancient culturalist perspective. Wolf's earliest discovery of the explicit theory is in the work of the eleventh-century Sufi philosopher, al-Ghazali (Farah, 1984, 91), who argued that in choosing a wife one should take care that

> she not be a close relative, as that would lessen desire. . . . For desire is excited by the deep emotions which result from sight and touch; emotions are strengthened by whatever is unfamiliar and new . . . what is familiar and seen continuously renders the faculties incapable of fully appreciating it, being affected by it, or becoming aroused through it.

In the eighteenth century the great Scottish moral philosopher Francis Hutcheson (1725, 192, italics in original) argued: "Had we no *moral Sense natural* to us, we should only look upon *Incest* as hurtful to ourselves and shun it, and never hate other *incestuous Persons,* more than we do a *broken Merchant;* so that still this Abhorrence supposes a *Sense of moral good.*"

And in the early nineteenth century the British utilitarian philosopher Jeremy Bentham (1864, 220), writing about the social prohibitions against incest, wrote:

> nature . . . agrees sufficiently well with the principle of utility. It is very rare that the passion of love is developed within the circle of individuals to whom marriage ought to be forbidden. There needs to give birth to that sentiment a certain degree of surprise, a sudden effect of novelty. . . . Individuals accustomed to see each other and to know each other, from an age which is neither capable of conceiving the desire nor of inspiring it, will see each other with the same eyes to the end of life; and this inclination finds no determinate epoch whence to begin.

Westermarck's most consequential precursor, however, was likely Charles Darwin, whose work he studied carefully. Darwin (1868, vol. 2, 104) wrote:

> Although there seems to be no strong inherited feeling in mankind against incest, it seems possible that men during primeval times may have been more excited by strange females than by those with whom they habitually lived; in the same manner as according to Mr. Cupples, male deerhounds are inclined towards strange females, while the females prefer dogs with whom they have associated. If any such feeling formerly existed in man, this would have led to a preference for marriages beyond the nearest kin, and might have been strengthened by the offspring of such marriages surviving in greater numbers, as analogy would lead us to believe would have occurred.

On the other side of the debate, the culturalist perspective that Freud embraced has a longer tradition and one weightier with authority. Incest prohibitions occur very widely and are by all indications quite ancient. They typically involve traditional accounts of the consequences of incest or of the origins of the prohibitions. Culturalist attempts at rational explanations of incest taboos, like Frazer's and Freud's, blend imperceptibly with myth and tradition.[15] In the premodern era skeptical philosophers like Hutcheson, by raising the possibility that moral sentiments often have a natural base (as opposed to resting strictly on divine or civil authority), joined the issue at a philosophical level. Hutcheson had his antagonist in Mandeville, who (like Frazer and Freud later) argued for a strict social construction of incest taboos: "Such [incestuous] Alliances are abominable; but it is certain that, whatever Horror we conceive at the Thought of them, there is nothing in Nature repugnant against them, but what is built upon Mode and Custom" (Mandeville, 1723, 331).

The Freud-Westermarck debate is thus the twentieth-century version of a classical one, but now informed, as it would increasingly be during this century, by evolutionary theory and by the burgeoning new biological and social

[15] This point was made effectively by Levi-Strauss (1963), who emphasized the importance of studying all versions of an evolving cultural myth, and wrote (217): "Therefore . . . Freud himself should be included among the recorded versions of the Oedipus myth on a par with earlier or seemingly more 'authentic' versions."

science fields. Freud banked heavily on the social-construction view of incest aversion, a view that, as Wolf notes, carried the day not only in psychoanalysis but also in anthropology and sociology throughout most of this century. This was the case despite the demonstrable fact that many of the proponents of this view based their reasoning on a blatantly faulty logic and/or gross distortion of what Westermarck actually proposed, suggesting a strongly entrenched culturalist prejudice.

Wolf offers as a prime example of this culturalist prejudice, of a type often repeated, the conclusions drawn by the influential British anthropologists Hose and McDougall in *The Pagan Tribes of Borneo* (1912). They noted that, among the Kenyahs, where adoption is commonplace and where intercourse between a youth and his sister-by-adoption (or vice versa) is not regarded as incestuous, nor the relation a bar to marriage, only one such marriage occurred over many years of contact. Yet rather than seeing this evidence of spontaneous sexual aversion between men and women who had been raised together as siblings as support of the Westermarck hypothesis, the authors (vol. 2, 197) conclude that

> the occurrence of incest between couples brought up in the same household is, of course, difficult to reconcile with Prof. Westermarck's well-known theory of the ground of the almost universal feeling against incest, namely that it depends upon sexual aversion or indifference engendered by close proximity during childhood. . . . It seems to us that the feeling with which incest is regarded is an example of a feeling or sentiment engendered in each generation by law and tradition, rather than a spontaneous reaction of individuals, based on some instinct or innate tendency.

Westermarck (1917, 752; italics in original) responded by pointing out the obvious fallacy in Hose and McDougall's argument:

> Messrs. Hose and McDougall . . . seem to know of only one instance of marriage between young Kenyahs brought up together as adopted brother and sisters, although such marriages are allowed. To maintain that cases of this kind are fatal to my theory seems to me as illogical as it would be to assume that the occurrence of a *horror feminae* in many men disproves the general prevalence of a feeling of love between the sexes.

Similarly, he responded to the Frazer-Freud argument in a way that ought to have been decisive:

> [Frazer's] argument implies a curious misconception of the origin of legal prohibitions. Of course, where there is no transgression there is no law. But Sir James cannot be ignorant of the variability of instincts and of the great variability of the sexual instinct, nor of the fact that there are circumstances in which a natural sentiment may be blunted or overcome. Would he maintain that there can be no general aversion to bes-

> tiality because bestiality is forbidden by law, and that the exceptional severity with which parricide is treated by many law books proves that a large number of men have a natural propensity to kill their parents? The law expresses the general feeling of the community and punishes acts that shock them, but it does not tell us whether an inclination to commit the forbidden act is felt by many or few. (1922, vol. 2, 203-204)

Let us also briefly review Freud's response, in the years following *Totem and Taboo,* to the ongoing challenge to his views. He strove to keep the Westermarck hypothesis out of bounds by attacking it while misrepresenting it as the *dominant* position of "science" and himself as the lone champion of an unpopular view, while neither responding to Westermarck's rejoinders nor referring to him by name. In his *Introductory Lecture 13* (1915-1916, 210), for example, he refers derisively to the "tremendous efforts [which] have been made to explain this horror of incest," notably those who "have maintained that, as a result of living together from early childhood onwards, sexual desire has been diverted from the people in question." The language of the first English edition (1924, 220), the one personally approved by Freud, is harsher, the efforts being described as "preposterous." In *Lecture 21* (1916-1917, 334-335) he writes:

> You will not be able to recall without a smile the pronouncements of science in explanation of the prohibition of incest. There is no end to what has been invented on the subject. It has been said that sexual inclination is diverted from members of the same family who are of opposite sex by the fact of having lived together from childhood.

And lest it be thought that the incest issue was confined to the early work or that it ceased to be a key element in his psychology, here are characteristic quotations from some late works:

> Since the penis owes its extraordinarily high narcissistic cathexis to its organic significance for the propagation of the species, the catastrophe to the Oedipus complex (the abandonment of incest and the institution of conscience and morality) may be regarded as a victory of the race over the individual. (1925a, 257)

> It is recognized that early infantile sexual life reaches its peak in what is known as the Oedipus complex . . . . A horror of incest and an enormous sense of guilt are left over from this prehistoric epoch of the individual's existence. It may be that something quite similar occurred in the prehistoric epoch of the human species as a whole and that the beginning of morality, religion and social order were intimately connected with the surmounting of that primaeval era. (1925b, 220-221)

Our construction of prehistory forces us to another explanation. The command in favour of exogamy, of which the horror of incest is the negative expression, was a product of the will of the father and carried this will on after he had been removed. (1939, 121)

And finally, from his ultimate work of social philosophy, *Civilization and Its Discontents* (1930, 104): "Its [civilization's] first, totemic, phase already brings with it the prohibition against an incestuous choice of object, and this is perhaps the most drastic mutilation which man's erotic life has in all time experienced."

Freud recognized, in other words, what was at stake in the debate over incest. As Wolf (1995, 19) precisely puts it, in a statement quoted by E. O. Wilson (1998, 179; italics in original), he

> saw all too clearly that if Westermarck was right, *he* was wrong. The possibility that early childhood association suppressed sexual attraction has to be denied lest the basis of the Oedipus complex crumble and with it his conception of personality dynamics, his explanation of neuroses, and his grand view of the origins of law, art, and civilization.

Wolf recognizes that the Westermarck hypothesis implies an appraisal of the relation of the individual to society profoundly different from the Freudian view, one that permits and promotes criticism of cultural institutions in ways that are foreclosed by Freud. He (1995, 19, quoting Westermarck, 1917, 738) goes on to make an elegant argument for the broader significance of tests of the Westermarck hypothesis:

> There is [also] the question of whether or not those universal rules that regulate the human passions exist to repress human nature or as an expression of human nature. And . . . there is the closely related question, debated by Hutcheson and Mandeville, of what the existence of the incest taboo implies about the origins of morality. The orthodox anthropological view is that morality is primarily a matter of obligation and duty—which is to say that morality is "built upon Mode and Custom." An alternative view, developed by Westermarck in his work on ethics and applied to the incest taboo, is that moral concepts "are ultimately based on moral emotions."[16]

[16]The concept of "moral emotions" is bound to seem strange to readers used to thinking either in the physicalist mode now embraced by technological psychiatry, of emotions as biologically based derivatives of instincts, as energetic and discharge phenomena, etc.; or in the modern emotivist mode, of emotions as underwriting morality but registering nonmoral qualities like pleasure-unpleasure (see MacIntyre's discussion in *After Virtue* [1981, chapters 2-5]). Both modes are characteristic of Freud. In Westermarck's (1917, 738) very different conception, "moral emotions . . . are essentially generalisations of tendencies in certain phenomena to call forth either indignation or approval." They are emotional reactions informed by and implying moral judgments, and could as well (perhaps more precisely if less elegantly) be called "emotional forms of moral judgment."

Tests of the Westermarck and Freud Hypotheses

Provided other factors are adequately controlled, "to disprove the [Westermarck] hypothesis, one must show that a representative sample of boys and girls who are reared together from an early age remain sexually attracted to one another" (Wolf, 1995, 16.) Correspondingly, to disprove the Freud social-transmission theory one would have to show that a representative sample of boys and girls reared together as siblings and with an absence of sexual prohibitions do, nonetheless, develop normal incest aversion.

Beginning in the 1950s a number of social scientists set to work on detailed studies of people living in cultural settings that constituted large-scale natural tests of these rival theories. The accounts (Irvine, 1952; Shepher, 1969; Spiro, 1954, 1955, 1956, 1958; Talmon, 1964; Wolf, 1966, 1968, 1970, 1995; Wolf & Huang, 1980) of these natural experiments—the *sim-pua* or "minor" marriage tradition in Taiwan and communal child rearing in the early Israeli kibbutzim—are landmarks of modern anthropological research. The significance of these natural experiments is explained by Wolf (1995, 21-22):

> The problem was that in all of the societies known to anthropology in Westermarck's time, the children normally reared together were siblings, making it impossible to determine whether apparent lack of sexual attraction for one another was owing to early childhood association or to the moral restrictions imposed by the incest taboo. That Freud was judged the easy victor in his debate with Westermarck was probably at least in part because his interpretation of dreams and other fantasies appeared to give him a way of revealing what lay beneath the attitude demanded by society. This gave him the advantage of being able to argue that when society is discounted, there is a natural attraction, not a natural aversion. Westermarck was never able to counter the claim that what he took to be a natural aversion was only a social artifact.

In other words, absent a suitable test of either hypothesis, Freud's seemed closer to being backed by empirical evidence while Westermarck's seemed purely speculative.

In the two natural experiments children were raised together either (in the Israeli case) without any cultural prohibition against sex or later marriage or (in the Taiwan case) with the explicit expectation that they would marry when mature. Both cases, therefore, provide an opportunity to observe how people raised together and exempt from a cultural incest taboo would experience each other sexually as adults. The predictions from the Freud and Westermarck theories provide the starkest contrast. Freudian theory predicts that such people, subject to incestuous stimulation as children but deprived of the necessary socialization, would grow up into incestuous adults or, alternatively, into adults with severe psychopathology (defective superegos and severe defensive deformations of personality). Westermarck's theory predicts that such children would grow up with normal incest aversion and no special psychosexual pathology.

The nature of the evidence from the two experiments is slightly different, for in the Israeli case the children were free to have sex with and/or marry their childhood sweethearts or not, while in the Taiwan case they were expected or coerced to marry, despite whatever (often strong) aversion they might feel. Thus the crucial variables in the Israeli case, where aversion was free to manifest in avoidance, were (a) indications of sexual attraction between adolescents and adults raised together as children, as evidenced by sexual affairs and marriages, and (b) indications of sexual and personal pathology in the children as children or as adults. In the Taiwanese case, where aversion was for the most part not free to manifest in avoidance of marriage, the crucial dependent variables were (a) indications of sexual satisfaction with the designated marriage partners, as well as (b) general indications of psychopathology, as in the Israeli case.

The Kibbutz Experience

Kibbutzim are communal settlements in Israel, part of a movement begun in the early 1900s, in what was then Palestine, by idealistic young Jewish European immigrants. Beginning with a small group intensely committed to a communistic and egalitarian agrarian way of life, the movement has grown and evolved into a loose federation of socialistic or quasisocialistic agricultural-industrial settlements with differing ideologies, in which approximately 4 percent of the Israeli population live. Kibbutzim are thus the most successful and persistent "Western" communes of the twentieth century. Their special interest for social science lies in the fact that, especially in the first several generations (later developments have led them to more closely resemble the dominant surrounding society), their social organization and especially their child-rearing practices challenged major sociological and psychological theories, notably about nuclear families, mother-child relations, and psychosexual development. For the kibbutz founders set about to deliberately destroy both reliance on private property and the nuclear patriarchal family, seen as a main source of sexism, authoritarianism, and inequality, with resulting distortions of personality. Many of the founders were explicitly anti-Freudian Marxists who saw the Oedipus complex as a product of bourgeois patriarchal society. While the guiding ideologies of these founders combined Marxism, anarchism, and Zionism, the mode of collective and coeducational child rearing developed in the early decades also corresponded quite well to a Westermarckian view of sexual development. As a way of promoting a collective consciousness with intellectual independence (these were not seen as conflicting goals) and undermining the destructive effects of property-owning nuclear families, children were raised from birth in "children's houses" and cared for by nurses, teachers, and each other, while contact with biological parents was minimal.

A good brief description of the common features of the kibbutz as it existed in the 1950s and early 1960s, when intense social-scientific interest was focused on the emerging "second generation" of young adults raised in this system, is provided by Talmon (1964, 491), one of the early researchers, who reported on three long-established and representative kibbutzim:

> The main features . . . are common ownership of property except for a few personal belongings and communal organization of production and consumption. Members' needs are provided for by communal institutions on an equalitarian basis. All income goes into the common treasury; each member gets only a very small annual allowance for personal expenses. The community is run as a single economic unit and as a single household. Husband and wife have independent jobs. . . . In most Kibbutzim children live apart from their parents and are looked after by members assigned to this task. They spend a few hours every day with their parents and siblings, but from their birth on they sleep, eat and study in special children's houses. Each age group leads its own life and has its autonomous arrangements.

Of particular interest from the point of view of the Freud-Westermarck controversy is the adult treatment of childhood sexual interests and behavior, which is extremely permissive. The children, living in small mixed groups close in age with nurses and teachers, are raised like siblings, with abundant opportunity to see, touch, and play with each other in all the activities of daily life, including toileting:

> [S]exual manifestations in young children are viewed as normal. Living and sleeping quarters are bisexual during this [early] stage. Children of different sexes sleep in the same room, shower together, play and run around in the nude and there is a considerable amount of wrestling, tickling, exploring, soothing and caressing between them. This close contact between the sexes continues until the second or third grade, and then decreases with age. Gradually, a sense of sexual shame emerges, and a growing distance between the sexes. (Talmon, 1964, 502-503)

This distance tends to increase until early adolescence, exacerbated by the earlier puberty of the girls, and then to diminish. The communal rearing and education continues through high school, after which the adolescents, now eligible for membership in the kibbutz, live independently. Adolescents are strongly discouraged from having sex in high school (and most abstain), but after graduation they "may engage in sexual relations with impunity and are given a free hand with respect to choice of mate" (503). "Mate selection is considered a purely personal and private matter and there is a strict ban against meddling in the process of choice" (499).

The striking finding from Talmon's study is that the young adults raised in this way are spontaneously exogamous. For the most part they become dedicated and hard-working members of the kibbutz and maintain friendships with peers but lose interest in them as sexual objects, turning (rarely, 3 percent) to adjacent peer groups, to the adult kibbutz population, or members who were socialized elsewhere and joined later (31 percent), to other kibbutzim (23 percent), or to the general society (43 percent) for lovers and mates. Of the 125 couples from three kibbutzim Talmon studied, "there was not one instance in which both mates were reared from birth in the same peer group" (492).

Other observers (Bettelheim, 1969; Rabin, 1965; Spiro, 1958) reported similar findings. Reviewing these data with a view toward refining and testing the Westermarck hypothesis, Shepher (1971, 228-237; summarized in 1983) thought it likely that the "Westermarck effect" operates maximally when there is continuous cosocialization from birth to six years, along the lines of an "imprinting" model. He therefore studied the marriage patterns of virtually the entire second generation of kibbutz adults (excluding 2.5 percent who lived in religious kibbutzim, for which data were unavailable; leaving 2,769 married couples from 211 kibbutzim), seeking to determine the early history of socialization. To the extent that he was able, he also investigated premarital sex among 42 second-generation adolescents from one kibbutz. His findings are even more striking. In the one kibbutz he studied in depth for sexual patterns, there was "not a single case of intra-peergroup (i.e., between children reared in the same educational group) sexual partnership" (1971, 217). The study of marriage patterns across the entire sample involved computer analysis and follow-up contact in cases suggesting marriage between cosocialized adults (he assumed that couples differing in age by less than two years were potentially members of the same socialization group). Of 60 such couples, 46 came from different peer groups. Of the remaining 14 "there were only 5 in which the spouses had been in the same peer group at any time before 6 years of age, and, of these, none had been socialized together during all 6 years" (1983, 59).

These findings appear to constitute a refutation of Freud's theory while lending strong support to Westermarck. An upbringing in which there is highly sexual intimacy between effective siblings, in the absence of prohibition and despite encouragement to marry—in short, a deliberate transgression of Oedipal norms—leads to a definite, spontaneous exogamous tendency at adolescence and progression to healthy adulthood rather than the deficiency of control predicted by Freudian theory.

The Taiwanese Experience

Arthur Wolf's research (Wolf, 1966, 1968, 1970, 1995; Wolf & Huang, 1980) is the result of the combination of an extraordinary set of circumstances and an extraordinarily perceptive and meticulous researcher. Unusual in his early appreciation of the Westermarck hypothesis, Wolf found himself as a young anthropologist in one of the few societies on earth (Hokkien-speaking peasants in northern Taiwan) that provided the natural conditions for testing it. This society had institutionalized multiple marriage forms, in one of which prospective husband and wife are also sociological brother and sister. These parallel marriage forms, combined with extensive household registers compiled by Japanese colonial officials during the period 1906-1945, provided remarkable conditions for testing the hypotheses. An ideal set of conditions would be

> at least two forms of marriage, one of which involved early and intimate association, while the other prohibited all contact between the parties prior to marriage . . . early and intimate association to be the only difference between the two forms of marriage . . . the process by which individuals were selected for the two forms of marriage to be essentially random . . . early association with their husbands or the absence thereof to be the only difference in the premarital experience of the women selected for the two forms of marriage . . . the general socioeconomic conditions under which people lived after marriage to be essentially uniform . . . [and] an objective means of measuring sexual attraction in a large population. (Wolf, 1995, 22)

Although these ideal conditions were not met, the actual circumstances of life in this part of Taiwan during these years approximated them closely enough that, through public records combined with fieldwork, Wolf has been able to provide an impressive series of experimental tests.

In this highly authoritarian society in which all marriages are arranged without consultation of the betrothed, there are two (patrilocal and uxorilocal) forms of "major" marriage (referring to bride and groom meeting as adults) and one form of "minor" or *sim-pua* ("little daughter-in-law") marriage. In the latter the designated bride is raised, usually from early infancy, in the home of her intended groom, typically several years her elder, the marriage taking place (often in the face of considerable reluctance of the betrothed) at adolescence.[17]

[17] While I use the present tense to describe this culture, *sim-pua* marriage as Wolf studied it is now largely a thing of the past in Taiwan, although it probably persists in rural enclaves on the mainland. Depending as it did on almost absolute parental authority and the conditions of village life, it began to break down toward the end of the Japanese occupation as economic alternatives provided young people the wherewithal to resist parental demands. By the end of the Japanese occupation in 1945 its incidence had dropped to 10 percent of patrilocal marriages (Wolf, 1970, 505), as opposed to nearly half in the first decades of the century. The Japanese and later the Communist Chinese attacked it as a backward feudal custom, and it was finished off in Taiwan by later social, political, and economic changes (Wolf, 1995, 215-220).

Thus the *sim-pua* and her husband are sociological siblings, and Westermarck's hypothesis predicts sexual aversion between them at maturity compared to major marriage, as well as generally normal psychic development.

There are significant differences between the two major-marriage forms. Patrilocal marriage is highly esteemed. The bride is assimilated into the household of her husband's family, takes his surname, and the children are considered part of his lineage. By contrast, uxorilocal marriage is a degraded form resorted to by poor men desperate for wives and by families who had failed to produce sons of their own. It more or less drastically contravenes the basic values of the kinship system and is regarded as morally suspect. Uxorilocal marriage consists of a spectrum of arrangements: at one extreme, the husband assumes his father-in-law's surname and agrees to work for his wife's family and have all his children assigned to his father-in-law's lineage; at the other, the husband retains all his rights as a father, simply agreeing to work for his father-in-law's family for a certain number of years.

Citing his own and others' (Fei, 1939; Okada, 1949; Wu, 1943) observations, Wolf provides an important cultural analysis of the reasons for the minor marriage tradition. Although there are some narrow economic advantages for very poor families they are clearly not decisive, offset as they are by economic and strategic disadvantages. Besides, minor marriage is prevalent among the wealthy. It is only understandable as an attempt to solve certain severe problems intrinsic to Chinese family life; notably the intense conflicts created between mothers-in-law and daughters-in-law. In this society sons are highly prized as heirs, sources of wealth, and security in old age, while women are officially inferior, fit only for menial labor and the bearing of (ideally, male) children. As mothers and mothers-in-law, however, they carry great authority within the family, able to discipline their children (including grown children) with impunity. The marriage of a son creates tremendous difficulties as its normative consequence, for the mother-in-law's status and influence are threatened. She is jealous and seeks to dominate the daughter-in-law so as to prevent her from stealing the son away, creating a vicious circle of strife that typically ends only with the death of the mother-in-law or the physical removal of the younger family. Given these conditions, marriage is heavily burdened with the need to balance tradition and novelty, obedience and transgression, accomplished largely by a split between official appearance and private behavior:

> The Chinese ideal of a distant and unemotional relationship between husband and wife recognizes the danger of a mother's jealousy. A man should never display any affection for his wife outside the privacy of their bedroom, and so far as possible he should avoid even speaking to her except to give orders. (Wolf, 1968, 869)

From certain points of view

> [i]t is the minor rather than the major form of marriage that comes closest to achieving this ideal. Raised from early childhood as a member of her future husband's family, the daughter-in-law does accept his parents as her own parents. She is first a daughter and only later and secondarily a daughter-in-law and a wife. (870)

Looked at in this way, the source of the difficulty for this society is nothing other than the incest taboo itself. To the extent it is adhered to, it prevents parents from doing what they would otherwise be inclined to do to promote domestic harmony: namely, marry their children to each other. Minor marriage is an attempt to circumvent the taboo by respecting the letter of the law (no sibling marriage) while creating effective siblings for marriage and thus keeping authority within the family. This is another way of understanding why it is such an important proving ground for the Freud-Westermarck controversy. As in the Israeli kibbutzim, the society (i.e., family and state authority) has, for reasons of its preservation and progress, set aside incest law, inviting and encouraging its young to do likewise. According to Freud's theory, such cultural laxity should reinforce their natural proclivities, resulting in severe psychological deformation as adults. According to Westermarck, they should do nothing of the sort but demonstrate a spontaneous aversion to what their elders have invited them to do.

In his early research Wolf took the minor form of marriage as the experimental condition and the major forms as its control, his object being to test the hypothesis that early intimate cosocialization diminishes erotic attraction at maturity. Since Kinsey-style direct reports of sexual experience were not feasible, he decided (1995, 36)

> to move one step further down the causal chain to easily observable, public events that are at least partly the result of sexual satisfaction or its absence—namely adultery, divorce, and fertility. [He] made three simple assumptions. The first is that if childhood association inhibits sexual attraction, minor marriages will give rise to more adultery than major and uxorilocal marriages. The second is that if childhood association inhibits sexual attraction, minor marriages will produce fewer children than major and uxorilocal marriages [remember this is a noncontracepting society in which children are highly prized sources of esteem, wealth, and security]. And the third is that if childhood association inhibits sexual attraction, minor marriages will be terminated by divorce more frequently than major and uxorilocal marriages.

In addition to official records he used classical fieldwork to gain information about incidence of adultery and illegitimacy. His work has expanded over thirty years from a single village and 300 marriages between 1900 and 1925 (1966, 1970) to twenty-six villages and two towns in two culturally distinct regions in the years 1905 to 1945, based on 164,000 years of marital experience (1995, 39).

Wolf's early findings from two locales (all these results are from Wolf, 1970, except as noted) were striking. Comparing 132 minor marriages with 171 major marriages (of both types), he found that 24 percent of the former ended in divorce or separation compared with 1.2 percent of the latter. Female adultery, uncommon and risky in this society, occurred with a frequency of 33 percent, compared to 11 percent in major marriages. Married men's use of prostitutes was three times higher in minor versus major marriages (1966, 889). Combining divorce and female adultery as indices of marital dissatisfaction, 46 percent of minor marriages ended in divorce or involved adultery compared to 11 percent of major marriages. And there was a striking difference in the fertility of marriages. Based on official records, major marriages were 34 percent more productive. Corrected for information about parentage (i.e., illegitimate children registered to father's lineage), the figure jumped to 51 percent. These figures probably underestimate the differences in coital frequency, given what is known about its relation to fecundability (Potter & Millman, 1985).

Wolf also discovered a group of forty-two women in the major marriage set who had been raised as *sim-pua* but ended up marrying uxorilocally or patrilocally, usually because of the death of their intended husband. Information about this group's marriages provided a natural control for a complex of possible psychological and social effects of the *sim-pua* experience that might well affect stability of marriage and fertility, such as adoption trauma or poverty. On all measures of marital dissatisfaction the differences between this group and the minor marriage group were as great or greater than demonstrated by the general population of major marriages. Wolf concluded that

> Although adopted daughters do experience trauma and deprivation and may represent a lower stratum of society, this is not the reason they bear fewer children, divorce their husbands, and sleep with other men. There is no evidence of unusual marital dissatisfaction as long as they marry a stranger; problems only arise when they are forced to marry a childhood associate. (514)

In his later work Wolf (Wolf & Huang, 1980; Wolf, 1995) refined his means of controlling for confounding variables and examined differences *within* the minor-marriage group according to age at adoption, so as to test the "critical period" aspect of the Westermarck hypothesis proposed by Shepher. To briefly summarize an impressive body of work, the results indicate that the bulk of the effect of early association on sexual dissatisfaction is traceable to experience in the first three years of life, suggesting strongly that this, not the six years thought by Shepher, is the critical period for the Westermarck effect.

Of special interest for anthropology and psychoanalysis is Wolf's discussion of the dependence of *sim-pua* marriage on the authority structure of the traditional Taiwanese family and the Chinese state. Reflecting on the prevalence of the practice and its rapid decline during and after the revolutionary upheavals of the pre- and postwar period, which substantially weakened (previously virtually absolute) patriarchal authority in the family, Wolf invites the reader to engage in a thought experiment. Consider, he asks, what conclusions an anthropologist would have likely drawn from the prevalence alone, as high as 80 percent in some districts, of the minor marriage tradition in South China. The following interpretation, he (1995, 215, quoting an imaginary anthropologist) suggests, would be likely:

> The interesting case of the minor form of marriage in China, by which husband and wife were reared together as intimately as most brothers and sisters, demonstrates beyond doubt that Westermarck was mistaken in arguing that childhood association inhibits sexual attraction. In some communities in South China marriages of this kind constituted 70 to 80 percent of all marriages and thus could not have entailed the dire consequences predicted by Westermarck.

It is easy, in other words, to be misled by cultural practices considered apart from the authority structure of the family and larger society. In the Chinese case these provided the warrant for parents to maintain an oppressive marriage institution that forced young people to behave contrary to their natural inclinations. As state-backed parental authority eroded, young men and women began rebelling against the institution in large numbers. The fact that *sim-pua* couples rebelled in various effective ways to attain a normal life, when provided the opportunity, and often in the face of great disadvantages and obstacles, suggests strongly that they were not the subhuman creatures predicted by Freudian theory but healthy and resourceful men and women.

The Israeli and Taiwanese experiments lend powerful support to Westermarck's hypothesis that the environmental requirement for activation of the incest-aversion instinct is early socialization of a friendly and intimate sort with peers and siblings—not the learning of incest taboos, as Freud would have it. When this condition is met, a strong aversion to incest arises spontaneously at adolescence, and people develop normally, perhaps even unusually healthily —after all, it takes unusual confidence and courage for a *sim-pua* bride or groom to rebel. In both the Taiwanese and Israeli cases we might say that the adolescents innately "knew better" than the adult society that encouraged them, for reasons of authority and cultural uniformity, to marry their (effective) sisters and brothers.

As difficult as it was for Frazer and Freud to believe, the existence of cultural prohibitions does not necessarily mean that the thing prohibited represents an instinctual inclination and that what separates man from beast or child is the learning of cultural prohibitions. In the case of incest, whether or not the taboo is universal, it appears to be unnecessary, at least to control incest (it obviously has other purposes, which I will explore in Chapter 4).

The outcome of *sim-pua* marriage exemplifies "the law of unintended consequences" in a way ironically complementary to the Victorian neuroses Freud suffered and studied: In both cases the society sought, to its detriment, to impose on its young people social disciplines that undermined their instinctual inclinations. Victorian child rearing sought to impose incest aversion precociously and unnecessarily, depriving children of needed intimacy, producing exaggerated and displaced moralistic conflicts in the form of neuroses, and damaging the capacity for adult love. The *sim-pua* form of marriage, developed to solve terrible self-imposed social difficulties, sought to force adolescents to marry their siblings. It brought about marital misery, infertility, infidelity, and breakup, and increased rather than decreased resentment of parental authority. One would be hard put to prefer one of these forms of psychosocial pathology over the other, but it seems folly indeed to infer profound laws of human nature from either of these specific European or Chinese modes of upbringing.

Parent-Child Incest

Both the Israeli and Taiwanese experiments bear on sibling incest. It is natural to ask whether there is any evidence from parent-child incest that substantiates the Westermarck hypothesis, which states that incest aversion is promoted by friendly intimacy with those with whom one grows up. In the kibbutzim this included a broad range of prepubertal sexual intimacy between peers. The formula relating childhood sexual activity to sibling incest aversion at maturity would therefore seem to be: "Incest in childhood prevents incest later." It is reasonable to assume that incest aversion works the same way between children and parents as between siblings, while its specifics have evolved in correspondence with those relationships. Thus, breast-feeding and related forms of intimate bodily care (all more or less "incestuous") might well exemplify the requirement for mother-child aversion; and perhaps nurturance and physical play for fathers and children. If that is so, we would expect that parent-child intimacy in early childhood would be a factor in inhibiting parent-child incest at puberty and adolescence, when children are at high risk of unwanted sexual contact. The one study which, to my knowledge, set out to test this prediction with respect to father-daughter incest provided confirmatory results.

In a well-designed study comparing men who had sexually abused their minor daughters with a control population, Parker and Parker (1986) tested the Westermarck hypothesis along with one derived from attachment theory to the effect that sexually abusive fathers are more likely to have experienced instability and deprivation as children. Their study indicates that both early deprivation in the father's family of orientation and lack of involvement in nurturant activities during the child's early years (through physical absence or otherwise), but not biological status, are causally related to later child abuse. Nurturant activities included diapering, washing, dressing, feeding, putting to bed, playing, reading, recreational outings, caring for when sick, and showing physical affection through kissing, cuddling, and holding. Contrary to a widely held belief (e.g., Finkelhor, 1979, 269), "nonbiological status of the father was not significantly associated with abuse *among those who were with their stepdaughters during the early socialization period*." (Parker & Parker, 1986, 541; italics in original) The differences in level of involvement were striking. For example, 36 percent of the abusers, compared to 5.6 percent of the nonabusers, were frequently absent from the home during the first three years of the child's life; and 5.4 percent of the abusers, compared to 37 percent of the nonabusers, were involved frequently in performing three or more child-care and nurturant tasks. (540) In a multiple-regression analysis Parker and Parker found that father involvement in child care and nurturance, along with parental treatment, contribute virtually all of the cumulative variance explaining abuse. This is further strong support for the Westermarck hypothesis.

The fact that mother-child bonding through feeding and bodily care is well ingrained in typical cultural roles, while paternal nurturance is relatively neglected, might account for the well-established fact that mother-son incest is the rarest form and father-daughter the commonest (van den Berghe, 1983, 96).

The Westermarck hypothesis also raises interesting questions pertinent to our attitudes toward sexuality. We might expect, for instance, that in a society where all childhood sexuality falls under the incest taboo, so that it is either prohibited outright or regarded as in need of correction (i.e., tolerated but considered morally and psychologically dangerous, as Freud did), some children (only children, for example, or children in particularly repressive families) will encounter special difficulty gaining the biologically necessary sexual experience during the optimal or "critical" period, and that this would lead them to seek compensatory "incestuous" experience afterward. To the extent such children uncritically accept the moral prohibitions and judgments to which they are exposed, they will become irrationally conflicted about their belated sexual interests. Such people would present in adulthood with sexual problems and conflicts we would recognize as "neurotic." Furthermore, one might expect such children to be stigmatized if not punished by society for their sexual interests, or be regarded as victims of inappropriate sexual advances, if they go about things passively. In a society such as ours where there is also considerable frank sexual abuse of children, it is an important problem to differentiate this population of children from those who are actually abused and exploited.

The two main sources of information bearing on this problem—clinical and survey data—provide ambiguous answers, as might be expected given the degree of theoretical confusion and conflicted social attitudes.

With regard to clinical data: Much evidence from psychoanalysis and psychotherapy attests to people's covert and overt longings for sexual recognition and contact, expressed indirectly in "transferences" to the therapist or in more direct form, and this has been variously interpreted and responded to. The Freudian position is that such expressions represent atavistic incestuous wishes resulting from failure to develop a proper Oedipus complex and therefore a proper degree of sexual repression. A psychoanalytic proposition derived from the Westermarck hypothesis is that such expressions more likely represent attempts to compensate for deficiencies of intimate experience in childhood and thus to correct the problem of sexual immaturity (Oedipus complex) that has followed as a consequence. Such an interpretation was first hinted at by Ferenczi (1985, 175) but without reference to Westermarck. Ferenczi saw the basic fault with the Oedipal formulation: "Incestuous fixation does not appear as a natural product of development but rather is implanted in the psyche from the outside." This perspective has been highly controversial within psychoanalysis (Haynal, 1988; Hoffer, 1991; Vida, 1994) and will undoubtedly remain so, challenging as it does the very foundation of Freudianism.

With respect to the second source of information, survey researchers have pointedly ignored the Westermarck hypothesis, and this is true even in recent studies. The classic studies by Kinsey and associates (1949, 1953) do not mention it. Kinsey found sibling and parent-child incest rare (1948, 558), although Ramey (1979, 1, citing personal communication) alleges that his institute suppressed contrary data. Two recent influential surveys purport to show that pathological adult-child incest is rampart in our culture. But Russell's (1984) does not mention Westermarck, and Finkelhor (1979, 92) dismisses him in much the same uncomprehending and biased manner as early anthropologists:

> data [like Shepher's] would suggest that sexual avoidance between siblings would be quite routine, as long as they were brought up in fairly close proximity. Our finding of a large number of incestuous involvements,

however, would suggest that such a mechanism was weak, easily by-passed, or nonexistent.

To fail to recognize that Westermarck's hypothesis predicts sexual aversion *at maturity* as a result of intimate experience during childhood is remarkable blindness, and Finkelhor's study demonstrates the risks of mere head-counting from a narrow theoretical and legalistic perspective. Discounting Westermarck obliges him to disallow the category of *desired* sexual contact at any age of childhood, the implication being that desire or intention is irrelevant in a legal minor.[18] His definition of incest (which includes mutual masturbation, exhibition, and the mere "invitation or request to do something sexual" [178]) therefore disregards whether the contact is desired or not, because "[t]he taboo on incest in our culture applies to all sexual contact between proscribed parties" (84). It also disregards whether the respondent judged the experience positive (51-52).[19] This exceedingly broad definition probably accounts for his finding a prevalence of incest among minor females 75 percent higher than Russell's comparable study (28 percent, of which 1.3 percent is father-daughter [Finkelhor, 83, 121] versus 16 percent, of which 4.5 percent is father-daughter [Russell, 184, 186]). Russell (1984, 181) excludes as nonabusive desired contacts with relative peers (subject less than five years younger than partner).[20]

I have focused on this very flawed study by Finkelhor because it illustrates the distorted outcomes to be expected in the field of sex-abuse research when the Westermarck hypothesis is ignored. Legalistic thinking like Freud's and Finkelhor's (incest is what society prohibits, and society would not pro-

[18] Note, however, that Finkelhor does not actually limit his report to legal minors. For the incest part of his study he set no upper age limit on reporting. Since 25 percent of his study group of college students were over twenty-one and 18 percent over twenty-four (42), his figures include an unspecified number of legal adults, although he states that his conclusions are "based almost wholly on experiences occurring before age eighteen" (86).

[19] Finkelhor considers all reported incidents "traumatic" whether his subjects judged them so or not. His respondents rated childhood sexual experiences on a scale from 1 (positive) to 5 (negative). He (99) calculated a "mean trauma score" for experiences with partners younger than the subject and 0-4, 5-10, and 10+ years older. For the girls (N = 245), the average rating was actually on the positive side of neutral (2.9 and 2.8) for the first two groups, 3.8 (mostly negative) for the third, and 4.2 (negative) for the fourth. This suggests that the closer the partner was to a peer, the more positive it was likely to be. Trauma and "positive experience" are usually regarded as opposites, but here positive experiences are judged to be more or less traumatic, reflecting his obvious bias. Since the last two groups must have contained all the forty cases of sexual experience with a father, stepfather, mother, or other adult family member or friend (data on p. 87, assuming cousins to be children and brother-in-law to be adults), it is highly likely that separate treatment of those experiences would have put the remaining contacts with younger or older children in the positive column—hardly support for his trauma hypothesis, and more in keeping with the logic of Westermarck's theory.

[20] Russell (1984, 191-192) discusses two other differences in method that might contribute to the striking disparity: Finkelhor's higher age limit and her (Russell's) use of interview versus questionnaire, promoting fuller reporting. Note, however, that these effects would operate in opposite directions, tending to cancel each other out, suggesting that the different *definitions* are crucial to the prevalence findings.

hibit it unless it were bad and dangerous) is circular, guarantees that social prejudices will be reinforced, and makes it difficult to gain a psychological or moral perspective on social rules in this area of human experience. While the Westermarck hypothesis predicts that childhood intimacy of various kinds with peers and parents is normative and necessary for proper sexual development, this needs to be better defined for our culture and not simplistically confused with the serious problem of sexual abuse. By conflating desired with unwanted and positive with negative sexual experience Finkelhor may actually be providing a measure of that portion of incestuous or nonincestuous sexual activity that is not only nonabusive but healthy for later maturity. Differentiating this activity from abuse would enable researchers to discover, through in-depth and longitudinal study, whether it in fact refutes or lends support to the Westermarck hypothesis.

Criticism of the Evidence and Confusion about Theories

A number of legitimate questions have been raised about the empirical evidence in both the kibbutz and Taiwanese cases (for a good overview see Leavitt [1990]). To the extent that these questions can be answered empirically, further clarification of the data will do so. In order for this to result in real understanding, however, a more difficult aspect of the debate over theory and evidence will have to be addressed.

There is in the literature a remarkable confusion concerning the terms of explanation—that is, about which data are relevant and what the competing theories imply for observable behavior. That this is a serious problem can be demonstrated by a few examples. The influential psychoanalyst Bettelheim (1969, 238) formulates the phenomenon of incest aversion among kibbutzim peers in Freudian terms, indicating that he misunderstands the theoretical problem completely. "Such a far-reaching *repression* of feelings about having one's body observed and about observing others leads to alienation from the erotic feelings roused in one's body." He seems not to recognize that in invoking the concept of repression, which in Freudian terms means instinctual conflict and Oedipal anxiety and guilt, he is begging the question altogether; for the Westermarck hypothesis predicts that children raised together in intimacy will experience, as part of the normal development of their sexual instincts, a (primary, as it were, as opposed to secondary) *lack of interest in their peers,* not a precocious development of Oedipal repression. Bettelheim's error illustrates the great difficulty Freudian thinkers encounter in conceiving of a person without an Oedipus complex.

Spiro also confuses these issues, for the same reason. In commenting about the extraordinary finding of the absence of peer marriage and, apparently, sexual relations, among the young kibbutz sabra (native-born Israelis), that is, the post–high school adolescents and young adults who are under no societal taboo, he suggests as an explanation that as adults they "have spontaneously evolved their own incest taboo" (348). This explanation is predicated on the condition that "if psychoanalysis has taught us anything, it is that siblings *do* have reciprocal sexual interests." But psychoanalytic teaching is exactly what is being tested. Spiro confuses adult and child sexual interest and, like Bettelheim, instinctual inhibition and cultural prohibition.

Kaffman (1977), whose observations of sexual freedom in kibbutz adolescents have been used to cast doubt on the Westermarckian interpretation, perpetuates the same confusion and thus fails to understand which data are relevant. For example, he writes that "the suggestion of absolute sexual abstinence within the group is less than exact" (216) because occasional sexual relationships between peers are reported and the partners seem to be without guilt. But a biosocial mechanism would hardly be expected to be absolute; it is precisely the point of the Westermarck mechanism that it gives rise to aversion (which can obviously be overcome in various ways), not guilt, which tends to be a function of social prohibitions.

The Sociobiological Consensus

The findings from Israel and Taiwan, along with a great deal of evidence from animal studies that indicate that incest-aversion mechanisms are predominant throughout the animal world,[21] have been crucial in promoting a consensus among social scientists concerned with human sexuality of the essential correctness of the Westermarck hypothesis.

In my view one of the most balanced and comprehensive statements of this consensus and the problems it opens up comes from Norbert Bischof (1972, 1975, 1985), a Swiss ethologist and psychologist. In reviewing the Freud-Westermarck debate he compares the anti-incest instinct to a well-recognized type of instinctual self-protection: certain birds' instinctual avoidance of insects with black-and-yellow stripes, as if they were all poisonous wasps. Bischof (1975, 59) argues convincingly that

> Westermarck therefore advances a legitimate argument, biologically speaking, when he assumes that nature recognizes early-childhood familiarity as a sufficient clue for consanguinity, just as black and yellow stripes stand for poison, the biologically unnecessary inhibition against marrying an adopted sister being tolerated just about as readily as the bird's abstinence from a meal of hover-flies.

Such biologic legitimacy cannot be claimed for the Frazer-Freud argument.

[21] I will not delve into this body of work here. The interested reader will find abundant references to it in the writings of Bischof, Fox, Parker, van den Berghe, and others.

He (1975, 41) focuses attention on Freud's "presumptuous" argument (in Freud, 1913, 123-124) that

> the findings of psychoanalysis make the hypothesis of an innate aversion to incestuous intercourse totally untenable. They have shown, on the contrary, that the earliest sexual excitations of youthful human beings are invariably of an incestuous character.

This argument was taken up and expanded in the direction of ethology by Levi-Strauss (1970, 18), who called incestuous mating "a natural phenomenon found commonly among animals." Bischof (42, italics in original) shows that this influential idea is completely at odds with reality. In fact,

> *in the whole animal world with very few exceptions no species is known in which under natural conditions inbreeding occurs to any considerable degree.*[22] Among "bonding-motivated animals, . . . that is, animals having the ability to recognize each other *individually,* and the *inclination to affiliate* with acquainted conspecifics . . . *nature systematically avoids* [incest].

He supports this conclusion with a great deal of empirical data from mammalian species, organized according to social and conjugal structures: solitary, male-cohort, polygynous, monogamous, and polygamous. All these social structures demonstrate the presence of incest barriers, which utilize one of two groups of mechanisms. In the first, family bonds are dissolved at sexual maturity. In the second, sexuality is suppressed in those individuals who remain with their families after puberty.

We are also indebted to Bischof for demonstrating the biological falsity of an argument commonly used to support the functionalist interpretation of the incest taboo. According to this argument, primitive humans came to understand the biological reason for the taboo because incest led to defective offspring. Our abhorrence of incestuous mating is a racial memory reinforced by the present-day fact of genetic defectiveness. However, Bischof (1975, 40-41) shows that a higher rate of defective progeny from inbreeding obtains only in populations that are stably exogamous, not ones that historically inbreed. It is true that "the proportion of unfavourable to favourable characters for recessive genes is indeed higher than for dominant." However, "the disparity is caused by selection acting constantly upon the dominant genes, whereas in the

[22] In fact there are exceptions to the general rule of outbreeding and they tell us interesting things about the evolutionary history of the species. For example, in the naked mole-rat, an insect-style social structure has evolved, involving sterile workers, a single reproductive queen, and a few drone males. In that species colony members share 85 percent of their genes from sibling and parent-child inbreeding. (Sherman et al., 1991) It appears to be the case that inbreeding is only detrimental in a species that, in effect, values individuality (for its "adaptive plasticity" and survival value) to the extent that it has established outbreeding and genetic variation as its normative practice, which is the case with virtually all mammals and birds (Bischof, 1972, 14, 24).

recessive pool, sheltered by the dominant alleles, all sorts of litter can collect unpenalized." Thus "an inbreeding depression would be a temporary phenomenon only, as natural selection would soon cleanse the—now manifest—recessive gene pool." In other words, defective offspring cannot be invoked as an explanation of the incest taboo. Although the benefit of incest aversion might be reinforced by the fact of defective progeny, this effect would only obtain in already stably exogamous cultures. The evolutionary advantage of exogamy, in terms of genetic diversity, can only be expected to operate on a very large time scale, not perceptible to us. In Bischof's (ibid.) words, "If, as Levi-Strauss (1970, 15) assumes, mankind has developed from an ancestry regularly practising incest, there would indeed have been no eugenic reason suddenly to forbid this."

Finally, Bischof turns to a consideration of these ethological findings for an understanding of human beings. Two questions naturally arise: "first, whether 'inner' inhibiting mechanisms of the kind discussed can be shown to exist in man, too; if so, second, given a background of such mechanisms, how are we to understand the development of corresponding cultural norms" (1975, 59). His basic conclusion is that such mechanisms as exist almost universally in the mammalian

> world are integral parts of the genetically fixed instinctive structure, and it would be astonishing if there were not at least rudimentary traces left in man. (1972, 24)

> The more or less radical emancipation of adolescents of both sexes from the child's referential structure of security and obedience—the surfeit with the established order, the lure of the distant, of the exotic, the forbidden, the dangerous—all this is common knowledge in developmental psychology. . . . [T]here can be little doubt that these phenomena are due by and large to maturation, although social forces can facilitate, inhibit, or channel them. (1975, 59-60)

To summarize this discussion of empirical tests of Freud and Westermarck, it is much more likely than not that Freud's theory of incest aversion is wrong. Westermarck's theory of a complex, developmental, anti-incest instinct that requires specific environmental input at crucial stages of childhood (in the form of closeness and freedom with parents and siblings) in order to manifest properly in adolescence, is likely correct. We should be skeptical in the extreme about the Oedipal theory lest we confuse, as Freud did, effect with cause, adult with childhood sexuality, and inadvertently promote the ideology of authority that is so woven into the fabric of Freudianism.

Freud-Westermarck and the Sociobiology Debate

Because evidence for the Westermarck hypothesis has lent support to the possibility that there are other complex behavioral instincts, the Freud-Westermarck debate has become a prominent part of a larger debate in the social sciences over human sociobiology, the research program devoted to discovering such instinctual components of behavior and social organization. This program, which is commonly attributed to E. O. Wilson (in his 1975 *Sociobiology*) has evoked passionate opposition, comparable to the criticism leveled at Chomsky's theory of generative grammar as an instinctual root of human language and cognition, for some similar reasons: critics believe it is fundamentally misguided and culturally prejudicial. Many of these critics are scholars of the first rank, holding views on society with which I am in deep sympathy. In this section I attempt to provide a brief, critical overview of their main arguments against human sociobiology, because my sympathy with their position is outweighed by my conviction that they are wrong. While a very incomplete survey, I believe it addresses the main intellectual issues.

Critics are concerned, for one thing, about the potential misuse of sociobiological theories to support reactionary social ideologies, while being aware of the dangers of stifling research (see, for example, Allen, 1978; Gould,1978; Kitcher, 1985, 1-11; Lewontin, Rose, & Kamin, 1984; Menzies, 1985). They point out that the assumption that "culture coevolved with genes, the two tending to converge on fitness-maximizing consequences" (as in van den Berghe, 1983, 98; see also Wilson, 1998, chapter 7), begs important questions about "whose fitness" is in question; it is simplistic, and likely to promote conservative complacency about the present state and direction of society ("Panglossian" is Gould and Lewontin's apt term) (Daly & Wilson, 1983; Gould & Lewontin, 1979).

I believe that potentials for misuse are indeed great, but that this serious concern is secondary to questions about whether the theories are good ones. Theories, especially grand and seductive theories of human nature and society, are inherently freighted with political and social significance, and evoke strong passions.

With regard to the substance of sociobiological theories, these critics have put forward several arguments in support of the idea that cultural phenomena cannot, in principle, be elucidated by biological theories. I believe these arguments are wrong in general and with regard to Freud-Westermarck in particular, and will discuss two of the most influential, as formulated by the philosophers Kitcher and Williams: namely, Kitcher's (1990) "paucity of mechanisms" argument and Williams's (1983) "representation argument." The first states that without much more knowledge than we have of intervening mechanisms, sociobiological theories are likely to be very wide of the mark, which would be a bad thing. The second is an echo and elaboration of Frazer's argument that cultural prohibitions would be redundant in the face of biological inhibitions.

To consider Kitcher first, he cites the great complexity of and huge ignorance about intervening entities and mechanisms in genetics, evolutionary biology, developmental psychology, and history. He (1990, 102, italics in original) insists, for example, that for sociobiology to succeed we need "to know the ways in which various forms of behavior are bound together by connections among their proximate mechanisms" and to "delineate the structure of the causal trees that link the genes to aspects of the phenotype (possible facets of morphology and physiology as well as behavioral traits). If we are entirely ignorant about this structure, then there is a very real danger that we shall focus on the wrong *explananda*." Without this knowledge, "specifications of the selective advantage of a particular piece of behavior are, at best, stabs in the dark." Inclined to doubt the existence of dedicated biological mechanisms in areas as complex as incest avoidance and to prefer a theory of general intelligence, he (1990, 100-101, italics in original) argues that there are "obvious limits on the power of selection to shape an individual phenotypic trait" and that "what is fixed or maintained by selection will be a *behavioral spectrum* or some underlying disposition that is implicated in each of the elements of a behavioral spectrum."

In insisting on detailed intervening mechanisms Kitcher succumbs, I believe, to an inductivist fallacy that flies in the face of facts. While it is probable that future discoveries in genetics will impose constraints on evolutionary theorizing, the present ignorance of genetic mechanisms is no reason to dissuade us from speculation. Certainly some or many of these speculations are stabs in the dark, and mistakes will be made, but inductivist caution—that is, insisting that theories be created by generalizing from observed facts—is no proof against them. To take our specific case as an example, the Westermarck hypothesis, which seemed far more speculative than Frazer's and Freud's when first proposed, posits an entity that satisfies the constraints imposed by present knowledge of behavioral genetics, while the same cannot be said for Freud's theory of incest, however much it was generalized from clinical facts. Nor is it the case that sophisticated and compelling theories about intervening mechanisms, and relevant data bearing on these mechanisms, do not exist. A number of them are reviewed by Parker (1976, 291 ff).

Kitcher seems to believe that theories that emerge from detailed knowledge of intervening mechanisms gain thereby some protection against the danger, inherent in all theorizing, of focusing on the wrong *explananda*. However, knowledge of mechanistic details (which are never, in any case, divorced from theoretical assumptions) often provides a false sense of assurance that a good general theory can be developed by induction from particular facts. This is simply not true. Good general theories often spring from inspired speculation in the absence of much knowledge of mechanisms, and bad theories from abundant knowledge. Particularly with the institutionalization and commercialization of science, and the interlinking of warfare and technology in the modern industrial state (Galbraith, 1971), the direction of scientific investigation is often determined by motives other than gaining knowledge, including feasibility, profitability, and political-military advantage. But we know certainly from history that some of the most inspired and influential theories have arisen in the absence of factual details from almost pure poetic speculation. In the sixth century B.C. Anaximander, in the total absence of observable facts, proposed a theory of the earth's free suspension in space, with an explanation of its stability, which prefigured the work of Aristarchus, Copernicus, and Newton. The earliest statements of atomic theory were made in the fifth century B.C. by Leucippus and his pupil Democritus with virtually no knowledge of the fine structure of matter. Darwin's remarkably productive evolutionary theory was developed in the absence of any knowledge of genetic mechanisms, the work of Mendel not being rediscovered until later.

To take an example from among many on the other side of the coin, although the currently popular "medical model" of psychiatry springs from a wealth of detailed knowledge of neurochemistry and neurophysiology, contains appealing and influential biochemical hypotheses of psychosis, depression, and anxiety, and supports huge academic, medical, and pharmaceutical organizations, it is a quite bad theory because its superficial and reductionistic assumptions leave it largely disconnected from the important realities of the mental states they seek to explain. One negative practical consequence of this state of affairs is that the overall success rate in treating severe mental illnesses in hospitalized patients in the United States has regressed tremendously from the late eighteenth century, when doctors in the early New England "retreats" had little knowledge of brain mechanisms but operated under a theory of "moral psychiatry" informed by general humane and philosophical principles (Bockoven, 1963; Cohen, 1998). Some of the best arguments for doubting and worrying about modern reductionistic theories of psychiatry and the poor outcomes they produce are, in fact, put forth by Kitcher's intellectual colleagues (Lewontin et al., 1984, chapters 7 & 8).

Let us move on to consider Williams's "representation problem." He begins (1983, 555-556, italics in original) with the idea that evolutionary theory has interconnecting normative and explanatory implications for the study of human beings and society. With regard to the former, he cites

> the standard objection [attributable to G. E. Moore, 1903] which holds that no [normative] lessons can be drawn at all, at least in any directly logical way, since any project of deriving ethical content from premisses of evolutionary theory commits the "naturalistic fallacy," an error which is today often equated with that of trying to derive *ought* from *is*.

The *ought-is* or *ought-can* problem touches on the concerns voiced by many critics of sociobiology, insofar as claims that human beings cannot live in a certain way could "coherently yield *constraints* on social goals, personal ideals, possible institutions and so forth" (556, italics in original). Williams recognizes that the idea that human beings cannot do certain things is an extremely vague form of statement, which "will not matter so long as one is clear about the level at which the formula of *'ought* implies *can'* is being applied" (557, italics in original); this application will involve matters of interpretation and education, social policy, political action, individual choice, and so forth. This is a sensible warning about the simplistic application of psychobiological findings to morality and public policy. For example, the fact that men and women are biologically primed for different roles with respect to raising children or earning a livelihood should have limited if any significance in deciding issues of adoption or custody or in promulgating laws and policies governing employment, considering the panoply and overriding importance of nonbiological requirements of parenthood and work.

It is with regard to the connections between the normative and explanatory implications of evolutionary theory that Williams perceives a "representation problem." It has two parts, a lesser one dealing with content and a greater one with function. Noting (557) that in humans "virtually no behavioural tendency which constitutes genuine action can just show up in a cultural context 'as itself,' " Williams formulates the content part of the problem as follows (557, italics in original): *"how is a phenotypic character which would present itself in other species as a behavioral tendency represented in a species which has a culture, language, and conceptual thought?"* With regard to the more serious problem of function, Williams (560) argues that it is the notion of a norm that gives rise to it. He recasts Frazer's (1910, 97) argument ("what nature itself prohibits and punishes, it would be superfluous for the law to prohibit and punish") as a serious "necessity problem" rather than a self-evident rhetorical trope. It is a problem of the relation of biological inhibition to cultural prohibition:

> The most, it seems, that a genetically acquired character could yield would be an inhibition against behaviours of a certain kind; what relation could that have to a socially sanctioned prohibition? Indeed, if the inhibitions exists, what *need* could there be for such a prohibition? If the prohibitory norm is to be part of the "extended phenotype" of the

species, how could we conceive, starting from an inhibition, that this might come about?

Williams goes on to argue (561, italics in original) that in the case of the incest taboo, in which a cultural prohibition seems to arise out of a biological inhibition,

> there are behavioural drives the function of which is to avoid inbreeding. Such a drive, however, has to be operationalized in some other way, since the animals do not have any direct knowledge of the matters relevant to inbreeding; the inhibition against mating has to be triggered by the recognition of or reaction to some property adequately correlated with the kin relationship, such as being an individual with which the animal has been brought up. It is *this* inhibition that is allegedly displayed, in the well-known case, by those brought up together in a kibbutz. But we have not yet reached the incest taboo.

At least in such cases, which do not represent a mere "raising to consciousness" of the inhibition, Williams sees a fundamental divide between the underlying inhibition and its corresponding prohibition, such that once the prohibition is in place, the biological inhibition would cease to have causative or explanatory significance. It would cease, thereby, to function as a motivation in the mind.

In Williams's view (561, italics in original), a cultural prohibition

> can have come about, in fact, only given human knowledge of relevant facts—presumably, of the ill-effects of in-breeding. . . . It turns out that we have to appeal in any case to something like a rational collective agency, directed towards avoiding recognized and agreed evils, and that *already* provides an adequate explanation—a fairly traditional one—of the incest prohibition.

This idea is extremely important because, although not identical to Freud's theory, it is congruent with it, and constitutes a rationale for the Freudian "break between the pre-cultural and the cultural" (562), which has been so persuasive.

It is not difficult to demonstrate, however, as Sesardic (1998) has done, that the Frazer-Freud-Williams problem of necessity is a pseudoproblem; and the demonstration is extremely relevant to the Freud-Westermarck debate and to psychoanalysis in general. Sesardic notes (416–417) that Williams is employing a

> crude picture of human behavioral dispositions. . . . The idea that inhibitions absolutely stamp out a behavioral variant which is their object flies in the face of almost everything we know about our own psychology and about evolutionary biology in general. Even the most deeply

> rooted and biologically vital inhibitions are occasionally overridden by sufficiently strong counteracting causes, under atypical conditions or in atypical individuals.

But there is a more decisive argument. Not only is natural selection "exactly expected to bring about such loose, tendency-like, exception-allowing dispositions, rather than inflexible, foolproof and never failing inhibitions" (417), but also, in humans, it is reasonable to expect that

> to get prohibitions going it is actually not necessary that the prohibited behavior be at least sometimes encountered nor indeed, for that matter, that it be possible at all. It is entirely sufficient that the forbidden action be *thought* possible. A confirming illustration that readily springs to mind is witchcraft which was prohibited and severely punished although it did not exist, and was in fact always impossible (416, italics in original).

Here, of course, Sesardic is extending arguments put forward by Westermarck himself in response to Frazer and Freud.

Sesardic's most important argument addresses the necessity problem directly. He argues decisively, I believe, against Williams's idea that a biological inhibition would cease to function as a mental motive in the face of a cultural inhibition supplied with "knowledge of relevant facts." This idea represents a real failure on Williams's part to understand the difference between conscious and unconscious motives and to understand how behavioral inhibitions, and instincts in general, are likely to register in the mind and be responded to by an animal capable of reflection and symbolic thought. For just as the thought of something can be sufficient to trigger a prohibition, so is it completely unwarranted to believe that humans in developing their ideas *informing* a prohibition will have, as a precondition, "knowledge of relevant facts," and therefore that a conscious prohibition would supplant the unconscious, instinctual inhibition as a motive—as opposed to being a justification or rationalization of the ongoing unconscious motive. For most people, it is only necessary to *assume* they have knowledge of relevant facts in solving an important problem (in the case of behavioral instincts, to explain why they are motivated to do, think, or feel things *automatically and unconsciously*), for them to act upon their knowledge. Thus Williams's "traditional" explanation of the incest taboo fails for precisely the same reason that psychoanalysis had to be invented: It fails to take unconscious (in this case, instinctual) motives into account. As Sesardic (1998, 422, italics in original) puts it, "it still remains completely open how this [instinctual] aversion will be presented to the minds of its possessors. Obviously, there is no guarantee that it will be *correctly* presented."

In the case of incest aversion as conceptualized by Westermarck, the stranger the connection between the biological object (people to whom one is sexually indifferent in adulthood) and the behavioral object that comes to trigger the inhibition (childhood housemates), and the more widely separated they are in time, the more difficult will be the problem of understanding how the instinct functions (i.e., the relevant facts). It is both a tribute to human intelligence and an embarrassing source of fallibility that this type of difficulty has never restrained people from promulgating theories and acting upon them (e.g., "avoiding recognized and agreed evils") when confronted with a problem. We may be innately highly intelligent creatures, but the shaping of that intelligence into rational and scientific forms (of which "knowledge of relevant facts" is a key part) is a late and still tenuous stage of cultural development.

I would take Sesardic's argument further and suggest that in guarding himself against the naturalistic fallacy Williams has fallen into an equally problematic "rationalistic fallacy." In seeking to avoid biological reductionism he has fallen into cultural reductionism. Williams mistakes a quintessential, language-based human activity, ratiocination, for a very particular and rare quality of ratiocination: namely, rational understanding (of which scientific thinking is a specialized form), which is all too elusive a process, perhaps especially when it comes to ourselves. It is a truism that cultural prohibitions are functions of ratiocinative human activity, but that is a far cry from "knowledge of relevant facts." The debate over incest aversion despite sophisticated theories and abundant evidence, with all the confusion about the relevance of demographic, biological, and clinical data, illustrates this problem.

Thus, while Williams in correct in perceiving the difference in thought quality between biologically informed inhibitions and cultural prohibitions, he is very wrong in regarding the divide as wide as he does and in believing that (in cases where cultural prohibitions arise from biological inhibitions) the prohibitions replace inhibitions in any profound epistemological sense. Confusing cognitive form with content, he overstates the case for an ineluctable mismatch between the cognitive content of inhibitions and prohibitions, and misjudges the nature of the break between the precultural and the cultural.

To summarize, the arguments and existing evidence do not prove Westermarck right (evidence never does, except provisionally), but he has withstood experimental tests while Freud's theory has been refuted. Moreover, Westermarck's hypothesis is not only biologically but philosophically legitimate.

Historicism

As we saw in the discussion of Oedipalism, the lawlike regularity that Freud imputes to the historical development of culture is derived by analogy and homology from the process he came to believe occurs in individual development, and which is a mainstay of his psychology. The psychology is epitomized by his paradigm of neurosis: the child's desire to touch his or her genitals—external prohibition—acceptance of the prohibition out of "love" for the prohibitor—repression of the desire, with resulting conflict and ambivalence. As we have also seen, that paradigm is heavily laden with instinctivist theory and social- and moral-philosophical assumptions, notably about the need for and role of authority in parent-child relations and in society and thinking generally. The whole structure of thought is hugely circular.

In the absence of a sound evolutionary biological rationale, Freud's phylogenetic theories must be considered to rest on a *historicist* explanation—that is, one in which historical processes are assumed to be lawlike, giving them great weight in determining future events.[23]

While historicist sociological reasoning has been most often, in modern times, associated with Hegel, Herder, and Marx, Freud's inspiration comes rather from the social contract theorists of the British empirical-utilitarian tradition. Freud's Oedipal theory shares with philosophers like Hobbes and Hume the view that the transition from a state of savagery characterized by unbridled aggression, greed, and licentiousness to a rule-determined civilized existence came about by primitive people's invention of society, the rules of which are often referred to as "artifices." It is commonly recognized that Freud's social-constructionist view of morality falls squarely within the liberal tradition spawned by the dominance of the market as a social institution, in which balancing various "passions and interests" becomes a main way of thinking about the individual's relation to society, but his specific indebtedness to the architects of this tradition, and especially to Hume, has not been adequately recognized.

I write this mindful of a number of references to the Hume connection in philosophical critiques of Freud. The commentators who are known to me have, however, missed the most important points of the connection. A good example is Gellner (1985), who, while recognizing (212) strong parallels between Freud's emotivism and Hume's, as well as the curious ease with which, in both theories, the supposedly wild instinctual nature of human beings is rendered conservative and staid (104), sees Freud as predominantly Nietzschean and anti-Humean in his implicit beliefs. Similarly, Marcuse, in *Reason and Revolution* (1941, 20-21), severely criticized Humean empiricism as "an attack upon the conditions of human freedom." However, in his later *Eros and Civilization* (1955), which is largely a defense of Freud through Marxian

[23] I employ this term, following the usage of Popper (1943, 14), to characterize a form of utopian social thinking that combines a fearful overemphasis on change with a belief in inexorable laws of destiny. For a further comment on Freud's historicism in the context of political and social change, see pp. 156–158.

reinterpretation, he fails to note the strong Humean influence in Freud or to mention Hume at all.

While Hume emphasized the property-rights aspects of modern social conventions, Freud's version emphasized obedience to patriarchal authority. I will make the argument for a strong derivation of Freudian from Humean psychology in Chapter 5, in the context of a discussion of the so-called "ego psychology." But a foretaste of the argument will be useful here to appreciate the strength of the influence.

A major conclusion of Books 1 and 2 of Hume's *Treatise of Human Nature* (1739-1740) is one that became quintessential Freud: moral concepts are really only emotionally determined perceptions, which we humans confuse with ideas: "Morality . . . is more properly felt than judg'd of; tho' this feeling or sentiment is commonly so soft and gentle, that we are apt to confound it with an idea" (470). Furthermore, moral concepts are not "natural," derived from innate knowledge, but rather are "artifices," social rules invented, in the first instance by primeval people, for the convenience of living in social groups: "Our sense of every kind of virtue is not natural; but . . . there are some virtues, that produce pleasure and approbation by means of an artifice or contrivance, which arises from the circumstances and necessity of mankind" (477).

These artifices or cultural conventions, centered on ownership and exchange of private property, are derived from natural principles, in much the same way as the Oedipus complex, in that they are motivated by passions (for property rather than sex), informed by the understanding that realistic satisfaction of these passions requires their restraint under social conditions: "Whatever restraint they [the artificial laws of property justice] may impose on the passions of men, they are the real offspring of those passions, and are only a more artful and more refin'd way of satisfying them" (526). Subsequently, these conventions are given moral attributes, which are in the nature of linguistic conventions (522) and pretenses (523)—that is, other artifices—in order to facilitate the cultural enforcement and transmission of these rules by socialization, education, and government.

A large part of Book 3, *Of Morals,* is devoted to Hume's historical argument. After discussing the varieties of selfishness, vanity, envy, and aggression that would have made group life impossible for protohumans, he comes to the conclusion that it was, uniquely, the invention of private property that must have rescued man from his "savage and solitary condition" (562):

> When they [primitive men] have observ'd, that the principal disturbance in society arises from those goods, which we call external, and from their looseness and easy transition from one person to another; they must seek for a remedy, by putting these goods, as far as possible, on the same foot-

> ing with the fix'd and constant advantages of the mind and body. This can be done after no other manner, than by a convention enter'd into by all the members of the society to bestow stability on the possession of those external goods . . . . By this means, every one knows what he may safely possess; and the passions are restrain'd in their partial and contradictory motions. (489)

This imagined social convention, which becomes a force in the minds of individuals through the combined action of continuous cultural reinforcement and behavioral evolution (it would take social Darwinism to make this latter implication explicit), serves the same function in Hume's psychology as Freud's primal horde theory does in his and has the same weaknesses.

For Freud later (and this must be viewed as an attempt to refine Hume), the culture-defining step is the internalization of Oedipal guilt from the sons' murder of the clan leader, creating patriarchy. His statements of assumptions, virtually identical to Hume's, are given largely in his two books devoted to anthropological speculation, *Totem and Taboo* (1913) and *Civilization and Its Discontents* (1930). Beginning with the assumption that "Aggressiveness . . . reigned almost without limit in primitive times" (1930, 113), he proposed that

> Human life in common is only made possible when a majority comes together which is stronger than any separate individual and which remains united against all separate individuals. This replacement of the power of the individual by the power of the community constitutes the decisive step of civilization. (95)

Thus when he wrote, ostensibly in response to Marx, that "aggressiveness was not created by property" (113), he was denying what he actually believed: Hume's theory, which he substantially appropriated, while changing the emphasis from private ownership to the patriarchal authority that enforces such ownership. Even this qualifier is questionable, however, for, as we will see later, Freud quite explicitly embraced Hume's arguments about private property.

Freud's guiding assumption that society opposes nature is, in other words, squarely within the Humean tradition. By disallowing innate moral knowledge, this doctrine makes the child totally dependent on parents and teachers for all such knowledge and so inclines its adherents to idealize the society they know. All of animal society and prior or different human societies tend to be regarded as inferior and savage. It is a view that can be maintained only at the cost of great selective inattention to anthropological and archaeological evidence, much of which demonstrates an unusual degree of social cohesion and cooperation in premodern societies. Kropotkin's famous *Mutual Aid: A Factor of Evolution* (1902) remains one of the great scholarly collections of this evidence and sources of critical argument against the Humean view.

The typical portrait of Freud as a lonely, radical thinker obscures the fact that his reaction to many sophisticated social theories of his day was regressive and antagonistic, in keeping with his Humean approach. Compare his historicist views of the moral system with the sophisticated historical and cultural perspectives of a leading contemporary. The influential British sociologist Leonard Hobhouse shares with Westermarck the assumption of an "instinctive element in human morality" (1906, 15). For Hobhouse, however, it is evident both that a person's moral system has a genuinely instinctual basis and that its development in the individual cannot be understood apart from the history, ways of life, material culture, and political organization of the society to which that person belongs. Development from primitive to modern culture has involved progressively greater influence of reflective thought over necessity and pure historical contingency. He recognized that material and technological advance does not always entail ethical advance, often bringing with it stagnation or regression, indicating that the relations between culture and morality are extremely complex, largely unconscious and unforeseeable, and poorly understood—anticipating the "law of unintended consequences": "Nowhere is the feat of escaping from one's own shadow harder than in the world of ethical and religious thought" (18). "If, indeed, we were to look at the conduct of modern society in some relations, and in those relations only, we should be apt to say that it cloaked under fine words actions not less savage than those of our rude and barbarous ancestors" (24).

Unlike Freud, that is, Hobhouse did not confine himself to sexual morality but was sensitive also to the ethical damage that hypocritical economic and social theories and practices are capable of wreaking:

> Purely economic changes, for example, will tend to raise one class and depress another. A community in which comparative equality has reigned may give way to one divided between rich and poor, and from such a division some form of class morality is almost certain to arise. . . . Such causes as the accumulation of capital and the rise of large urban markets have at times made slave labour especially profitable, and slavery has accordingly received a great extension, while the class of free citizens has declined. (21)

He was sensitive also to the position of women as a test of civilized morality, and to many of the contradictions within modern society as pertains to women:

> In the English law of Blackstone's day, for example, a married woman can scarcely be said to have had a legal personality, so great is the number of her disqualifications . . . ; and many of these disqualifications last on down to the present generation. If we turn to the oldest code of laws

in the world, the recently-rediscovered laws of Hammurabi, we shall find that few of these disqualifications applied to married women in Babylonia some 2000 years before Christ. (32-33)

Hobhouse was not a doomsayer. He recognized that a sophisticated society has the means to recognize if not to completely understand potentially negative effects of material change and to create social policies to counteract them. By these means it may elevate to the level of conscious thought and action "the element of the unconscious in social life" (22). Thus, just "as the nonethical changes of society affect the standards of conduct, so ethical ideas may in their turn react upon social organization. Such a reaction has made a large part of the history of the modern world" (22).

Freud would have done well to take a lesson from Hobhouse, for such sophisticated concepts as the "unconscious in social life," of the ethical consequences of material changes, and of the feedback between material-technological change and ethical considerations informing social policy were all quite alien to his historicist way of thinking. Operating with a crude dichotomy of individual and society, he regarded mental dysfunction as a failure on the individual's part to adequately internalize the moral standards of modern society, which despite his early reservations about sexual morality he came to regard as exceptionable only in their stringency. He registered no curiosity about problems that were obvious to observers like Hobhouse, such as the rise of wage slavery, the constrictions of freedom, the debasement of women, and the relations of these outcomes to a market-organized society. It is fair to say that Freud was glamourized[24] by modern society and "the great world-dominating nations of white race upon whom the leadership of the human species has fallen" (1915d, 276).

The historicist quality of Freudian thought is reflected in the boundaries of present-day Freudian inquiry. Just as Freud had little use for the historical investigations of thinkers like Bachofen, Morgan, and Engels when they led to reasonable speculations that patriarchy might be a relatively recent cultural invention, so among present-day Freudians is there a dearth of interest in the actual, much-developed, history of patriarchy and gender role, for which Lerner's (1986) seminal text is essential. Just as Freud ignored critics of the modern creed, so is there a similar lack of interest in the psychological and sociological foundations of institutional modernity, for which Polanyi's (1944) historical analysis of the free-market system and MacIntyre's (1981, 1988) critique of modern liberal philosophy are essential. Such works lead to critical perspectives on the current political-economic-intellectual order, which pose

[24] I use this word in the primary sense of bewitchment or enchantment, especially by occult learning *(Oxford English Dictionary)*.

a direct challenge to key assumptions of Freudianism. By contrast, Freud's adoption of Hume and antagonism to Marx has made psychoanalysis into a rationale for capitalism, seen as a "natural" social order providing necessary discharge opportunities for man's greed and aggression. Thus we find Freudian rhetoric serving as a seemingly weighty rationale for "psychoanalytically informed" defenders of modern capitalism, of which a good example is the recent work of Heilbroner (1993), in which he assures us that capitalism is "a social order that draws its acquisitive energies from the unconscious substratum of behavior" (160). Lest we naively think that this unconscious stratum that fuels our greed might be modified through changes in society, he invokes the spirit of Freud to tell us just what the limits are:

> Empathic parenting and supportive institutions can undoubtedly instill many social routines other than our own, but they cannot produce "liberated" behavior—that is, behavior free of sublimated rage, denials of many kinds, and actings-out of fantasies of oppression . . . . These infantile yearnings are never overcome, only expressed in many disguises. (159)

It is also true that socialist-oriented psychoanalytic thinkers like W. Reich and Adler (in their early days), Fromm and, probably most influentially, Marcuse (1955), embraced Freudianism as a doctrine critical and subversive of capitalist society. This section would be incomplete without at least mentioning this trend, for many readers have no doubt been introduced to psychoanalysis through these writings and may find my discussion in this section somewhat puzzling.

To take Marcuse as the leading example (see also Cohen, 1998-1999, for a brief critique of Adler's work): his approach is based, I believe, on a generous but mistaken reading of Freud that concentrates on the spirit of social criticism from his earliest work (which Marcuse calls [1955, chapter 1] the "hidden trend" of Freudianism) and neglects the extreme reactionism of his middle and later work.

Like some other socialist thinkers, Marcuse sought to forge links between Marx and Freud. Without going into a detailed critique of these efforts here, it is relevant to note in this context the key idea with which he forges this link, that of "surplus repression." Marcuse sought to modify Freudian theory in two ways. First, he interpreted repression as a function of the capitalist social-economic system and its effects on consciousness. This is an interpretation that Freud would have fervently denied. Second, making an analogy with Marx's idea of surplus value as the principal weapon of capitalist domination, he sought, by introducing the notion of a variable "surplus repression," to rationalize Freud's view of sexual repression. According to this view, surplus repression is the excessive susceptibility to repression of people living under capitalism—that is, the portion of repression above and beyond that which constitutes the inherent repressive cost of capitalism. This surplus derives, in effect, from the individual's failure of critical capacity with respect to the effects of this social organization. Such individuals sacrifice more of self, freedom, and capacity for pleasure than they have to.

I believe that Marcuse's ideas are important but do not elaborate Freud so much as suggest a different psychoanalysis altogether, in which critical social and political awareness is necessary in order to minimize repression—an implicit and very important point of view, but one radically at odds with Freud. Lacking a sound critique of Freud, Marcuse seems not to have recognized the contradictoriness of his own thought, and how much of an anti-Freudian he actually was.[25]

Essentialism

Finally, there is in Freudianism another tendency or artificial perspective—essentialism—that severely constricts critical thinking. This perspective is intimately linked to the three others and is partly intellectual, partly political. It takes the form of a conviction that Freud's particular view of instinct and therefore of repression constitutes the essence of psychoanalysis.[26]

Freud (1914a, 16) claimed that "the theory of repression is the . . . most essential part" of psychoanalysis. When he wrote this he had in mind sexual repression, for aggression was not yet included in his instinct theory and in fact was treated very differently. As we have seen, he embraced *particular* and problematic theories of instinct and sexual repression among those available, committing psychoanalysis to its defense. This commitment fueled, and continues to fuel, resistance to thoughtful criticism of the repression concept.

The resistance to criticism is nowhere better seen than in the extraordinary gap, in scholarly psychoanalytic writing, between the ostensible importance of repression theory and the lack of concern for its coherence. The gap is especially striking with respect to a problem that Freud recognized but that modern Freudians have neglected—that of *primal* repression. This concept is designed to account for repression's origins and causes (Cohen & Kinston, 1984; Frank, 1969; Frank & Muslin, 1967; Kinston & Cohen, 1986; Madison, 1956, 1961).

---

[25] For an interesting psychoanalytic appreciation of Marcuse's work I refer the reader to Robinson (1969); and for a discussion of its severe problems, to MacIntyre (1970).

[26] Perhaps another caveat is in place here. The view I describe as "essentialist" in this section is foresworn by many contemporary Freudians, but their attempts to revise Freud's theories typically do not achieve real significance because of a failure to appreciate how intimately interwoven it is with the whole instinctivist-Oedipalist-historicist agenda of his psychoanalysis, so that changing one perspective without addressing the others is insufficient. Critical examination of these attempts at revision must be postponed to a future volume, for it depends on the adequacy of my critique of Freudianism. In this section I will focus on what I consider the most important and problematic aspects of the essentialist viewpoint, the failure to develop a proper theory of "primal repression."

Freud maintained that the repression encountered in everyday clinical work with neurotics, termed *repression proper,* is a secondary phenomenon that depends on the prior occurrence of a *primal repression* of thoughts, images, or memories bound to an instinct. This hypothesis is stated as follows:

> We have reason to assume that there is a *primal repression,* a first phase of repression, which consists in the psychical (ideational) representation of the instinct being denied entrance into the conscious. With this a *fixation* is established; the representative in question persists unaltered from then onwards and the instinct remains attached to it. . . . The second stage of repression, *repression proper,* affects mental derivatives of the repressed representative, or such trains of thought as, originating elsewhere, have come into associative connective with it. (1915b, 148; italics in original)

Yet the theory of primal repression is extremely confused. Freud held different views of it at different times and the significance of the concept has not been agreed upon since.

Kinston and I, discussing primal repression, noted (1984, 412) that a "striking characteristic of [the analytic] literature is the way that one aspect or another of Freud's views on repression are uncritically endorsed while the rich theoretical problems and contradictory formulations which he bequeathed are sidestepped." We noted that only one author, Madison (1956), had drawn attention to the extraordinary neglect of primal repression and that few practicing analysts even concern themselves with the subject. Classic texts like those of Fenichel (1945), A. Freud (1936, 1966), and Nagera (1969-1970) do not mention it. For the most part, if Freudian scholars tackle primal repression at all, it is to justify ignoring it. Writings in this vein (of which Brenner's [1957] is a prime example) are exercises in evasion and circular reasoning. Brenner simply asserts that the mechanism of primal repression is the same as that of repression, a statement of essentiality and infinite regress that ignores even the basic logical necessity Freud found for introducing the concept (in [1915a, 148]). In short, primal repression, a problem that follows ineluctably from repression theory, appears to be a great embarrassment.

Among philosophers interested in psychoanalysis, Ricoeur (1970, 139-140) seems to be the only one to have explicitly noticed this problem:

> what we take to be the primal expression of an instinct [in Freudian theory] is in fact the product of a fixation; the relation between expression and instinct never appears to us except as one that has been established, sedimented, "fixed." In order to attain an immediate expression one would have to go back beyond this primal repression. . . . As far as I know, however, Freud never stated the conditions under which one could go back beyond primal repression.

The reason for this embarrassed confusion, silence, and denial with regard to what ought to be a central theoretical concern is now easy enough to identify. In Ricoeur's terms, Freudians cannot state the "conditions under which one could go back beyond primal repression" to the "immediate expression" of an instinct because *there is no* "immediate expression," that is, *the supposed incestuous instinct does not exist.* The supposed instinct represents a misconstruction of the origins of neurosis. Meanwhile, the conditions that actually produce neurosis, including the typical *subjective experience* of being in the grip of uncontrollable instinct—which are largely the social, political, economic, and moral conditions in families and societies—are unexamined and systematically excluded from Freudian inquiry.

Among other reasons, in other words, repression theory in Freudianism is incoherent because the origin of neurosis is attributed to a nonexistent entity, belief in which shares the same misunderstandings that give rise to neurosis. In such a system, the failure of critical reflection about the self, that lies at the heart of neurosis, can never be properly tackled. This is the source of the embarrassed confusion about primal repression.

Actually, Freud was not altogether unaware of these severe difficulties with repression theory. As we will see in the discussion (in Chapter 7) of psychic trauma and traumatic neurosis, he had some awareness that those phenomena might actually be examples of neurosis arising *de novo,* thus addressing the circularity of repression theory, and made some valuable but very incomplete suggestions.

Conceptually, the problem of primal repression bears the same relation to psychoanalytic theory as does the problem of so-called "primitive accumulation" for economic theory. That problem was best stated by Marx, in one of the late chapters of *Capital* (1889, 736-737), in a passage whose relevance to psychoanalysis will be immediately apparent:

> We have seen how money is changed into capital; how through capital surplus-value is made, and from surplus-value more capital. But the accumulation of capital presupposed surplus-value; surplus-value presupposes capitalistic production; capitalistic production presupposes the pre-existence of considerable masses of capital and of labour-power in the hands of producers of commodities. The whole movement, therefore, seems to turn in a vicious circle, out of which we can get only by supposing a primitive accumulation (previous accumulation of Adam Smith) preceding capitalistic accumulation; an accumulation not the result of the capitalist mode of production, but its starting point.
>
> This primitive accumulation plays in Political Economy about the same part as original sin in theology. . . . Its origin is supposed to be explained when it is told as an anecdote of the past. In times long gone by there were two sorts of people; one, the diligent, intelligent, and, above all, fru-

> gal elite; the other, lazy rascals, spending their substance, and more, in riotous living. . . . Thus it came to pass that the former sort accumulated wealth, and the latter sort had at last nothing to sell except their own skins. . . . Such insipid childishness is every day preached to us in the defence of property. . . . In actual history it is notorious that conquest, enslavement, robbery, murder, briefly force, play the great part. In the tender annals of Political Economy the idyllic reigns from time immemorial. Right and "labour" were from all time the sole means of enrichment, the present years of course always excepted. As a matter of fact, the methods of primitive accumulation are anything but idyllic.

The problem is quite the same for the psychoanalytic understanding of neurosis, that has (in the Freudian scheme) repression of Oedipal desires at its core. For where do these desires, and this repression of desire, come from, apart from the neurotic system itself? As we have seen from examining the instinctivist and Oedipalist perspectives (e.g., the fable of the "touching phobia," with its just-so story quality) the answers furnished by Freud in terms of biology, anthropology, and psycho-sexual development of the individual are anything but satisfying. A solution, or even a critical approach, to the conundrum of primal repression might provide us a way out of the impasse.

In our reexamination of repression theory, Kinston and I (Cohen & Kinston, 1984) acknowledged its incoherence and put forward a theory that accords better with the facts of clinical work. We suggested that, contrary to Freud's view, secondary repression should not be regarded as a normative and essential aspect of psychological development. Rather, it is a pathological form of forgetting and, more important, a failure of critical attitude regarding the impact of (usually early) incomprehensible and traumatic experiences. Secondary repression represents one of several potential outcomes of primal repression, which is a state of being overwhelmed by such experiences. In the (secondary) repressive response, the person attempts to limit this damaging effect by accommodating to rather than opposing the experiences and their effect. This produces the typical neurotic outcome of irrational guilt, personality constriction, and diminished concept of self.

The healthiest outcome of primal repression, of course, is to adequately understand and effectively deal with the trauma. This results in critical awareness without secondary repression. *Critical awareness is thus the "negative" of neurosis,* to borrow Freud's trope. In keeping with this solution of the problem of primal and secondary repression, Kinston and I proposed a novel categorization of patients: healthy individuals (who sometimes seek psychoanalysis as a result of or in preparation for a particular stress), neurotic individuals, and cumulatively traumatized individuals. In the 1984 and two subsequent articles (Kinston & Cohen, 1986; 1988), we described clinical approaches to psychopathology that take into account the variable presence and extent of secondary repression. In the final chapter of this book I return to the idea of critical reflection as the antidote to neurosis by proposing that we conceive of clinical psychoanalysis as a "thinking cure" rather than a talking cure.

Conclusion

The major theories of Freudian psychoanalysis, which comprise its social-constructionist view of the human moral system—those of instinct, sexuality, aggression, and behavioral evolution—rest on dubious assumptions that they share with the irrationalist wing of modern liberal empiricism. These theories function to justify implicit ideologies of modern society rather than as coherent and testable ideas. The resulting psychology promotes the internalization of these cultural ideologies rather than freedom and responsibility for critical inquiry.

The burden of proof is not met by Freudianism with respect to its theory of moral development. Debate about the patriarchal, property-oriented, and statist ideologies that constitute so much of Freudianism's hidden agenda needs to become a main part of its manifest agenda if psychoanalysis is to develop into a rational discipline.

3

EXTENDING WESTERMARCK:
A Legitimate Sociobiological Basis For Psychoanalysis

The beginning is the most important part of the work.

—Plato, *The Republic, Book 1*

It is one of the characteristic prejudices of the reaction of the nineteenth century against the eighteenth, to accord to the unreasoning elements in human nature the infallibility which the eighteenth century is supposed to have ascribed the reasoning elements. For the apotheosis of Reason we have substituted that of Instinct; and we call everything instinct which we find in ourselves and for which we cannot trace any rational foundation. This idolatry, infinitely more degrading than the other, and the most pernicious of the false worships of the present day, of all of which it is now the main support, will probably hold its ground until it gives way before a sound psychology, laying bare the real root of much that is bowed down to as the intention of Nature and the ordinance of God.

—J. S. Mill, *The Subjection of Women* (1869)

Instinct and Society

If we follow Freud's intuition in approaching psychoanalysis by way of instinct, while recognizing that he had instinct all wrong, then Westermarck ought to be a corrective for some of the worst errors of Freudianism. How would a Westermarckian approach to instinct change psychoanalysis?

Broadly speaking, it would radically change the way we think about interactions between instinct and culture, individual and society, in the development and functioning of mind. There is not inevitable conflict between instinct and social prohibitions, nor a great divide between pre-culture and culture relived and fought out in each individual's development. Instinct is a source of knowledge, not necessarily less sophisticated or complex than social reasoning, and not some raw force to be subdued. Concepts of conscious and unconscious mental experience would need to change accordingly.

In the sociobiological model, many cultural institutions and forms of institutionalized behavior are based on (implicit or explicit) theoretical understandings of our instincts. Behavior pursued in light of these understandings is in the nature of experiment. Like other behavior based on approximate understandings, it is likely to have major unintended consequences, either because the understanding is plain wrong or because the world has changed and the understanding does not take important new factors into account. All child rearing, for example, is an experiment, whether or not we realize it, and however "conservative" (i.e., conforming to cultural norms) our parenting is. What Fox calls the "Freud effect" represents a largely unsuccessful experiment in repressive child rearing that promoted neurosis and crippled the capacity for adult love, just as the Taiwan experience represents a largely unsuccessful experiment in sibling marriage, promoting large-scale marital discord and hatred of parents.

To take a rational view of our behavior as parents is to recognize the experimental nature of the enterprise of parenthood, be prepared for all manner of unintended consequences, and use these consequences to understand the real, as opposed to predicted, effects of our actions, construct new theories, alter our behavior, observe its effects, and so forth, in a continuous effort to learn from experience. Informed by such an appreciation of instinct, culture, and behavior, psychoanalysis would become a self-critical discipline complementary to an autonomous sociology, anthropology, economics, and political science.

If the Westermarckian view of the sexual instinct were to prove true of instincts in general, a quite untraditional perspective on child development within families and societies would open up. Relevant questions from a sociobiological point of view would be: What are the deep structures of behavioral instincts, that is, what inborn knowledge do they imply and what theories of the self and the world might they support? What environmental support do they require, at what stages of life? To what extent do modes of child rearing, education, and socialization promote or hinder the person's maximal development of innate potentialities for understanding and exploring his or her self and the world? How much plasticity is there in development? Under what conditions, in other words, can compensatory or therapeutic experience make up for deficiencies of optimal experience after the foreclosure of critical periods?

In addressing such questions, the human capacity for symbolic memory and thought would play an enormous role. It is sensible to think that the crucial differences between animals and humans, and presumably between protohumans and humans, are differences in cognitive capacity, not instinctual prohibitions. The general-versus-special-case problem that I identified in psychoanalysis can be specified in terms of this insight. Our capacity to think about our instincts confers upon us the power to foster, enhance, or prohibit their expression. Our capacity to think critically about our instincts confers the power to construct theories about them. We have the potential for testing many of these theories and modifying them when possible in light of current conditions. Such experiments in living would be most significant in areas of human sexuality, aggression, and conflict. This is one of the great challenges of sociobiology, which some of its more fearful critics have not sufficiently recognized: To understand the biological roots of social behavior is not to be ruled by biology but to be able to free ourselves of biological determinism where possible.

In other words, Westermarck cautions us not to fall into the trap of thinking, as Freud did, that because we share instincts and biology with our animal predecessors, we share with them also their fixity of expression and developmental timetables. The logic of instincts is different in animals and humans. The "rules" of animal society obey an instinctual logic that is directed toward achieving an aggregate biological result—in the case of incest, avoidance of incestuous mating and healthy propagation of the species. The fact that human social structures and rules utilize language and thought makes them prone to errors of interpretation and to infiltration by purely social motives but also renders them accessible to processes of reflection, testing, and correction.

The pervasiveness of incest taboos suggests that human societies have generally understood the necessity of incest aversion while failing to understand how it works, or perhaps having lost an earlier understanding. Typically, the misinterpretation is in the direction of attributing far more importance to socialization than is warranted, in keeping with the perceived needs for authority structures to legislate what in any case most people would do.

By way of illustration, imagine a society of philosophical birds, seeking to understand their own obscure yet compelling urge to avoid wasps. After much discussion in the trees, they infer the biological reason: the wasp's deadly sting. This knowledge is celebrated—first in homely rituals within the nest, then in temples officiated by High Priests of Wasp Avoidance. Over time, however, the birds come to believe that the priests and their temples protect them from a shameful and primitive tendency to be attracted, even fascinated, by the deadly wasps; that without the temple rituals and priestly offices they would surely perish.

This parable is instructive but limited by the fact that birds avoid wasps from birth, whereas human (and birds too, for that matter) avoid incestuous objects only from the point of sexual maturity onward, a much more difficult phenomenon to understand.

A psychoanalysis informed by Westermarck's understanding would emphasize the maturational aspect of the sex instinct, which in humans is bound to become intertwined with other maturities. And it would seek to understand social standards and institutions in light of these natural maturing tendencies. It would not, for example, assume that long-lived social institutions and beliefs warrant the inferences about human nature that Frazer and Freud made. The origins, meanings, purposes, and effects of these social forms would be sought on a case-by-case basis. As to phenomena that Freud correctly identified in himself and others as sources of immaturity and pathology—incestuous inclinations persisting into adulthood—it would ask how and why one's natural tendencies to outgrow these inclinations are thwarted. What conditions of social life promote that outcome?

At a clinical level, these questions shift the focus of analysis onto factors in the life of the patient that promote or retard psychosexual maturation. The assumptions would be the reverse of Freudianism: The person is assumed to have the instinctive inclination and innate knowledge to mature. The broad aim of clinical treatment with regard to psychosexual development would be to identify and reduce whatever influences have interfered with those innate capacities.

In order to get a preliminary idea of the issues that such psychoanalysis would be called upon to deal with, let us consider first how other human maturational capacities are bound to affect the expression of the sexual instinct.

Instinct in Light of Language and Thought

Words reflect thought. The English word "instinct" reflects thinking that created a category within the larger universe of motive. It seems to have originated in the Late Middle Ages, derived from the Latin gerund *instinctus,* meaning prompting or instigation, from the verb *instinguere,* to prick, presumably derived from the Greek *stichein,* to prick. It found its way unmodified into German *(Instinkt),* where it exists alongside the Germanic word *Trieb* (from *Trieben,* to push), which came to have a somewhat more general connotation, as does the English equivalent, "drive." All these terms refer to knowledge that is inborn and genetically coded, pushing or pricking us from below.[27]

In considering behavioral instincts from a Westermarckian point of view, we must recognize that there are obvious differences between them in cogni-

[27]A number of psychoanalytic scholars, of whom Bettelheim (1983) is perhaps the best known, seeking to deny Freud's instinctivist errors, have made overmuch of the fact that he typically (although neither consistently nor rigorously) used the Germanic *Trieb* to refer to human instinct and the Latinism *Instinkt* to refer to animal instinct. They blame Freud's English translators for rendering his language overly scientistic by translating both words indiscriminately into the English "instinct." This is an attempt to evade a substantive argument with a narrowly semantic one. No good argument has been presented, nor, do I believe, does one exist, to make us to believe that the usage of these words alters the basic sense of Freud's thinking.

tive content and level and that these differences have major implications for how we register and think about them. Maturational instincts like incest-avoidance are bound to register in the mind differently than appetitive or reflexive instincts, such as eating and pain-avoidance. Freud's and Frazer's argument ("It is not easy to see why any deep human instinct should need to be reinforced by law. There is no law commanding men to eat and drink or forbidding them to put their hands in the fire.") misses this important point by conflating instincts of different types and levels of complexity, and considering sexuality an appetitive instinct.

Eating and pain-avoidance are highly automatized behaviors linked to readily perceivable negative consequences. They lend themselves to being adequately understood, for most practical purposes, in terms of simple causal theories such as "stimulus produces response": eating satisfies hunger, pain-avoidance reduces injury. This fact has major advantages and liabilities. Stimulus-response theories lend themselves to generalization via similarity or proximity, as in so-called (but misleadingly called) "conditioned reflex" learning. In classical animal conditioning a neutral stimulus such as a bell, paired with the arrival of food, will later elicit salivation even in the absence of food. In that case, the animal has, sensibly enough, generalized his theory of instinct (food relieves hunger) to a neutral stimulus that predicts the arrival of food. If the bell is then presented without the food, it will take some time, in the face of repeated negative outcomes, for the animal to discriminate the two conditions—to, in effect, critically assess its old theory and construct a new one better suited to the new reality. The seemingly unexceptionable theory of instinct has made for unconscious efficiency but also made it harder to notice exceptions—which we might consider a normal and relatively harmless form of dogmatism.

People, like animals, can be "conditioned" to do irrational or self-destructive things based on obedience to meaningless signals because of their historical linkage to gratifying or aversive stimuli. Techniques of rhetoric, advertising, propaganda, and brainwashing exploit the normal cognitive weakness for such indiscriminate learning.

But when applied to a complex maturational instinct like sexuality, the problems of simple causal theories multiply. If we are inclined to have trouble distinguishing a bell from food that was presented simultaneously and is no longer, how much more difficult must it be to properly understand an instinct that generates a response *ten to fifteen years* after the stimulus—even apart from the variety of social motives that impinge on it. Not allowing for this complexity of instinct, Freud could not begin to understand how it actually functioned.

Inevitably, sexual maturation, coinciding as it does with the beginning of social and legal adulthood, takes on complex meanings in which society has an interest. These interests, and not the instinct itself, account for what Frazer and Freud could not understand, that is, "why any deep human instinct should need to be reinforced by law." Westermarck, on the other hand, was well aware that this reinforcement is typical—that multitudes of religious and civil proscriptions and prescriptions have existed and do exist to regulate and reinforce what various societies consider proper sexual behavior, *as though* sexual pleasure and unpleasure were insufficient mechanisms. He was not misled by this fact into simplistically treating the sexual instinct as pure appetite.

Prominent among the social motives impinging on sexual maturation are the natural interests of those in authority to maintain that authority by exaggerating their importance. The idea that any complex social behavior must be socially learned is ideally suited to this end and is preferred over other explanations. Rulers tend not to be philosophers. Maturational instincts constitute a perfect instrument for the authoritarian attitude because their results are fairly predictable while their mechanisms are obscure. Social authority can claim responsibility for the benefits while shedding responsibility when things go wrong—can, in effect, privatize power while socializing liability. Such authoritarian attitudes vary from culture to culture and time to time, and social change does not always progress in the direction of diminishing it.

The anti-incest instinct, maturing during adolescence, manifests in reversals of the way we respond to childhood sources of satisfaction and enjoyment—the typical "surfeit" with and turning away from the status quo. Of inordinate importance, and contributing to the difficulty of understanding it, is the fact that *one may heed its urges or not without evident, and certainly without immediate, harm.* The sexual instinct inclines the individual to separate from childhood ways and embrace adult aims, but this inclination can be substantially rejected. This would appear to be true for animals as well, but the modern human condition, with its pluralism of poorly understood political, ideologic, and economic interests contending for the allegiance of individuals, is far too complex for the anti-incest instinct to provide much specific guidance.

Under conditions of modern life, therefore, overall maturation is given an impetus by sexual maturation but the individual has great freedom in both directions—to refuse that impetus as well as to challenge officially sanctioned sexuality. Moral and intellectual maturation requires judgment of issues quite removed from, but complexly interrelated with, sexuality. A culture tends to promote sexual maturity only to the extent that it is compatible with *its* standards, which are likely to be conflicting and confused and repellent to many individuals. Under these conditions "transgressive" sexuality is a natural vehicle for rebellious spirits—from Villon and Abelard through Sade to Wilde and Genet, Djuna Barnes and Angela Carter—to mock and provoke the status quo while exploring new esthetic and philosophical territory.

The mental consequences of failure to mature are correspondingly complex and hard to foresee. Sexual repression would appear to be an instinctually enforced consequence of failure to mature but one that can take many symbolic forms, as psychoanalysis has demonstrated.

Achieving sexual maturity in modern society is therefore a task the complexity of which is barely indicated by these reflections. One thing is reasonably certain. Almost invariably in actually existing modern societies urges to mature psychosexually will engender social and intrapsychic conflict for many people, especially those who take issue with cultural norms and values.

All these aspects of the sexual instinct have great clinical significance. The central theoretical problem that Freudianism sets for itself is the success or failure of the learning of an anti-instinctual tendency, which in its view is at the crux of moral character and optimally takes place between the ages of two and six. In this view, the Oedipal transformation of infantile sexuality should be complete by the latter age. From a Westermarckian point of view, this is an unrealistic and unnecessary expectation that seeks to prescribe something the child cannot properly understand and that therefore is likely to interfere with intellect and maturation. In other words, Oedipal psychology (the Freud effect) is an unintended negative consequence of a well-meaning but mistaken interpretation of human sexuality.

In terms of psychoanalytic procedure, the Freudian conception calls for the analyst to render conscious the supposed incestuous childhood "complex" in order to free the patient from childhood sexual attachments and promote his or her maturity. This means of achieving maturity is dubious for all the reasons discussed. The "Oedipus complex" in childhood is a precocious bit of antisexual social learning, not an evolutionary imperative as Freud thought.

Incestuous motives and fantasies in childhood are normative and of no pathogenic significance. It is only their persistence into adulthood as a guiding sexual and mental orientation that causes difficulty for maturity, and this is a consequence of the subversion of an instinct, not its expression. In a psychoanalysis informed by Westermarck's hypothesis the focus would be on the person's ease or difficulty in understanding and adapting one's instinctual anti-incestuousness to the conditions of one's life and society—no easy task, but at least one that utilizes the patient's innate capacities and knowledge.

Precocity, Delay, Extension: Implications for Child Rearing and Therapy

Westermarck also provides a corrective to Freud's assumptions of an evolutionary psychosexual precocity, with important clinical implications. Freudianism attributes conflict over incestuous impulses to psychosexual precocity, thereby justifying precocious repression. Westermarck makes us realize, however, that there is nothing precocious here and that incestuous features are a normal aspect of *immature* sexuality. Childhood sexual interests in peers, siblings, and parents are *destined to undergo not repression but transformation* through the maturation process. It is human cognitive capacities that undergo a precocious maturation compared to less evolved animals. For example, the language instinct is genetically programmed to mature between the ages of two and six (Pinker, 1994). A healthy child actively uses these capacities to explore the world in increasingly complex ways, and this naturally includes his or her sexuality and the environment's response. It can hardly be an accident that this period of extraordinary cognitive development is the same period assigned by Freud to the efflorescence and "resolution" of the Oedipus complex.

Given his preconceptions, Freud was bound to regard nonrepressive ways of responding to the child's sexual development as dangerously permissive, leading to failures in superego development. In a Westermarckian view, by contrast, parents would be encouraged to allow their children to experience a full flowering of their immature sexuality and to help them understand its creative, intellectual, and artistic possibilities, secure in the knowledge that it will naturally mature into adult forms. Such an attitude would incline parents to expend their educative efforts not in areas where the child would develop naturally on his or her own but in areas not under instinctual control, where failure of development would be genuinely harmful, and that could therefore benefit from mature guidance. Arguably, such an attitude would go a certain distance toward propelling us out of the stage of socialization-based child rearing, which is the dominant mode worldwide, to the next stage, conceived by DeMause (1974) as a "helping" mode.

In DeMause's powerful conception, various types of psychopathology reflect the persistence in society of historically outmoded forms of child rearing, which are typically not perceptible until an advance has taken place. From the perspective of the helping mode, the construction of which is under way in some segments of society, neurosis reflects the persistence of the socialization mode, with its emphasis on precocious sexual repression, just as more severe forms of pathology represent remnants of historically earlier and more primitive modes.

The human condition modifies the developmental timetables of our animal ancestors in the direction of delay and variability as well as precocity. Cognitive complexity extends maturational opportunities as well as possibilities for failure, so that adolescence is an infinitely more challenging and creative matter than in the animal. If the human anti-incest instinct matures at adolescence, the question is raised as to how long the "window of opportunity" for psychosexual maturation stays open. How critical, in other words, is the critical period for obtaining the experiences necessary for maturation? Can they be had later, an in what form?

The human adolescent seeks new territory intellectually, morally, and spiritually, not just geographically and sexually. He or she seeks to avoid incest psychologically, by gaining freedom from the strictures of the family circle and received ideas. Institutionalized forms of the incest taboo, on the other hand, promote more or less irrational social control.

We can, in principle, understand and reassess our unconsciously driven choices at any age, and undoubtedly within limits, make corrections. This loosening of the connection between chronology and maturity is in an important sense the biological condition that makes psychoanalysis possible. The adult who comes to *realize* that he or she has failed to make the adolescent separation and affiliation with the larger world has more chances to do so. We know very little as yet about biological limits on mental maturation, and this is an area to which psychoanalysis, in concert with other disciplines, should be able to contribute.

Psychoanalysis as Psychology and Philosophy Combined

Having pointed out the many oppositions between Freud and Westermarck, it is also true that there are areas of compatibility and uncertainty. For example, while conceding that society's regulation of sexuality imposes on the young precocious and unnecessary burdens of conscience and undermines their maturation, one might yet argue that this is a necessary compromise at our stage of cultural development. The argument would run something like this: The Oedipal, or puritanical, view of sexuality justifies society's moral education of its young, reflecting the fact that human societies accord their young status as sentient and moral beings. Human societies cannot be content with a final and aggregate result but properly concern themselves with young individuals, and the shaping of sexual attitudes is an important part of that undertaking. In the West, puritanism has been a significant and, according to some serious thinkers (notably Max Weber) progressive force in cultural evolution. Was it? If so, is it still?

These considerations pose interesting, researchable problems that suggest that a psychoanalysis informed by Westermarck need not be as far apart from Freudianism as first appears. Exploring this bridge would raise other important questions. What other natural moralities besides anti-incest are there and how do they develop? What are the benefits and detriments of attempting to instill them precociously in children? A considerable body of child-development literature (see the bibliography in Wilson [1993] for a good sampling) suggests that there are many natural moralities, but we know very little about them.

The main point of this chapter is that language, symbolic thought, and cultural interests make satisfaction of the anti-incest instinct a vastly (perhaps infinitely) more complicated matter in humans than in animals. The anti-incest instinct must find expression as a complex psycho-socio-politico-maturational tendency.

Freudianism has usefully made us aware of the symbolic equivalences between sexual, intellectual, and moral qualities, and has made of our sexual struggles a grand metaphor for conflicts of all sorts. Incest and incest-aversion, sexual repression and freedom from repression, are important things in themselves as well as metaphors for a wide range of human qualities and endeavors. But metaphors have limits, and the limits of the Freudian metaphor are largely determined by its inadequacy in representing our sexual natures.

Freudianism errs badly by accepting uncritically the assumption of actually existing societies that *they* are what stand between sexual morality and immorality, the survival of the individual and the survival of the society. Psychoanalytic help requires thoughtful criticism of the social influences with which one has been brought up. It requires critical thinking and *reciprocal* freedom between analyst and analysand to explore conscious and unconscious prejudices. Ideally, it is an activity that combines a psychology of the unconscious with moral philosophy.

Working toward a Rational Basis for Moral Action

To the extent that moral agency in Freudianism rests, on one hand, on a mechanistic view of personality and, on the other, on the acceptance of authority *qua* authority, it provides an unsatisfactory standard for those people for whom reason is the necessary and sufficient condition for moral character and happiness.[28]

The clinical corollary of the reflections of this and the previous chapter is that a successful psychoanalysis ought to empower the individual to change from reliance on a dogmatic or religious type of morality to one based on his or her reasoning capacities with regard to the values, virtues, and traditions important to that individual. This therapeutic transformation corresponds to the historical and philosophical distinction between a faith-based morality, as represented predominantly in our culture and era by the Christian tradition, and a morality based on human reason, represented by the Aristotelian tradi-

---

[28] I am using these terms in the sense of the *Nicomachean Ethics* (Aristotle, ca. 325 B.C.), according to which happiness *(eudaimonia)* is the state experienced by the person whose life activity is guided by reason toward achieving the good *(agathos)* for him- or herself and in general, that is, according to the virtues of character—continence, prudence, courage, justice, magnanimity, and friendship. Although using similar language in typical English translation, the concepts are quite different from the corresponding Freudian notions. Aristotelian *eudaimonia,* for example, has little to do with the notion of happiness as maximum pleasure yield, the notion accepted by Freud.

tion, which has never, despite close to a thousand years of effort by religious philosophers, been fully assimilated into their religions.[29]

The practical application of these concepts may be illustrated by the following brief account of forty psychoanalytic sessions conducted, over a year's time, along their lines.

Sexually passionate and daring in her youth, yet frigid with her husband, a smart and affectionate man who loved her deeply and who was the love of her life, a woman sought help for bizarre paranoid and phobic symptoms—that her husband would die while on a business trip and her children in their sleep, that she might harm them accidentally, and so on.

A source of marital unhappiness, her sexual frigidity had an ironic aspect to it, like her other symptoms. Her husband was the only man she had been deeply in love with. Together they had two wonderful and healthy children, and she was as happy in her married and family life as she could imagine being. Yet the passion of their courtship and early marriage had deteriorated because of her sexual indifference. This was a curious reversal for her, who in her youth, when she turned from an ungainly girl into a beautiful woman, had sought love through passionate and often indiscriminate sexual affairs. Yet about this part of her life she felt only shame and guilt.

With some initial reluctance she was able to recognize that her fears corresponded to some profound negativity and irrational guilt in her own personality, making it difficult to believe or accept that she was worthy of her actual good fortune. Already with this recognition and the shift in emphasis it created, her fears began to abate. We continued to explore the grounds of her profound negativity.

When I learned about the circumstances of her early life, it seemed obvious that this nexus of emotional experience must have to do with a pattern of crazy sexuality and hypocritical morality in her family, from which she had not freed herself. Her father was clearly a corrupt and lost man, an ordained Lutheran pastor who did not practice what he preached, but led a closeted sadomasochistic homoerotic existence. He cruelly chided his daughter for her lack of comeliness. During the course of my patient's growing up, his hypocrisy was gradually revealed. She discovered her father's lewd behavior and his stash of sadomasochistic literature, was treated lewdly by him, and her parents' marriage dissolved. Stripped of his ecclesiastical function, her father

[29]Although it is commonly taken for granted, including by scholars as skeptical and perceptive as MacIntyre (1981, 1988) that the latter tradition was successfully assimilated into the former, notably through the work of Aquinas, the more persuasive analysis of Jaffa (1952) argues that this assimilation was never complete, and that Aristotle would have been horrified by the willingness of Christians to accept something as impossible and destructive to human agency as the notions of personal immortality and a perpetually inaccessible divine intelligence. My personal and clinical experience suggests strongly that, for most people in our culture, this issue is as far from settled as it is difficult to articulate.

was reduced to pathetically explaining his failure as a parent and human being through psychobabble and psychiatric jargon (he had "attention deficit disorder," said his therapist, and was victimized by his own past). My patient not only retained a certain sympathy and "love" for her father, despite her conscious hatred and contempt for his past behavior and ongoing attempts to manipulate her; but following contacts with him she was liable to fits of irrational guilt, often expressed in intensified symptoms. The Oedipal dynamics are easy enough to infer, and were easy to identify and for her to recognize. But the crucial question was why she continued to accord this obviously corrupt and failed man any moral authority whatever.

My patient was inclined to explain her sexual life and its problems in this way: As a teenager and young woman she had been desperate for affection and tenderness, which she sought through sex. Sex was only the degraded means to a higher end, without value in itself. Having gained the greatest object of her desire she now wanted only tenderness; she wanted to please her husband but had genuinely lost any sexual interest for herself. With some difficulty she came to understand the contradictions embodied in this attitude, which actually portrayed a moralistic antisexuality typical of a scared and repressed preadolescent: "If you really love me, you won't need to make love to me." She recognized too that there must be some connection between her sexual and intellectual inhibitions. She was trained as a lawyer, but practiced only briefly. She aspired to write, and had written all her life, yet never shared her poems or stories with anyone or sought to develop her writing in any systematic way or have anything published. Thus, we came to the stage of asking: What is the common theme and central point of all these neurotic inhibitions, self-hatreds, and confusions, from the standpoint of moral character?

My patient was able to recognize that, inadvertently, she was becoming a hypocrite like her father—loving her husband but not wanting to make love to him and in effect punishing him for his sexual interest, as she did her children for their vitality; denying her own previously intense sexuality for unconvincing moralistic reasons; not following her intellectual passions; and retaining an obedience toward a father she consciously despised, who was somehow at the hub of this web. I therefore challenged her as to the grounds for continuing to believe in the dictum "honor thy father" in her particular case. At the same time I proposed to her that her sexual activity in her teens and twenties was more than a desperate search for affection. It was also part of a courageous and complex rebellion against what she understandably perceived to be a hypocritical and male-dominated sexual world. With as much pride as embarrassment she told me of various exploits from that era that had the point of demonstrating to men that anything they could do, she could do better.

As to "honor thy father," it was, she explained, the result of being raised a Lutheran pastor's daughter. But what did she know of Lutheranism, beyond the churchgoing and the moralistic prescriptions? Very little, it turned out, or of the Christianity of which Lutheranism is an offshoot, let alone of pre-Christian moral philosophy. She began to read, and was fascinated and disturbed. Was her Christianity any more than a conditioned reflex, based on fear rather than rational belief? She suddenly was no longer sure, and started to think and discuss these issues critically with her husband and a few close friends. The more she realized that moral life requires strength of character and intellect, not obedience to childhood dogmas, the more her symptoms faded away. Even her old sexual fire was coming back. It appeared to her now, with chagrin, that she had been sleep-walking intellectually during college and law school, and that it was time to awaken.

4

FROM INQUIRY TO ORTHODOXY

> I would like to believe that people have an instinct for freedom, that they really want to control their own affairs. They don't want to be pushed around, ordered, oppressed, etc., and they want a chance to do things that make sense, like constructive work in a way that they control, or maybe control together with others. I don't know any way to prove this. It's really a hope about what human beings are like—a hope that if social structures change sufficiently, those aspects of human nature will be realized.
>
> —Noam Chomsky, prefatory quote in M. Albert & R. Hahnel, *The Political Economy of Participatory Economics* (1991)

> If, as even the DSM-III [Diagnostic and Statistical Manual of the American Psychiatric Association] has recognized, all behavior involves a social dimension, then the work of psychology cannot limit itself to the abstract plane of the individual but must also confront social factors, which form the arena for the expression of all human individuality.
>
> —Ignacio Martin-Baro, *Writings for a Liberation Psychology* (1994)

> We invoked what we believe to be the three constitutive facts in the consciousness of Western man: knowledge of death, knowledge of freedom, knowledge of society.
>
> —Karl Polanyi, *The Great Transformation* (1944)

Early Psychoanalysis and Its Moral Tensions: Self-Preservation

In his early work, Freud flirted with ideas of innate morality but rejected them in favor of a theory reaffirming the amoral and antisocial character of instinct. A critical review of this intellectual history is central to my inquiry and will touch on the clinical, theoretical, and social influences at play during this period.

From its beginnings until about 1915 psychoanalysis possessed a concept —self-preservation—that at least could accommodate the notion of innate moral knowledge. In the theory of this era, self-preservation is one of two great instinctual forces; the other is libido. It was sometimes referred to as a singular "ego instinct" or "self-preservative instinct" and sometimes as a collective—"those other instincts, which have as their aim the self-preservation of the individual" (Freud, 1910, 214). Aggression is derived from this instinct in that it is, normally, elicited by threats to self-preservation rather than being an instinct in its own right.[30] Thus a "central thesis" of the theory is that the "prototypes of . . . hate are derived not from sexual life, but from the ego's struggle to preserve and maintain itself" (Laplanche & Pontalis, 1973, 18-19).

By itself, without specifying for or against what the self is being preserved, self-preservation is a morally ambiguous concept. Self-preservation at any price is generally not considered an unmixed good. Preserving oneself while sacrificing or dishonoring one's beliefs, values, family, friends, or fellow citizens is generally regarded as at least weak and at worst despicable, although often excused if done under great duress. But sacrificing oneself or risking self-sacrifice to preserve others or for important principles is generally and properly honored as the height of courageous virtue. Society does not usually bestow its honors on cowards. Thus it was the social context, the relation between self-preservation and social aggression, for example, that gave the concept of self-preservation its moral significance. And it was clear from the clinical situations to which Freud initially applied the concept that he intuitively had such considerations in mind, and that the concept encompassed not only bodily and material self-interest but moral goods like rationality and justice. Used in this way, *instinctive* self-preservation bears implications antithetical to the social-constructionist view that society imposes moral values on the inherently selfish and amoral individual.

Theoretically, however, self-preservation became in Freud's hands an increasingly ambiguous idea that could not differentiate between material and moral good. It was given up altogether in 1920. Why was this? Understanding Freud's reasons for giving up the concept will further help us understand the trend to a materialist-reductionist orthodoxy in the early years of psychoanalysis.

The self-preservative instinct was intended to represent the biological source of one basic aim of human existence, often in conflict with the other basic aim of participating in group life and the survival of the species. Freud postulated that self-preservative motives originate in and remain attached to

[30] This conception of aggression is the psychoanalytic equivalent of the so-called frustration theory of aggression, as developed by Dollard, Miller et al. (1939). It is because Freud later radically rejected this conception that those authors pointedly deal only with the pre-1920 theory in their borrowing from psychoanalysis.

particular physiological systems and organs, driving the person to seek organ-specific forms of satisfaction, of which the paradigm is the satisfaction of hunger. These motives are contrasted with sexual motives, which ultimately subserve the survival of the species. The conflict between self-preservation and libido was thus intended to represent the biological source of the moral tension between selfishness and altruism. Freud sought to explain a large range of neurotic symptoms in terms of this opposition. The sexual instinct, he believed, remain much longer under the sway of the "pleasure principle," while the former, tied to satisfaction by real external objects, are subject to early discipline by the "reality principle" and become agents of that principle, therefore entering into conflict with the sexual instincts (1911, 222-223). Conflicts arising in the mind between organ-based, ego-instinctual needs and the symbolic uses of the organ for libidinal satisfaction can account, for example, for certain neurotic disturbances of organ function, notably hysterical "conversion" symptoms such as blindness (e.g., 1910), paralysis, analgesia, and so on.

However, the phenomena of aggression and assertiveness that Freud intuitively explained by the ego instinct indicate that the aspects of self that he was addressing went far beyond physical reality and the world of external objects and in fact represented independently existing moral factors. The interesting problems of aggression in family or political settings always pertains to its meaning: What is being fought against? Is protest against injustice legitimate and constructive, or gratuitous? These problems will be abundantly clear when we turn to one of Freud's cases. But they were precisely the problems and meanings that Freud could not allow in his theory.

Freud's difficulty in recognizing the moral complexity of the parent-child relationship contributed to his abandoning the self-preservative instinct. In effect, he could not believe, any more than in the case of incest-aversion, that a human instinct could possess the complexity required to explain his intuitive observations. Wedded to a simplistic view of instinct as appetite and discharge, he ruled out the possibility that the satisfaction of physical needs might represent an early example, not a paradigm, of a much broader developmental array of moral needs.

What is needed to live well—the intuitions leading to knowledge of what is valuable or essential, and necessary to preserve— is something that *matures* with age and experience, certainly different for the infant, the young child, the older child, the adolescent, and the adult. Freud's attempt to *derive* such a complex developmental and moral motive as self-preservation from hunger—based on the belief that "all the organic instincts that operate in our mind may be classified as 'hunger' or 'love' " (Freud, 1910, 215)—is extremely implausible. Hunger is not a complex maturational instinct. It is one of the simpler, appetitive instincts and therefore unsuited to derive a complex moral and developmental function. Perhaps even more than the anti-incest instinct, an instinct of self-preservation implies ideas with which Freud was uncomfortable: that a self might seek from birth that which supports its integrity, autonomy, and sociability, rather than that which is destructive of those qualities. Such a self would possess some innate understanding of these moral differences. As in the case of sexuality (libido, love), the problem is with a too-limited definition of instinct and the corollary assumption that society only, through its teaching and discipline, tames the innately amoral, discharge-seeking, natural individual.

The incompatibility between these assumptions and the clinical phenomena the theory was designed to explain became quickly manifest in Freud's extreme difficulty in applying the theory. Laplanche and Pontalis recognize the huge gaps that separated Freud's intuitive clinical use of self-preservation from his inadequate theoretical derivation. They (1973, 147, quoting Freud [1910, 213]) observe, for example, that

> no sooner had the concept of the ego-instincts been introduced than Freud noted the attachment of these instincts [in opposition to the idea that they remain attached to particular organ systems and modes of satisfaction] . . . to a specific group of *ideas,* a group "for which we use the collective concept of the 'ego'—a compound which is made up variously at different times." . . . This plainly makes the term "ego-instincts" ambiguous: these instincts are considered on the one hand as tendencies *emanating* from the organism . . . and directed towards relatively specific external objects (e.g., food); on the other hand, however, they are viewed as attached to the ego as if to their object.

Laplanche and Pontalis (147) note, therefore, that despite the great importance Freud theoretically attached to the conflict between ego- and libido-instincts in the genesis of repression, and the greater closeness of the ego-instincts to the sense of reality, making them a prime candidate for repressing agents, "in the interpretations of the conflict offered by Freud the instincts of self-preservation are practically never seen to operate as the motor force of repression." And

> in the clinical studies published before 1910 the ego's place in the conflict is often emphasized, but no mention is made of its relationship with the functions necessary for the preservation of the biological individual. Later, after the self-preservative instinct has been explicitly posited in theory as an ego-instinct, it is still rarely evoked as an energy of repression.

The conclusion to be drawn is that the self-preservative instinct was a concept that had great intuitive appeal to the clinician in Freud but which he could not creatively use to account for relevant phenomena because of his philosophical and theoretical beliefs. His fundamental convictions that the moral system is created by a socialization process that disciplines amoral instincts confined him to a theoretical derivation that could not begin to account for the psychogical and social realities he set out to explain.

Had Freud been more open to Westermarck he would have been freed to frame coherent questions and make clearer psychoanalytic observations about instinctive self-preservation. He would have been able to develop sounder theories and test them clinically. But by abandoning (in 1920) the self-preservative instinct he moved in the direction of dogmatic assertion, and the resulting theories became more and more divorced from common sense.

Freud's difficulty in making clinical use of the self-preservation concept in a rigorous way to accommodate complex strivings of the self can be illustrated by his handling of a typical case of the period.

The Example of Dora

"Dora" is the fictional name of a seventeen-year-old girl whom Freud (1905a) treated in 1900. She was brought to him by her father, who hoped she could be cured of a worsening mental condition involving depression, irritability, suicidal ideas, social withdrawal, nervous coughing, headaches, and fainting spells. These symptoms constituted a marked personality change in a girl formerly bright, energetic, and engaged with the world. Freud's diagnosis was hysteria.

Dora's condition had developed in the context of a difficult family situation. Her father, a successful businessman to whom she had been close, was having an affair with a young married friend of the family. Although overtly solicitous of his daughter, he was quite self-involved, deceitful in his attempts to cover up the affair, and even promoted an affair between Dora and his lover's husband as a means of camouflage.

Freud's analysis was confined almost completely to Dora's libidinal conflicts, as reflected in two dreams he extensively interpreted. He was able to show that she harbored unconscious fantasies indicating conflicted sexual desires in relation to her father and his lover, and toward the man who had tried to seduce her. He showed also that these fantasies were implicated in some of her symptoms, some of which cleared up when the fantasies were interpreted. The case report is remarkable for the complete absence of any reference to self-preservative issues or conflicts, illustrating Laplanche and Pontalis's point. Although Dora's situation was rife with problems of aggression and conflicted judgment, Freud did not use the theory of self-preservation to account for them.

Dora broke off the treatment after three months, seemingly dissatisfied with his approach. She returned fifteen months later, after having confronted the guilty parties. In other words, having received no help or guidance from Freud in managing her problems with judgment and aggression, she used her own best judgment to deal with the situation. She seems to have expected that Freud would at least be interested in her handling of the matter and want to discuss it with her. At this point, however, he revealed his authoritarian bias by declining to work further with her, seeing her action as neurotic "revenge" (121-122).

The treatment was clearly incomplete and the clinical results indifferent, as Freud acknowledged. Nonetheless, he felt that it was a reasonable validation of his major theses.

This case is both celebrated and notorious. As one of only a handful of detailed Freud cases, it has become a clinical paradigm for Freudianism because of the detailed analysis of the dreams and hysterical symptoms. Later analytic scholars like Erikson (1962) and Lacan (1952) have commented on the case extensively. It has also been the object of intense scrutiny from feminists and other critics, who see in Freud's handling of Dora evidence of frightened misogyny, social naïveté and hypocrisy, and deceit and malevolence toward patients. (See the essays by Rose, Ramas, Gallop, Cixous & Clement, and others in the volume edited by Bernheimer & Kahane [1985]; see also Esterson [1998], Kanzer & Glenn [1980], Lakoff & Coyne [1993], Mahony [1996], Sprengnether [1990], and Wax [1999, chapter 7].) Historical research has shown that the long-term clinical outcome of the case was quite negative, leaving open the possibility that the treatment was not merely incomplete but actually destructive (Deutsch, 1957).

The case nicely illustrates the phenomena that Freud had difficulty understanding because of his convictions about the social-constructionist nature of human morality, here displayed with disturbing consequences. Although the ego-instinct theory could have easily been developed to understand Dora's particular problems, he forced himself into a much more convoluted channel. His report shows the presence of libidinal conflicts but it is also laced with accounts of complex but unconscious perceptions, cognitions, and ethical judgments that contributed to Dora's mental struggles. These included, prominently, judgments of the intellect, character, and moral integrity of the major players in the sexual-political family drama in which she was caught up.

Dora seemed to have little difficulty with her assessment of her mother, an obsessive nag. She had set herself for many years against her influence, and Freud concurred with her negative judgment (20). Given that situation, her energetic and engaged father was bound to take on intensified importance during her growing-up years. When she was preadolescent and he fell in love with the beautiful young acquaintance, it engendered the most painful and confused feelings, which, lacking direct expression, were in part expressed through hysterical symptoms. Her father's infidelity to her, as expressed in his deceit and manipulation, was an incomprehensible blow. As Freud described it, her state of mind involved elements that had been more or less unconscious but were not too difficult to infer and clarify—intense resentment of her father as well as admiration and envy, attraction to as well as hatred of the husband of her father's lover, who had made sexual advances to her, and very conflicted feelings toward the woman herself, who had formerly been her friend. Clarifying such attitudes and judgments could obviously have been very important to the analytic work.

Dora wished she had the equanimity of her older brother, who felt that they "even ought to be glad, perhaps, that [father] has found a woman he can love" (54). But she could not bring herself to forgive him. Freud realized that her father's character flaws, as well as her unconscious complicity, contributed to Dora's difficulties in forming a clear judgment and acting with full and deliberate consciousness. But it is anything but clear what Freud's idea was of a healthy stance and a proper course of action.

Thus, it is difficult to assess to what extent problems of unconscious judgment, purpose, and intention became part of the analytic process or were just Freud's personal reflections. If they were discussed, it seems almost certain that they were not given much weight. For example, in Freud's view, Dora's father was indeed a liar, "one of those men who know how to evade a dilemma by falsifying their judgment upon one of the conflicting alternatives" (34). But whether or not Freud shared his views with Dora, he did not consider them very important, to judge from his rebuff of her when she sought further treatment. He felt that her confrontation of her father was a species of "acting out" that impugned the sincerity of her wish for more treatment. His clinical behavior matches his dominant theory, in which the individual depends on paternal authority to develop control over instincts and it is therefore neurotic to rebel overmuch, however corrupt the authority. Dora was therefore, in his view, not acting morally and freely, but neurotically, in demanding an explanation from her father.

The Elimination of Self-Preservation

Not even Freud's harshest critics could expect a pioneer clinician to have success with every case. But a clinician-researcher who claims to be developing a scientific method of treatment should at least approach his cases as necessary experiments, tests of his theories. As striking as is the clinical failure of the Dora case is its place in Freud's intellectual history. For his answer to the kinds of difficulties encountered in the case (and others from the period, we must assume) was, *in complete contradiction to the evidence,* to give up entirely on the concept of self-preservation. Changing course radically, he simply (but after a complex detour into "ego psychology" discussed in the next chapter) eliminated it from his theory.

In the rearranged instinct theory that emerged with increasing conviction after fifteen years, aggression was defined as a basic instinct rather than as a response to threats to the self. This shift created the famous (but mislabeled) "dual-instinct theory" of 1920 in which incestuous sexuality and aggression are the twin pillars of mental motivation. I discuss this theoretical shift at length and in historical context in Chapter 8, and the reader who is not familiar with the new theory may want to preview that chapter for a perspective on the comments that follow—which focus on the *effect* of this shift on the psychoanalytic possibilities represented by the self-preservation concept.

In making this shift, Freud all but eliminated the possibility of autonomous moral agency from the mind. Ridding theory of the troubling ambiguity of the self-preservative instinct, it brought psychoanalysis to a unified view of instinct and also into harmony with many modern views of morality as based not on any consideration of the good but on a multiplicity of selfish interests and passions in conflict with each other and with social demands.

Freedom from the constraints of an instinctual self-preservation left Freud in a position to speculate grandly about the transformation of instinct into ego, biology into psychology. In an important sense this theoretical shift parallels his assumed defeat of Westermarck. But in both cases Freud freed himself from the constraints of biology only by contriving a fantasy biology that he could treat as he wished. It also put Freud the clinician and social thinker who strove for human betterment in an awkward position. After rejecting self-preservation, he sought to hold on to an autonomous moral agency in the mind by expanding "libido" to include the "Eros of the poets and philosophers" (1920, 50), and specifically (1932, 212) the Christian concept of brotherly love (agape), which he had earlier, consistently, dismissed as wishful thinking. Even had that effort been well thought out (which it was not), it would have been an inadequate solution to the twin problems of innate knowledge and natural morality. For example, while the Catholic doctrine of Natural Law figures complexly in Christian moral philosophy, it holds that only through supernatural intervention (revelation) can man compensate for the imperfections of his fallen nature and limited reason. So embracing Christianity makes psychoanalysis less receptive to a rational approach to these problems.

Perhaps more important, the dual-instinct theory stifles investigation of the social causes of repression, removing psychoanalysis further from social reality. In the new theory the role of such causes is restricted proportionally to the expanded requirements of the superego system, based now on a belief in twin instincts that follow the same highly reductionistic logic. This contributes, perhaps, to the fact that, in the era of the 1920s through the 1940s, Freudianism, following the big leap of its aging master (Freud died in 1939), took on an increasingly defensive and churchlike character. It fell to certain post-Freudian thinkers to attempt to revive the inquiry into instinctive self-preservation that Freud had abandoned.

For these reasons, the advent of the dual-instinct theory represents a watershed, in which the instinctivist Oedipal argument attained hegemony over the entire domain of analytic inquiry. This hegemony, and not the more widely discussed relinquishment of the "seduction theory," is the true defining moment of Freudianism as a self-contained theory. Freud understandably regarded this development as crucial for the consistency of his system and held unwaveringly to it, whatever its irrationalities. It is the pre-1920 period of speculation followed by severe contraction that Guattari (1995, 48) must have had in mind when he wrote

> Freud's genius, or perhaps his madness, was to have hit upon the emergence of a subjective continent which philosophy, the history of religions, and literatures had only explored from a distance. Then he forged theoretical instruments, devised analytical techniques and encouraged the creation of schools and international institutions, so that questions that were originally exposed quickly closed up again.

The Crisis of Moral Meaning and the Beginning of Orthodoxy

Freud's self-preservation theory was an intuitive one, constructed to explain certain major facts of neuroses. If one seeks to understand the lives of neurotic individuals, as Freud did, it is hard to avoid the conclusion that they, like Dora, struggle with conscious and unconscious aggressive reactions to protest and protect themselves against damaging influences, prominent among which are the limitations and hypocrisies of their family lives as children. They have difficulty managing these reactions and behaving effectively to the extent that they are irrationally insecure and guilty and the aims of the aggression are obscured and repressed. Freud intuitively recognized this aggression as a valid expression of one's self-preservative nature. In fact, he (1914b, 92) found it "quite impossible to place the genesis of neurosis upon the narrow basis of the castration complex" (i.e., explanations solely in terms of repressed sexuality and the Oedipus complex). Yet he could not do the same when it came to *theory*. He could not part with the stereotyped instinctivism that we have found to be at the heart of his Oedipal theorizing. This led him to dismiss his observations that self-preservative *judgment* is routinely repressed in neurosis.

These contradictions intensified in the years 1914-1920, a period of intense questioning. As clinical experience increased, so did Freud's reservations about explaining neurosis on the narrow Oedipal basis. In his theoretical papers of 1915 he expressed serious doubt about the extent to which libido theory could account for repression. On top of this was the impact of the war. Like the Holocaust for the next generation, the First World War was an awakening to unsuspected social realities, which could not but affect how psychoanalysis saw individuals in society. Clinical and political realities were both enormously influential in determining the direction of psychoanalysis during this turbulent time.

The difficulties in Freud's theory reflected a heavy but disguised weighting of conservative social and political thinking. A large split existed between attitudes toward sexual and nonsexual protest against social morality. In the area of sexuality he favored a degree of liberation from hypocritical sexual morality, while viewing with the greatest skepticism any wider protest against family and cultural mores—those "common ideal[s] of a family, a class or a nation" (1914b, 101). Yet clinical experience showed that repressed protest against such norms, as much or more than the sexual protest, was a major factor in neurosis.

At a cultural level, certain political and social ideals embraced by Freud and so many of his generation were proving very problematic. Specifically, the free-market economic order of which he thought so highly ("the extensive community of interests established by commerce and production" [1915d, 288]), by destabilizing national economies and social structures contributed directly to the Great War and to the greatest barbarity the modern world had seen up to that time (see Polanyi's classic 1944 work, *The Great Transformation,* for an exposition of this argument and extensive bibliography). Adherence to these ideals and their underlying rationales led Freud to an intellectual dilemma, especially acute during the interwar period. Either there was something terribly flawed about them, or they were correct but humans were perverse beasts who could not be effectively civilized under the best of circumstances.

Freud handled this dilemma by radically changing his theory in the direction of the second alternative, in several complex stages over a number of years, and these changes entail a radical shrinking of perspective that has continued to afflict psychoanalysis. In order to understand the changes and the thinking behind them, it will be useful to examine the various challenges to his theory that occupied him during these years and his reactions to them.

Repression of Self-Preservation

The first challenge was posed by clinical observations of the type illustrated by the Dora case. It is not just libido but natural self-preservative tendencies that are repressed in neurosis: the neurotic individual does not adequately perceive, remember, think about, and judge harmful circumstances. In light of these observations and inferences it became impossible to maintain the classic cuts between ego and id, and conscious and unconscious, with their assumptions of beneficent socialization. Freud first addressed the problem systematically in theoretical papers, notably the "metapsychological" papers of 1915.

The most consequential observations are trenchantly formulated in the third paper of the series, on the nature of the unconscious and repression. Freud wrote (1915c, 192-193): "it is not only the psychically repressed that remains alien to consciousness, but also some of the impulses which dominate our ego—something, therefore, that forms the strongest functional antithesis to the repressed." This problem corresponds exactly to the split between the two instinct theories. Freud is here recognizing that the "higher" functions of the personality that ought to subserve its self-preservation, and not just libido, succumb to repression. The point is obscured by a bit of Freudian rhetoric that contrasts "alien to consciousness" with "repressed," when they of course mean the same thing.

As we have seen, he had up to this point, in keeping with his ideas about the requirements of civilized life, attributed unique importance to libido. What is destined to become repressed is that which belongs to our archaic libidinal heritage. He had insisted (1910, 215) that "our civilization . . . originates mainly at the cost of the sexual component instincts." At a clinical level, Freud, therefore, had believed that the *one* constant feature of the repressed was its sexual content. Whatever else is repressed and adds to the unconscious meaning of neurotic symptoms, a sexual content is always present and has special importance: "At least one of the meanings of a symptom is the representation of a sexual phantasy, but . . . no such limitation is imposed upon the content of its other meanings" (1905a, 47). The 1915 statement expresses his discovery that repressed *nonsexual* content, as represented by the person's need to perceive, remember, think, and judge, is equally important in any real neurosis.

Freud registered these contradictions as *a theoretical problem* while maintaining the almost exclusive sexual emphasis in his clinical work, as we saw in the Dora case. But by 1915 he was noticing the repression of moral judgment in neurosis and raising questions about the connection between sexual impulses and the larger pool of repressed ideas. Are sexual impulses indeed uniquely important causes or are they simply part of complex social and moral situations, in which perceptions and judgments along with sexual inclinations are repressed?

The clinical problems behind the 1915 papers are the common human realities corresponding to the theoretical split and moral tension between libido and self-preservation: in the case of Dora, the fear-driven inhibition or repression of perception, knowledge, judgment, and action, at times of serious disillusionment with parents or other authorities, which typically come to a head in adolescence. These social and moral realities are characteristic of virtually all analyses, as far as I can tell. Neurotic patients are made anxious by and repress thoughts and judgments about their early lives and life in general that are actually morally sound and potentially liberating. They are confused as to where their true interests lie. As a consequence they either do not see, or battle ineffectually against, the various conditions that enslave them.

An Evolving Orthodoxy

"Dual-instinct" is a misleading designation for the post-1920 theory, for, by treating both sex and aggression as highly reductionistic instincts Freud actually eliminates the dualistic moral tension of the libido/self-preservation model. This elimination-by-definition was followed by a complex series of theoretical shifts that he made in the years 1914-1920.

An exploration of Freud's social and moral philosophies is needed to comprehend these complicated shifts, and this will be undertaken in Chapters 5, 7, 8, and 9. In what came to be his exclusive view, the moral universe of the child is determined by what are conceived to be purely appetitive biological needs, by definition amoral and asocial, to control which inhibitions are conveyed from the social environment. The *all-important social inhibitions* "imposed from without" (1914b, 100) and internalized are what Freud referred to as "the conditioning factor of repression" (93). This factor depends on the person's attachment to "the common ideal of a family, a class or a nation" (101), the generalized form of the motive problematically characterized as "the child's loving relation to the author of the prohibition" (1913, 29).

It is one of the great ironies of the Freudian tradition that, while aiming to develop a complex psychology of inner experience, it evolved so quickly (as Guattari noted) into a highly conventional social philosophy. During the period circa 1915-1920 Freud consolidated his view that *it is pathological to revolt against the common standards of socialization.* "The revolt," wrote Freud, "against this 'censoring agency' [an early term for superego] arises out of the subject's desire *(in accordance with the fundamental character of his illness)* to liberate himself from all these influences, beginning with the parental one . . . ." (1914b, 96, my italics) However misguided social education may be—and he saw this clearly, at least early on with regard to hypocritical sexual morality—revolt against it is pathological. An appreciation of this intellectual history helps us to understand why it is only some of Freud's early theories that provide anything approximating a coherent idea of the human moral system.

Freud did register some doubts about his evolving position:

> The disturbances to which a child's original narcissism is exposed, the reactions with which he seeks to protect himself from them and the paths into

which he is forced in doing so—these are themes which I propose to leave on one side, as an important field of work which still awaits exploration. (1914b, 92)

The implication of this veiled comment is that the "conditioning factors" to which the child submits may not be so innocuous after all. But by 1920 Freud will have dealt with this reservation by deciding that the person, innately destructive, was unworthy of such solicitude.

5

THE EGO-PSYCHOLOGY SOLUTION:
Freud's Subversion of Meaning

> It is no exaggeration to say that much of the seventh chapter of *The Interpretation of Dreams,* and indeed, of Freud's later "metapsychological" studies, has only become fully intelligible since the publication of the *Project.* Students of Freud's theoretical writings have been aware that even in his profoundest psychological speculations little or no discussion is to be found upon some of the *most* fundamental of the concepts of which he makes use . . . . The paucity of explanation of such basic notions in Freud's later writings suggests that he was taking it for granted that they were as much a matter of course to his readers as they were to himself.
>
> —James Strachey, Introduction to Freud's *The Interpretation of Dreams* (1953)

Ego Psychology: A Quasineurological, Associationist Theory of Consciousness

The need to understand situations like Dora's was, as Freud wrote in hindsight, a "disagreeable discovery" (1933, 69) because the elegant simplicity and seeming explanatory power of earlier formulations was lost. Clinical observation seemed to refute the theory that repressed libido caused neurosis, and with it (given his unwillingness to give more than token significance to instinctual self-preservation) his Oedipal social-constructionist theory of the self. Freud was no longer able to make repression of unacceptable libidinal impulses "the basis of far-reaching and inevitable conclusions" (1923, 18).

This is the yawning gap left by his narrowly instinctivist understanding of personality and sexuality combined with his inability, based on similar reasoning, to apply the self-preservation concept in a creative way. This gap was eventually filled by the "death instinct"; that is, by the concept of innate self-destruction. To go there directly, however, would take us way ahead of our story and leave out fifteen years of work in which a complex intermediary structure, now known as "ego psychology," was developed. No understanding of Freudianism would be complete without an appreciation of this work and its function as a bridge between the earlier and the later theories.

The theoretical challenge that lies behind this work is that "consciousness stands in no simple relation either to the different systems [of the mind] or to repression" (1915c, 192). Freud's response to this challenge, his effort to overhaul his theory, which occupied him for the last twenty-five years of his life, constitutes a body of work that, like his psychoanalytic anthropology, is impressive in its ambition, inventiveness, and erudition. Yet it results finally in an intellectual house of cards, excessively arcane and unstable while still failing to deal with the foundational problems. My aim in this chapter is to show the reasons for this highly critical assessment, while elucidating complex Freudian ideas, the sources of and interconnections among which have not generally been recognized.

The body of theory that came to be known as "ego psychology" was Freud's first substantial attempt at overhaul. Although now identified with the later, more famous works, *The Ego and the Id* (1923) and *Inhibitions, Symptoms, and Anxiety* (1926), its theoretical grounding is a series of "metapsychological" (i.e., highly theoretical) papers of 1915. In those papers Freud sought to provide a more complex view of repression and mental functioning, in keeping with the "disagreeable discovery." Rather than relying on simple dichotomies between conscious and unconscious, more or less corresponding to ego and id, the ego was to be considered a complex system with unconscious, preconscious, and conscious levels, capable of imposing repressive censorship at both unconscious-preconscious and preconscious-conscious boundaries. Theories of language, knowledge, and conceptual thought play a crucial role in these refinements, and so psychoanalysis post-1915 comes to resemble an epistemological system. Ego psychology with its linguistic and epistemologic refinements remains a major component of psychoanalysis to this day.

The key new concept proposed in the *Papers on Metapsychology* (1915a; 1915b; 1915c) is that for an instinctual "derivative" to become conscious in the fullest sense—that is, to be integrated into and used effectively in one's personality—it must become an idea that is verbally articulated and thought about. This concept has important roots in Freud's neurological and linguistic thinking.

As an economical way of critically discussing a large amount of theoretical material, I will present Freud's ideas in an unconventional way, which, however, best demonstrates their purposes, sources, and interconnections. I start with a discussion of his ideas about representation, thinking, and language, proceed to assess his views on the nature of consciousness, and end with a discussion of his social psychology. Running through these discussions as a connecting thread is my familiar main question: to what extent do Freud's ideas promote a view of human motivation and agency, especially moral agency, that coherently elaborates the basic psychoanalytic ideas (the exaggerated influence of unconscious mental processes and of childhood experience)?

Freudian Linguistics

In introducing linguistic concepts into his theory Freud sought to link psychoanalytic problems with classical epistemological ones. The striking features of this effort at linkage, evident if one makes the effort to search beneath his complex terminology for underlying assumptions and ideas, is how superficial his engagement with these problems was. Basically, he treated certain dubious linguistic ideas as proven and as merely needing to be integrated with *his* psychological theories. He did not think deeply or hard about language. Rather, he took a number of received but quite controversial and problematic theories as fact.

Virtually *all* Freud's ideas about language are set forth in a highly condensed, dogmatic fashion in his early *On Aphasia* (1891). They were carried over unmodified into the *Project for a Scientific Psychology* (1895b) and from there into all his later work.

Thus, when he re-approached the problem of language in 1915 (1915c, 194, italics in original), he wrote: "To [the existing theory] let us add that the existence of the censorship between the *Pcs.* [preconscious] and the *Cs.* [conscious] teaches us that becoming conscious is no mere act of perception, but is probably also a hypercathexis, a further advance in the psychical organization." Here is our first encounter with a Freudian coinage, *hypercathexis,* hugely important to the theory from here on. What does it mean?[31]

Hypercathexis is Freud's term for the *conformity of words with "things,"* derived from a certain strain of linguistic theorizing:

> What we have permissibly called the conscious presentation of the object can now be split up into the presentation of the word and the presentation of the *thing;* . . . the conscious presentation comprises the presentation of the thing plus the presentation of the word belonging to it, while the unconscious presentation is the presentation of the thing alone. The system *Ucs.* contains the thing-cathexes of the objects, the

[31] The ensuing discussion in the text elucidates the concept of hypercathexis. The meaning of the underlying concept, cathexis, is approximately "investment of mental energy." For a further discussion of these concepts see pages 117–118.

> first and true object-cathexes; the system *Pcs.* comes about by this thing-presentation being hypercathected through being linked with the word-presentation corresponding to it. It is these hypercathexes, we may suppose, that bring about a higher psychical organization and make it possible for the primary process to be succeeded by the secondary process which is dominant in the *Pcs.* Now, too, we are in a position to state precisely what it is that repression denies to the rejected presentation in the transference neuroses; what it denies to the presentation is translation into words which shall remain attached to the object. A presentation which is not put into words, or a psychical act which is not hypercathected, remains thereafter in the *Ucs.* in a state of repression. . . . [T]hought-processes, i.e., those acts of cathexis which are comparatively remote from perception, are in themselves without quality and unconscious, and . . . attain their capacity to become conscious only through being linked with the residues of perceptions of *words.* (1915c, 201-202, italics in original)

To relate this proposition to clinical issues—Dora's, for example—it implies that a main component of her pathology was not an absolute inability to think, but a selective inability to recognize and verbalize her reactions to disturbing influences, absent which they remained surd unconscious "things."

This linking of consciousness with verbal thought pertains to ancient philosophical problems, which had been revived as objects of intense interest and speculation in the several centuries prior to Freud. It draws upon the manner of framing those questions to which most of the great philosophers had contributed, and which are used to this day—most influentially Locke and Descartes, but also Bacon, Hobbes, Leibniz, Rousseau, Condillac, Diderot, Herder, Humboldt, Hume, and Adam Smith. At first glance, therefore, Freud's return to such problems would seem to herald a rapprochement with earlier traditions of thought and an elaboration of intuitions about the knowing, reflecting self that he had expressed in the early ego instinct idea but failed to develop.

Turning to the traditions from which Freud's ideas are drawn, however, we find these expectations disappointed on both counts. Such a rapprochement would have reduced the significance of Freudian ideas to a distinctly secondary role. Rather, he borrowed selectively from existing traditions, for the most part with neither acknowledgment nor critical discussion, avoiding serious questions about language and thought while attempting to preserve the main features of his libido-dominated psychology. His failure to acknowledge sources makes it difficult for students of psychoanalysis to locate Freud's apparently new ideas in ongoing traditions of inquiry and exaggerates the sense of originality.

In fact, Freud made use of a familiar and general framework of categories—words, objects of perception, and ideas—as well as some familiar theories, which he attempted to fuse with his own. Since this amalgamation bears much of the weight of ego psychology, it is worthwhile to examine it closely.

Words and Things: Indebtedness to Locke and Condillac

As is apparent from the 1915 excerpts, Freud made use of a philological and associationist approach to language. Consciousness is tied to the linguistic functions of linking "things" with words, which linkage constitutes a simple concept or "idea" and brings about a "higher psychical organization." This characterization of consciousness expresses on one hand the ordinary observation that verbally articulated ideas are a main content of consciousness, while hypothesizing that unconscious "thing-representations," denied word-representation, are a main content of the repressed unconscious. This approach to knowledge or "understanding" is a classic one, used most powerfully by Locke, who, like Freud, found that it was "impossible to speak clearly and distinctly of our Knowledge . . . without considering, first, the Nature, Use, and Signification of Language" (Locke, 1689, 401). Locke had challenged the earlier medieval-scholastic Adamic doctrine according to which the representation of things by words was only an apparent dualism, obscuring the real unitary nature of linguistic signs, a reflection of their divine origin. Locke's forceful and convincing refutation of the Adamic doctrine of privileged knowledge, and his exploration of the problematic nature of verbal representation, lies at the heart of the epistemological argument of his *Essay Concerning Human Understanding* (1689). In the words of the great historian of linguistics Hans Aarsleff (1982, 24), his critique of language that follows from this refutation "laid the foundation of the modern study of language." It is Locke's critique to which Freud implicitly refers by positing, as a major problem, the conformity, or lack of conformity, of word-representations with things.

Freud's use of this Lockean language, however, *omits reference to Locke's central epistemological problem,* which is the "cheat of words." "'Tis plain cheat and abuse, when I make them [words] stand sometimes for one thing, and sometimes for another" (1689, 492). Locke (406-407) (in this and all subsequent quotes from Locke and Condillac, italics are in the original), in other words, recognized that the common, unconscious habit of believing that words are as good as things is a serious but tenacious mistake. Words do not represent things in some way that provides privileged knowledge of their nature, but rather represent ideas, or propositions about things, events, phenomena:

> Though Words, as they are used by Men, can properly and immediately signify nothing but the *Ideas,* that are in the Mind of the Speaker; yet they in their Thoughts give them a secret reference to two other things. *First, they suppose their Words to be Marks of the Ideas in the Minds also of*

other Men, with whom they communicate. . . . Secondly, . . . they often suppose their Words to stand also for the reality of Things. . . . [T]hat is a perverting the use of Words, and brings unavoidable Obscurity and Confusion into their Signification, whenever we make them stand for any thing, but those *Ideas* we have in our own Minds. . . . To this Abuse, those Men are most subject, who confine their Thoughts to any one System, and give themselves up into a firm belief of the Perfection of any received Hypothesis. (497)

The "double conformity" of words and things reflects only the acceptance of conventional thought and provides us no guidance as to which ideas about things warrant belief, that is, constitute provisional knowledge: "There is no Knowledge of Things conveyed by Men's Words, when their *Ideas* agree not to the Reality of Things" (505). For ideas are the "Instruments, or Materials, of our Knowledge," and "Knowledge . . . all consists in Propositions" (401); that is, conjectures about reality, which must be thought about critically and tested against experience.

Freud makes all of these enormous issues seem unproblematic. His use of Lockean linguistic concepts is actually regressive, because it posits that the mere conformity of word- and thing-representations (therefore conventional opinions and ideas) constitutes an "advance in the psychical organization," the very notion that Locke passionately argued against. It can only be an advance if one believes that acceptance of received opinion, as opposed to thinking for oneself, is a higher psychic function. To relate this to clinical matters, in Locke's view Dora, for example, would have been seen as suffering the effects of the "cheat of words," in that she was excessively in the grip of this unconscious habit, placing excessive weight on conventional explanations of the things that disturbed and injured her despite her grave reservations about them. She could not trust her own judgment sufficiently to develop adequate explanations.

Hypercathexis is simply a Freudian version of the old notion of the "double conformity" of words and things, a psychoanalytic statement of the common habit *challenged* by Locke, and one that begs the crucial questions about the nature and purpose of consciousness, and about the truth and value of the ideas in our consciousness. In order to develop some sense of Freud's answers to the questions being begged—which will also explain why Freud treated linguistic formulations so offhandedly—we need to delve into his assumptions about the origins of words and the manner in which words become connected with ideas. This inquiry will provide an opportunity to critique a number of additional Freudian concepts that were introduced into the theory around this time and to further identify sources.

Origin of Words

First, what does Freud have to say about the origin of words? In *On Aphasia* (1891), he starts with the assertion that: "From the psychological point of view the 'word' is the functional unit of speech; it is a complex concept constituted of auditory, visual and kinaesthetic elements" (1891, 73). There are two components to Freud's attempt to account for the existence, meaning, and use of words, one of which purports to account for the learning of words with established meaning, the other purporting to explain the baby's "invention" of words through perceptual and bodily experience. Concerning the former, "We learn to speak by associating a 'word sound image' with an 'impression of word innervation.' When we have spoken, we are in possession of a 'kinaesthetic word image,' i.e., of the sensory impressions from the organs of speech" (73). Speech, then, is a function of cognition, of learning to articulate words and (as the 1915 quote [on pp. 105–106] made clear) to associate words with things. This is a low-level theory of language acquisition by pairing and says nothing about the crucial epistemological questions. Of the elements associated in this theory, one (the "sound image") clearly refers to phonetics, while the other (the "impression of word innervation") is an obscure concept that presumably has something to do with semantics, perception, and memory, but it is devoid of meaning, as far as I can tell.

Regarding the origin of words, Freud relies (completely without acknowledgment) on the influential theory of Condillac (in his [1746] *Essay on the Origin of Human Knowledge,* subtitled "a supplement to Mr. Locke's Essay"), which had long been available in German translation.[32] Condillac took the step, of which Locke stopped short, of making language central to a theory of knowledge, in part by presenting a hypothesis about language origins, a theory that complements the theories of innate linguistic competence and universal grammar, widely known and accepted in their day. In keeping with the "state of nature" theorizing prevalent in the eighteenth century, Condillac (1746, 172-173) suggested that the first words, and therefore the first word-based memories, arise from the social-communicative function of the "cries of nature":

> When they [early men] came to live together, they had occasion to enlarge and improve those first operations; because their mutual converse made them connect with the cries of each passion, the perceptions

[32] I am not asserting, nor do I have evidence, that Freud was directly familiar with Condillac's work. However, Condillac's thesis was taken up and debated by major thinkers in France, Germany, England, and Scotland, throughout the eighteenth century (Diderot, Rousseau, Turgot, and other Encyclopedists in France; Maupertuis, Herder, and others in Germany; Adam Smith, Monboddo, Priestley, Shaftesbury, Berkeley, and Hutcheson in Scotland and England), and it is hardly conceivable that Freud was not aware of his theory and of the "origin of language" debate through one or more of these sources.

> which they naturally signified. They generally accompanied them with some motion, gesture or action, whose expression was yet of a more sensible nature. For example, he who suffered, by being deprived of an object which his wants had rendered necessary to him, did not confine himself to cries or sounds only; he used some endeavors to obtain it, he moved his head, his arms, and every part of his body. The other, struck with this sight, fixed his eye on the same object, and perceiving some inward emotions which he was not yet able to account for, he suffered in seeing his companion suffer. . . . [T]he same circumstances could not be frequently repeated, but they must have accustomed themselves at length to connect with the cries of the passions and with the different motions of the body, those perceptions which were expressed in so sensible a manner. The more they grew familiar with those signs, the more they were in a capacity of reviving them at pleasure. Their memory began to acquire some form of habit, they were able to command their imagination as they pleased, and insensibly they learned to do by reflexion what they had hitherto done merely by instinct. . . . For example, he who saw a place in which he had been frightened, mimicked those cries and movements which were the signs of fear, in order to warn the other not to expose himself to the same danger.

Here is Freud's (1895b, 366-367, italics in original) version of Condillac's theory:

> In the first place, there are objects—perceptions—that make one *scream,* because they arouse pain; and it turns out as an immensely important fact that this association of a sound (which arouses motor images of one's own as well) with a perceptual [image], which is composite apart from this, emphasizes that object as a hostile one and serves to direct attention to the perceptual [image]. When otherwise, owing to pain, one has received no good indication of the quality of the object, the *information of one's own scream* serves to characterize the object. Thus this association is a means of making memories that arouse unpleasure conscious and objects of attention: the first class of conscious memories has been created.

Although Freud borrows Condillac's theory of word origins, he uses it in a radically different way, one that favors received opinions and conventional thought. Condillac assumed several things about human nature, the most important of which would be attacked by later theorists: an instinctive uniformity of gestural expression of mental states such as pain, fear, and joy; an instinctive human sociability; and an instinctive capacity for reflective thought. Because Freud fundamentally disagreed with the latter two assumptions, he could not follow Condillac's distinction between primitive, gestural language and sophisticated human language, any more than he could follow Locke's distinction between mere word-thing conformity and propositional thought leading to knowledge.

For Condillac the hypothetical nucleus of gestural and action-based speech is simply the initial raw material upon which the mind operates, and it tells us little about the truly interesting, important, and specifically human linguistic and cognitive capacities. Thanks to human beings' unique reasoning ability, the original gestural language suggests the possibility of developing other "artificial" signs. In other words, it is a model and no more: "the natural cries served them for a pattern, to frame a new language" (174).

> The use of those signs sensibly enlarged and improved the operations of the mind, and on the other hand these having acquired such improvement, perfected the signs, and rendered the use of them more familiar. Experience shews that these two things assist each other. (173-174)

He gives mathematical notation as an example of such a highly elaborated symbolic language for expressing propositions. In this he was following and expanding upon Locke (1689, 405), who also stressed the distinction between the natural, gestural language and the language of artificial signs used to express ideas:

> Thus we may conceive how *Words,* which were by Nature so well adapted to that purpose, come to be made use of by Men, *as the Signs of* their *Ideas;* not by any natural connexion, that there is between particular articulate Sounds and certain *Ideas,* for then there would be but one Language amongst all Men; but by a voluntary Imposition, whereby such a Word is made arbitrarily the Mark of such an *Idea.*

Locke and Condillac would likely have regarded some of Dora's psychosomatic symptoms, such as her compulsive cough, as the descendant in the adult of a crude "natural" speech derived from a child's cry that, precisely because it was never elaborated into intelligent and critical thought, remained an unconsciously dissociated element in her mind.

Freud's ideas, in marked contrast to Locke and Condillac, are rather simplistic, again emphasizing learning and imitation. In his view (1895b, 367), once the basic "association" between one's internal response to the object and the object itself, and thus the "first class of conscious memories," is established, "[n]ot much is . . . needed in order to invent speech." This "invention" follows the same pattern as the initial formation based on instinct and social mimicry, rather than, as in Condillac, totally different principles. For Freud, in other words, the rest of language follows as an almost trivial consequence of the basic act of language creation from the emotional gesture:

> There are other objects, which constantly produce certain sounds—in whose perceptual complex, that is, a sound plays a part. In virtue of the

trend towards *imitation,* which emerges during judging, it is possible to find the information of movement attaching to the sound-image. This class of memories, too, can now become conscious. It now still remains to associate intentional sounds with the perceptions; after that, the memories when the indications of sound-discharge are observed become conscious like perceptions. (Freud, 1895b, 366-367, italics in original)

Condillac, like Locke, recognized the foolishness and danger of this idea about inevitable associations. Commenting on Condillac, Aarsleff (1982, 29, my italics) writes that truly human language

> *begins when reason and reflection, taking their cue from vocal gestures, step in to suggest the deliberate creation of arbitrary, conventional signs* made according to need in the common interest of self-preservation. . . . It is impossible for knowledge to exist and expand without arbitrary, manmade signs which, when attached to the ideas initially suggested by communal need, put mind in control of knowledge. The signs become both a memory bank and a retrieval system, *serving equally the needs of private thinking and the ends of communication.* This firm linkage between signifier and signified is called the "connection of ideas"—*"la liaison des idées"*—which, *being an expression of reason and reflection, is also controlled by them in the ever-widening expansion of the repertory of signs and of ratiocinative possibilities.*

This principle of the purposeful "connection of ideas" is "altogether different from the irrational chance association of ideas, which for Locke was 'a kind of madness' " (ibid.). The reference to Locke is (1689, 395): "I shall be pardon'd for calling it [the association of ideas] by so harsh a name as *Madness,* when it is considered, that opposition to Reason deserves that Name, and is really Madness."

Here we have the crucial difference between Freud's epistemology and that of Locke, Condillac, and the rational empiricists who followed their inspiration. For them, language has innate origins that can account for much of its basic structure (it would await the work of Chomsky to revive and develop the ideas of universal grammar much further than was done in the eighteenth century) but can never account for its creative use in developing ideas, propositions, and knowledge. New knowledge is always conjectural and needs to be tested against experience. Thus, the connections between language and cognition, ideas and experience, are highly complex interactions. For Freud, however, knowledge is conventional, and therefore cognition *entails* language as a purely executive function.

Freud's version of the "origin of language" therefore also constitutes a regression from Condillac's theory, in the direction of the old Adamism. Freud could not permit too much room in his concept of language for creative or critical thought because of his devotion to conventional Oedipal meanings.

He thus favored a highly constricted view, one that can explain little beyond the acceptance of conventional opinions and ideas.

The fact that this view has, unfortunately, become something of a psychoanalytic dogma explains why psychoanalysis has contributed so little to understanding language as a cognitive system, in spite of its undoubted interest to writers, artists, and scholars for help with appreciating symbolic language use.

Things, and Ideas about Things

Finally, let us turn to Freud's concepts of things and ideas. The entity to which words refer, that which they signify, is the "thing-presentation" or "idea,"[33] an epistemological concept intended to be the elementary unit of *sensory-based knowledge.* In Freud's usage, "presentation" refers to a sensory registration in the brain (not necessarily localized in the manner assumed by the neurologists he was disputing in his 1891 monograph on aphasia): "In psychology the simple idea is to us something elementary which we can clearly differentiate from its connection with other ideas" (1891, 55-56). Freud seemed to be unaware, as in his handling of the ideas of Locke and Condillac, of the epistemological assumptions with which this statement is freighted. This is reflected in the matter-of-fact but inaccurate way he refers to related concepts as unexceptionable findings of "philosophy." Referring to Mill's *A System of Logic,* he (1891, 78, my italics) wrote:

> According to philosophical teaching, the idea of the object contains *nothing else;* the appearance of a "thing," the "properties" of which are conveyed to us by our senses [visual, acoustic, kinaesthetic], originates *only* from the fact that in enumerating the sensory impressions perceived from an object, we allow for the possibility of there being a large series of new impressions being added to the chain of associations.

The concept that ideas about "things" can be fully accounted for (by a process of induction, for example) by the sensory impressions received from that thing, of course, far antedates Mill. It is the core assumption of the reactionary branch of empiricist epistemology, best represented by the work of Hume, for whom all knowledge comes, not from propositions, but from sense perception.

As famously put forward by Hume as a first principle of his *Treatise of Human Nature* (1739–1740, 4, italics in original), "*all our simple ideas* [from which complex ideas are derived by combination] *in their first appearance are deriv'd from simple impressions* [sensations, passions, and emotions], *which are correspondent to them, and which they exactly represent.*" In this statement he was fol-

[33] In Freud's original German the term was *Objektvorstellung, Dingvorstellung,* or *Sachvorstellung.* This is translated by Stengel (in Freud, 1891) as "idea or concept of the object," and later by Strachey (e.g., in Freud, 1900, 296; 1915c, 201), in an attempt to reveal the underlying epistemology, as "object-presentation." For a discussion of these terms and their translation, see Laplanche and Pontalis (1973, 448) and Strachey (in Freud, 1915c, 201, n1).

lowing Locke superficially. But although Hume is often thought of as an elaborator of Locke, he actually demonstrated the very habit of thought that Locke abhorred and challenged, in which people assume an unproblematic empirical basis for the "double conformity" between their words and the things to which their words refer. Believing that all knowledge derives from sense perception on one hand and social learning on the other, and is therefore purely conventional, Hume (415) also believed that reason is a paltry factor in human life, that "is, and ought only to be the slave of the passions, and [that] can never pretend to any other office than to serve and obey them." Hume's version of empiricism is a reaction against Locke, and the one that Freud embraced.

Because this version furnishes the entity (the thing-presentation) that anchors the Freudian concept of associations, and is thus in considerable measure at the heart of Freud's 1915 theory of consciousness, it is necessary to pay some critical attention to it.[34] Here too, we might keep in mind the clinical problems, exemplified by the case of Dora, that these linguistic and cognitive concepts are supposed to illuminate. What are the "things" (phenomena) that Dora sensed, and about which she needed to develop articulated ideas, in order to preserve herself and promote her maturing into an adult woman?

The Humean assumption, which Freud embraced, that knowledge of "things" is something elementary provided by sensation, is most certainly egregiously wrong. Popper (Popper & Eccles, 1977, 121), presents the strongest refutation of it:

> This idea is not merely mistaken, but grotesquely mistaken: we have only to remember the ten thousand million neurons of our cerebral cortex, some of them (the cortical pyramidal cells) each with "an estimated total of ten thousand" synaptic links (Eccles, 1966, 54). These may be said to represent the material . . . traces of our inherited and almost entirely unconscious knowledge, selected by evolution.

What seems, on naive observation, to be a direct result of sensation, is in fact informed by this wealth of complex and unconscious genetic knowl-

[34] Hume was driven by his empiricist doctrine to deny the very existence of a self. In the section "Of Personal Identity" of his *Treatise* (1739-1740, 251, italics and capitalization in original) he argues against "some philosophers, who imagine that we are every moment intimately conscious of what we call our SELF"; and he says of these philosophers that "Unluckily all these positive assertions are contrary to that very experience, which is pleaded for them, nor have we any idea of *self* . . . . For from what impression cou'd this idea be derived? This question 'tis impossible to answer without manifest contradiction and absurdity. . . ."

While denying the self as a primary entity, Hume in his psychology sought to derive the self as a social construct, through a theory of the interests and the social emotions they produce, notably pride and shame. Freud seems to have been ambivalent about whether selves exist as primary entities, as shown in my discussion (in the previous chapter) of the fate of his theory of self-preservation. After the demise of this theory, he was thoroughly Humean in his approach, seeking to explain how the self emerges through the play of interests and emotions in socialization.

edge. Careful observation of human infants in interaction with their human and inanimate environment brings this idea home. One of the most striking recent observations is that reported by Meltzoff and Moore (1977), who demonstrated in newborn infants complex, differentiated responses to human facial and manual gestures, previously thought impossible. Such findings indicate that infants are guided from the beginning of life by what is best described as innate knowledge, impossible to "infer" from their sensory experience. The same is true of their active interest in and responses to the inanimate world.

This insight is of course the same one that underlies Chomsky's (e.g., 1965) revival and extension of universal and generative grammar, as a framework for contributing to the linguistic side of cognitive science. For him, the key linguistic observation that refutes the Humean doctrine (and which far antedates him, as he readily acknowledges) is the very young child's rapid acquisition of extremely complex "rules" for generating grammatically comprehensible sentences that cannot possibly be "inferred" from his limited and personal exposure to spoken language. It is rather strange but true that Freud, the neurologist and the psychologist interested in unconscious processes, approached the brain as a complex processing machine but not as a storehouse for an extraordinary amount of genetic knowledge, most of which is unconscious.

Hume's theory of "things" and "ideas" about things rests fundamentally on an acceptance not only of the privileged authority of sense-perception but, as MacIntyre (1988, 281-325) has shown, on the acceptance of the attitudes of the privileged segments of his society, especially as regards property. Reflection about the inadequacy of the sense-perception theory of knowledge indicates why these two aspects of Humeanism (induction from sense perception and conventional social knowledge) go together. The former theory *requires* the latter and vice versa. For if we indeed had to rely on our sense perceptions alone for knowledge of things, we would all be imbeciles.[35] To compensate for this inevitable imbecility, both Freud and Hume posit, in effect, that knowledge of things *actually* comes from accepting conventionally held beliefs and theories. But basing knowledge on conventional beliefs is another form of imbecility—not thinking for oneself ("madness," in Locke's terminology). The common feature, in other words, of both aspects of Humeanism is *belief in authority,* to protect again the difficulties of thinking for oneself.

[35] In his *History of Western Philosophy* (1945, 673), Bertrand Russell put the problem of Hume in similar terms: "The growth of unreason throughout the nineteenth century and what has passed of the twentieth is a natural sequel to Hume's destruction of empiricism. It is therefore important to discover whether there is any answer to Hume within the framework of a philosophy that is wholly or mainly empirical. If not, there is no intellectual difference between sanity and insanity. The lunatic who believes that he is a poached egg is to be condemned solely on the ground that he is in a minority . . . ."

Tying these reflections back to Dora's dilemma, it is fair to say that her problem, with respect to the "things" (phenomena) in her family that were causing her difficulties lay in relying too much for explanations on the conventional opinions of those influential people around her and not on her own innate and developing capacities for judgment, aided if necessary by someone who could help her with that development. She was, in effect, too much of a Humean and could not have been helped by learning to be a better Humean (i.e., a Freudian).

Pseudointeractionism

I have shown that in three distinct and crucial respects, Freud's assumptions about language, thought, and consciousness constitute in fact a reaction against the rational-empiricist ideas of Locke and Condillac. Freud thinks (1) that the conformity per se between words and things constitutes a sufficient basis for a "higher psychical organization," (2) that the origin of language in the "cries of nature" constitutes an adequate basis for understanding all human language, and (3) that our ideas about the "things" of the world, and therefore thought in general, can be fully explained by our sensory impressions of them in conjunction with conventional social understandings. These three interpretations share the feature of rejecting what thinkers like Descartes, Locke, and Condillac found essential as a basis for acquiring knowledge—the *interaction* between ideas and experience, under the aegis of human beings' innate capacity for reason and storehouse of knowledge, so as to fashion language and understandings in light of experience and decide on their value in representing reality, *including moral and social reality.*

Freud uses the language and form of interactionism and rational empiricism, but in the substance of his thinking rejects true interactionism under the sign of reason, retaining only the communicative, socializing function of language. He thus in effect argues for the acceptance of conventional ideas and opinions as the basis for acquiring knowledge. For this reason, Freud's language and cognitive theories may be labeled "pseudointeractionist," and this, along with "cryptointeractionist" reasoning (in which interactionist explanations are in fact relied upon, while being obscured), is a feature that characterizes his neurological thinking as well, which is another source of ideas for the ego psychology.

Freudian Neurology: A Pseudo- and Cryptointeractionist Theory

It is frequently argued, and with some justification, that the main sources of Freud's inspiration for his 1915 revisions were not philosophical (in fact, he often expressed contempt for philosophy) but natural-scientific reasoning based on clinical observation and grounded in his background as a neurological thinker of some sophistication. It is true that many of the ideas discussed in the previous section have parallels in Freud's neurological model of the mind, as presented in *On Aphasia, Project for a Scientific Psychology,* and chapter 7 of *The Interpretation of Dreams,* and many students of psychoanalysis base their confidence in its rationality on this foundation. It is necessary, therefore, to examine these sources for the neurological roots of the ideas that entered into the 1915 ego-psychological revisions. I feel that a word of warning and apology is due here for the next few pages of rather turgid theory. However, it offers essential background for understanding what otherwise remains excessively mysterious in Freud. (I recommend Pribram and Gill's excellent book on the neurological theory, *Freud's 'Project' Re-assessed* [1976] as a companion source.)

As we have seen, a version of associationism, the conformity between words and things, is at the heart of the 1915 theory of consciousness and, in turn, of the ego psychology. The reasons for the associations are largely stated in Freud's neurologically inspired writings. What are the entities involved, and how do they enter into regular correspondence?

Neurological Sources of Freudian Associationism

Freud's neurological system is presented in full in his 1895 *Project for a Scientific Psychology,* a work that was not published in his lifetime but communicated only to his close confidant Wilhelm Fliess. Nonetheless, as immediately appreciated by Freud scholars upon its publication in 1950, it informed much of his subsequent theorizing. It is in this work, for instance, that the concept of "hypercathexis" is introduced, as an explanation of consciousness through language use and selective attention. Cathexis (Strachey's translation of the German *Besetzung,* a word meaning "that which occupies or possesses") is a concept designed to bridge neurology and psychology by referring simultaneously to the quantity of energy that "fills" neural tissue and the effects of such neural activation on mental activity. As noted by the neurophysiologist Karl Pribram and the psychoanalytic theorist Merton Gill (1976, 16, 63) in their commentary on Freud's text, cathexis, from a neurophysiological point of view, is to be identified with the measurable electric potential (voltage) of nerve tissue, a phenomenon familiar to physicians in the late nineteenth century. Later, in the form of "libidinal cathexis," the term took on primarily psychological significance, as "concentration or accumulation of mental energy in a particular channel" *(Oxford English Dictionary).*

The psychological concept of *hypercathexis* referred at first to selective attention to indicators of "reality" and later (as we have seen) to the special attention due language as the prime indicator of *social* reality. It is a part of what Freud described as the "biological rule of attention," which runs: *"If an indication of reality appears, then the perceptual cathexis which is simultaneously present is to be hypercathected"* (1895b, 371, italics in original).

In hypercathexis, certain parts of the brain (not anatomic structures but cells of a certain type, presumably distributed throughout various anatomic structures and constituting the nuclear "ego"), specialized to receive neural inputs both from the viscera and from sensory organs, stimulate other parts that are responsible for the experience of consciousness, through a process of selective reinforcement guided by certain "indications of quality" (1895b, 360-363). The aspect of hypercathexis emphasized in the 1915 emendations—attention to words—signifies a heightened awareness on Freud's part of the importance of speech and thought in conveying social reality. To adequately understand and critique the source of this idea in neurological theory, we need to examine the theoretical structure of the *Project,* where they are set forth in some detail.

In the *Project* Freud tackles the so-called "mind-body problem" in ways that illustrate his difficulties with mind-body interaction.[36] Although many of the explanations actually depend upon interaction between mind and body or mind and external reality, this central fact is obscured by reductionistic theories couched in purely physicochemical terms. Because of this *denial of interaction,* complex mental phenomena such as values, choices, and personal theories, which are irreducible to physicochemical mechanisms, are denied independent existence.

Two factors seem to account for this strange state of affairs. The main one is Freud's commitment *in principle* to a reductionist program of explanation. This commitment kept him from seeing the need for theories of higher mental phenomena that he was well aware of and in fact described; and it is a main cause of the circularities that still plague psychoanalysis. The second is his contradictory belief that he was in fact articulating, at least in specific areas, an interactionist point of view. In fact, he did so only in the sense of defending a purely mental *treatment.* In this context he (1905b, 284) made the following strong statement: "The relation between body and mind (in animals no less than in human beings) is a reciprocal [i.e., interacting] one." And in the same paragraph he refers to the "independence" of mental life. But the statement is not consistent with his articulated theories of psychological development, which are strongly reductionistic, that is, anti-interactionist. Overall, Freudian theory is therefore best described as a confused mix of pseudointeractionism and cryptointeractionism—sometimes nominally interactionist but actually

[36] There are good reasons, articulated, for example, by Chomsky (1996, 38-45) and Strawson (1959), for thinking that the very notion of a mind-body, mental-physical dichotomy is a scientifically inadequate framework for psychological theories that aspire to account for any higher mental functions. The dichotomy, however, has meaning in ordinary thought and constitutes a venerable, serious, and ongoing tradition of inquiry, within which psychoanalysis has an established place. Rather than engage in debate over the ultimate scientific value of this tradition, therefore, it will be more productive to examine Freud's ideas in the context of mind-body theorizing.

reductionist, sometimes nominally reductionist but actually interactionist. Separating the wheat from the chaff will shed further light on the incoherencies of Freudianism and on the directions psychoanalysis needs to follow if it is to be put on a sound footing.

Freud for the most part and throughout his career believed that his theory was a materialist and therefore reductionist one, albeit incomplete, and this is abundantly clear in the *Project*. Throughout his later work he expressed confidence that at some future point the reduction of psychology to biology and thence to chemistry and physics would be fully realized: "We must recollect that all our provisional ideas in psychology will presumably some day be based on an organic substructure . . . special substances and chemical processes which perform the operations of sexuality and provide for the extension of individual life into that of the species." (1914b, 78)[37]

His view of consciousness and reality-testing, with which the *Project* is primarily concerned, is a physical theory of mental events, in the tradition of nineteenth-century psychophysical theorizing that derives ultimately from La Mettrie, the famous author of *L'Homme Machine* (1747). "Since all the faculties of the soul depend to such a degree on the proper organization of the brain and of the whole body," La Mettrie (48) argued, "apparently they are but this organization itself, [and] the soul is clearly an enlightened machine." Freud was so taken, in fact, with the automaton-like quality of his *Project* theory that he (1895a, 129) wrote elatedly to his confidant Fliess that it was finally

> possible to see from the details of neurosis all the way to the very conditioning of consciousness. Everything fell into place, the cogs meshed, the thing really seemed to be a machine which in a moment would run of itself. The three systems of neurones, the "free" and "bound" states of quantity, the primary and secondary processes, the main trend and the compromise trend of the nervous system, the two biological rules of attention and defence, the indications of quality, reality and thought, the state of the psycho-sexual group, the sexual determination of repression, and finally the factors determining consciousness as a perceptual

[37] Reductionism is, of course, a branch of materialist philosophy that remains popular to this day, best articulated by Oppenheim and Putnam (1958). Its leading critics have, however, pointed out that there is no single instance of reduction of one scientific field into another. The reduction of chemistry to physics, often cited as the paradigm of scientific reduction, is far from complete and is unlikely to ever be complete. The comparatively most successful case of reduction from one level to another within a scientific theory is that of Young-Fresnel optics to Maxwellian electromagnetics, and even in that case the reduction is not complete (Popper, 1974). The failure of reductionism as a philosophy has not deterred reductionist thinking of extremely crude and improbable sorts in a wide variety of fields. This is currently a dangerously popular (in my view) trend in psychiatry, where a crude reductionism (from psychology through biology to chemistry) has been seized upon by many psychiatrists eager to promote simplistic, drug-based treatments of psychological conditions. It will be many years, if ever, before the outcome of the present-day misguided enthusiasm for such treatment is rationally evaluated.

function—the whole thing held together, and still does. I can naturally hardly contain myself with delight.[38]

Theory of Consciousness

In the *Project,* ideas about speech representations are part of a general theory of consciousness as an adaptive biological function. Consciousness depends on the capacity of the brain to perceive "indications of quality," which is differentiated from variations of "quantity," Freud's term for measurable physicochemical processes (electric current and potential) in nerve cells and represented by the letter Q.[39] Quality refers to sensory indicators of external reality. The person's ability to discriminate internal states from external world, real from hallucinatory satisfaction, is a crucial part of Freud's theory.

The neural basis for these discriminations consists of brain tissue specialized for reception of quantity and/or quality and involves mechanisms that determine whether that tissue is permanently altered by the passage of excitations (as is necessary for memory to occur, in the *psi* or ego neurons) or unaffected by such passage (as in the *phi* or perceptual neurons, and the *omega* or consciousness neurons).

> Consciousness gives us what are called *qualities*—sensations which are *different* in a great multiplicity of ways and whose *difference* is distinguished according to the relations with the external world. Within this difference there are series, similarities and so on, but there are in fact no quantities in it. (Freud, 1895b, 308, italices in original)

To account for the experience of consciousness Freud ingeniously proposed that the brain can differentiate qualitative stimulation from quantitative. Peripheral *(phi)* neurons respond to level of potential and current, whereas central *(omega)* neurons respond to the frequency of excitation:

> I shall assume that all the resistance of the contact-barriers applies only to the transference of Q, but that the *period* of the neuronal motion is transmitted without inhibition in all directions, as though it were a

[38] This quote exemplifies the theorizing that I described as "turgid" earlier. It strikes me now that the turgidity consists of poor thinking combined with inflated rhetoric. Many of the ideas referred to in this quote will seem exotic to readers, including psychoanalysts unfamiliar with the detailed development of Freud's thinking. This is a problem I can only address partially here, out of considerations of length and the reader's patience. Readers who wish to familiarize themselves with the details of the mechanical theory will have to consult the original works, in conjunction perhaps with Pribram and Gill (1976) and Laplanche and Pontalis's (1973) dictionary of analytic terms. I will confine my observations to those aspects of the *Project* that are especially useful for understanding the 1915 ego psychology.

[39] Sometimes, but inconsistently, quantity is represented by the rather mysterious designation Q'_{η}, the differentiation of which from Q is not clear. Strachey, in his introduction to the *Project,* suggests (1895b, 289, 294) that Freud may have intended Q to mean quantity in general and Q'_{η} quantity of the intercellular order of magnitude. He reprinted these symbols as they occurred in the original manuscript, leaving it to the reader to interpret them.

> process of induction. . . . [T]he *omega* neurones are incapable of receiving $Q\dot{\eta}$, but . . . instead they appropriate the *period* of the excitation and . . . this state of theirs of being affected by period while they are filled with the minimum of $Q\dot{\eta}$ is the fundamental basis of consciousness. . . . The *psi* neurones too have their period, of course; but it is without quality or, more correctly, *monotonous*. Deviations from this psychical period that is specific for them come to consciousness as qualities. . . . Where do these differences of *period* spring from? Everything points to the sense-organs, whose qualities seem to be represented precisely by different periods of neuronal motion. (1895b, 310, italics in original)

Although this theory purports to provide a physicochemical mechanism for distinguishing "quality," that is something of a verbal trick, for the property to which it refers has nothing to do with the moral and intellectual referents of that word in ordinary discourse (i.e., the qualities of a person, the qualities of an idea) but to sensory qualities (color, hardness, etc.). *The theory is thus a specification in neurological terms of the Humean assumption that all ideas come from sensation,* an assumption which, as we have seen, is egregiously wrong.

Even if we were to grant that some *acquired* knowledge comes strictly through the senses (itself a dubious proposition), the theory has no way of accounting for the qualities that are most significant in human life. Dora's father's sensory qualities were of little significance to her, for example, in her growing up and in the life crisis that enveloped her as an adolescent. Because of their obvious irrelevance, a physical description of her father appears nowhere in the case report, and it makes no difference to us in judging Dora's situation whether he was tall or short, round or angular. It was indications of his moral and intellectual qualities, those qualities generally subsumed under the category of character—his honesty, the genuineness of his attempts to solve problems in his marriage and love life, and to balance them against concerns for his daughter, which in turn reflected his ideas and theories about what it is to be a man and a father—that were the crucial and confusing ones for Dora, and these qualities are completely unrepresented in Freud's theory. Freud does not even attempt to tackle the question, begged by his theory, of how important moral and intellectual qualities might be derived, at a neurological level, from sensory qualities. We are thus thrown back onto a pure socialization model, which centers on the person's unquestioned acceptance of qualities asserted or attributed. That, of course, was Dora's problem to begin with.

It will be objected that Freud's Humean, tabula rasa view of mind was supplemented by his instinct theory, which posits innate tendencies. Let us turn, then, to Freud's neurological instinct theory to discover what these tendencies consist of.

Neurological Theory of Instinct: The Helpless Baby

From the neurological instinct theory comes one of Freud's main interactionist explanations of the significance of parental attitudes and ideas on the mind of the developing child. A central phenomenon in mental development is the interaction between the helpless infant and his or her parents, and Freud's recognition of the huge influence of these early social interactions is one of his enduring contributions. These interactions become models for later intrapsychic experience conceived as cooperative and conflictual interaction between agencies of the mind, e.g., the id and the ego as inheritors of organic forces and social requirements, respectively.

The infant is helpless to meet its own needs because of its immaturity combined with the nature of biological instinct. Bodily needs, in Freud's view, generate unending arousal in the nervous system, which can be relieved only by "specific action" on the part of caregivers, in relation to which the infant is at first purely receptive and passive.

Central to the notion of the helpless baby is the concept of "secretory" or "key" neurons that "cause the generation in the interior of the body of something which operates as a stimulus upon the endogenous path of conduction to *psi*" (1895b, 320). The infant has no way of bringing about surcease from this stimulation. Pribram and Gill (1976, 44) point out that Freud's instinct theory "consists of a positive feedback mechanism, which, if there were no way to stop it, would lead to an ever increasing accrual of excitation." According to Freud, this otherwise uncontrollable excitation is stopped only as relations to other human beings are initiated:

> The removal of the stimulus is only made possible here by an intervention which for the time being gets rid of the release of Q_{η}' in the interior of the body; and this intervention calls for an alteration in the external world (supply of nourishment, proximity of the sexual object) which, as a *specific action,* can only be brought about in definite ways. At first, the human organism is incapable of bringing about the specific action. It takes place by *extraneous help,* when the attention of an experienced person is drawn to the child's state by discharge along the path of internal change [e.g., by the child's screaming]. In this way this path of discharge acquires a secondary function of the highest importance, that of *communication,* and the initial helplessness of human beings is the *primal source* of all *moral motives.* (Freud, 1895b, 317-318, italics in original)

This view of the helpless, tabula rasa baby, the biological side of the theory, is, as we have seen, both extremely unlikely and incongruent with readily observable facts. It neglects both the extraordinary innate knowledge the newborn infant has stored in its brain, which guides to a large extent his or her active interests in and responses to the animate and inanimate world. And the theory imposes severe and implausible limitations on learning, thinking, and moral development.

Although Pribram and Gill generally commend Freud's *Project,* they (1976, 44) point out that his neurological instinct theory, which employs only positive feedback, corresponds poorly to modern understandings of the regulation of instinctual behavior. Freud's theory, combined with his view of the social intervention that brings arousal to a halt, is a statement in neurological terms of his main convictions: that human beings are by nature unregulated animals, that they know "things" only through their senses, and that they are totally dependent on social intervention for moral learning.

Instinctual behavior, as Pribram and Gill point out (43-47), actually involves negative feedback as well as feedforward mechanisms (processes with a built-in capacity to ready the organism for adaptive activity)—that is, built-in knowledge of one's body and the world, not just a means to register arousal. Instincts are inborn *knowledge* and programmed *patterns of interaction.* In Chapters 2 and 3, I identified this problem in Freud's view of the sexual instinct, in part to show that relevant concepts were available to him to develop a biologically adequate theory of human sexuality. Because of his Humean misunderstanding of how sexuality actually develops at adolescence in animals and humans, he unwarrantedly exaggerated the need for external regulation, as he did with regard to so-called biological urges in general.

Consider next the implications of Freud's neurological instinct theory for learning, thinking, and moral development. In the course of providing help to the infant, the parent naturally and automatically provides not only important sensory and cognitive stimulation and practice, but experiences of approval and disapproval that introduce the infant to the socially appropriate behavior that will maximize the chance for relief, as opposed to prolonged distress or punishment. Such learning is viewed by Freud as the crucible for the acquisition of moral motives, the basis of the morality-as-socialization view: "The education and development of this original ego takes place in a repetitive state of craving, in *expectation.* It [the ego] learns first that it must not cathect the motor images, so that discharge results, until certain conditions have been fulfilled from the direction of the perception" (1895b, 369, italics in original).

This education is simultaneously an education in social reality, which Freud, presumptuously but typically, calls "the source of all moral motives"—the conditions under which instinctual urges may be expected to result in satisfaction as opposed to frustration, punishment, or shame, as determined by the judgment and responses of the parents.

It is obvious that when we speak of approval and disapproval and socially appropriate conditions of satisfaction, we are speaking largely of attitudes and theories (explicit or implicit theories of the self, for example, and contingent theories of child rearing) that are in part culturally determined and in part determined by the parents' particular conscious and unconscious views of such cultural norms. The function of parents, and mentors in general, is best served when they convey to their children or students an appreciation that they are largely vehicles for knowledge and tradition and that their knowledge is imperfect, as opposed to representing themselves as infallible authors of their theories. In this way they promote, along with whatever practice, training, and learning of cultural norms is provided, a capacity to think critically about what is provided, a wish to understand what works and what doesn't, what is good and what is bad, and to improve upon it. That quality in the parent or mentor is the hallmark of active, participatory, as opposed to authoritarian, child rearing and education—what DeMause (1974) describes as the "helpful" mode of child rearing as opposed to the socialization mode.

Freud's theory of instinct, the "body" part of his theory of child-parent interaction, therefore provides a false biological rationale for the tendency to authoritarian learning, from both the child's and the parents' side. From the side of the child, control of drives is always achieved through an absolute dependence on caregivers (knowledge from without), never through the maturation of innate tendencies (knowledge from within). Pribram and Gill (1976, 46), significantly, describe learning how to behave through interaction with others not as moral, as Freud would have it, but "adaptive" behavior: "It is in the regulation of neurochemical drive processes that the *Project* spells out the details of a mechanism by which internal change serves the adaptive function of relating to other human beings, in other words, how drive and drive gratification become integrated in an interpersonal context."

Unfortunately, Pribram and Gill do not critically discuss, any more than Freud does, the differences between adaptive and moral or truth-seeking behavior. To specify adaptation as an element of a psychology of the cognitive and moral systems requires asking "adaptation to what?" It would seem obvious that adaptation to one's limited circle of family, friends, and teachers in growing up ought to subserve the larger goal of adaptation to the world, the scope of which (i.e., the problems for which solutions need to be found) is bounded only by the perceptiveness and creativity of the person. This critical question is completely bypassed in Freud's theory.

From the side of the parents, because their attitudes and theories are treated as static representatives of the social world rather than a highly particular and inevitably degraded segment of potential experience, no attention is paid to the parents' side of the child-parent interaction. Important questions thus remain unasked: What are the attitudes and theories of parents and how are they acquired? How do people growing up decide which theories and attitudes to embrace and which to reject? These are questions that are hugely important in the decisions of people to have children and how to raise them, as any parent knows who takes the trouble to reflect about them. This inattention to the discretionary mental side of parenting contributes strongly to the social conservatism of Freudian theory, in which equating interests of the self with the interests of family and society is seen as exemplary of higher functioning, rather than as pathological narrowness.

Curiously (since Freud is known as the theorist of instinct *par excellence*), we find, as we found in our analysis of his treatment of sexuality, that it is his misunderstanding of the biology of instinct generally, which he confuses with a vague and inaccurate concept of arousal or stimulation, that is a main source of the problem. Because no attention is paid to the parents' mental life, treated as generic, one is left to infer that *their* ideas, attitudes, and values derive also from the biological necessity that they were subject to as children, and so on ad infinitum. The parents' purely mental states, a critically important element of the actual interaction between them and their children, are referred back in circular fashion to physicochemical mechanisms, rather than being accorded an independent existence.

Cognitive Theory: Associationism; Reproductive versus Observational Thought

As a consequence of his arousal-only instinct theory, which makes the baby completely dependent on its surroundings for knowledge of the world, Freud's theories of cognition and motivation are substantially pure socialization-learning models. For in his view *the earliest experiences of satisfaction provide the aim that is missing from the instinct,* which knows only arousal. They *create* a motivational system of primary "wishes" that, while strongly socially conditioned, functions afterward, and is regarded, as a proper instinctual system. The wishes comprising this system are the famous "id" motives, chief among which are wishes for incest and for parricide, which drive the so-called "primary process." The person, according to Freud, is ruled by these motives in that he or she forever after seeks their satisfaction.

In Freud's view the process leading to the formation of these wishes is the first, momentous, structuring of mind, which specifies the vague concept of association; that is, the conditions of the initial experiences of satisfaction are enduringly associated in people's minds with the "thing-presentations" of biological needs to form primary wishes. It is the association in the mind of the child between bodily needs and the stimulus qualities of the caretaking situation that constitutes a wish in the specific Freudian sense. In this way Oedipal conditions, a product of social learning, come to function as Oedipal instincts. This is the nucleus of a large body of theory based on the person's enduring motivation to recapture conditions in the external world that resemble, and in the ideal case are identical with, the original conditions of satisfaction. Clearly, this theory is the source of the obfuscation that I identified earlier (see pp. 22–23), on purely logical grounds, between internal and external, love and compliance, and effect and cause.

This body of theory places great emphasis on a division between two broad categories of mental activity, conceptualized as *reproductive* mental activity, or primary process, on the one hand, and *observational, cognitive,* mental activity, or secondary process, on the other. Reproductive thought seeks to recapture the original conditions of satisfaction, whereas observational or cognitive thought, modeled upon a "biological rule" of "primary defense" (1895b, 322, 371-372), inhibits the reproductive tendency to allow the person to scan the environment to assure that only that measure of reproduction is achieved that is compatible with the limitations of current reality.

The problems of this view of motivation and cognition are problems inherent in associationism generally, in that it eliminates a possible simple explanation by a mysterious definition. A process that is understandable as the forming of expectations and theories—the theories of self and the world that people develop in response to their childhood circumstances—is hypostatized into entities (primary wishes) with mysterious properties, much as in Pavlovian theory the dog's understandable expectations are labeled "conditioned reflexes," associationist entities without explanatory substance. This Freudian reification actually embodies a preference: to render cognition subservient to the conservative tendency to reproduce early conditions of life, so as to prove and re-prove early theories. This leaves out of consideration the contrary but far more interesting tendencies, equally evident in people, to *test and disprove* their early theories. Freud would later (in [1920], 38-43, for example) consider those creative and mutative tendencies, which he earlier ascribed to the self, unreal. The complex, infinitely creative, and barely understood processes of knowing are in this way limited and degraded according to the implicit instrumental theory that people only want to know what they already think they know—a common enough human tendency but hardly one, I think, worth elevating to a law of nature. On the other hand, the history of human thought ought to teach us, if it teaches us nothing else, that understandings of the self and the world come about in the most varied, surprising, and idiosyncratic ways; that most of the great understandings in the history of human thought are speculative and counterintuitive in the extreme; and that the spontaneity, individuality, and creativity of scientific and philosophic thought would be utterly defeated by being guided by such a narrow program as Freud imagines. At the clinical level, Dora's efforts, against great odds, to revise the expectations of self and the social world into which she had been sadly indoctrinated as a child were defeated by this program, as translated into psychoanalysis by Freud, leading to the failure of her treatment.

Now let us turn to Freud's "rule" of primary defense, to understand further the psychoanalytic theory of cognition.

In the *Project* this rule is to begin with a neurological one. Internal arousal leads to inhibition of the *psi* system, the nuclear ego, so as to allow the person to scan the environment for those configurations that signal opportunities for limited and socially approved satisfaction of instinctual impulses. The whole panoply of normal and pathological defenses that constitutes much of the ego derives from this primary neurological mechanism. Pribram and Gill (75) summarize this theory as follows:

> Finally, the normal secondary *psi* processes of delay become established. These make possible a continuing comparison between the excitations originating in the memory structures of *psi* and those initiated in *phi*. The results of these comparisons between experienced wish and the perception of reality lead, by a process of neural inhibition—i.e., of delaying premature discharge, to the ordered growth of the network of neurons in *psi* which when cathected become the will. This normal operation leading to specific action is called, as we have seen, the secondary process; when it fails, because, for some reason, the balance between facilitation and inhibition is tipped against the latter, more primary wishful processes, invoking primary and even *reflex* defence, are brought into operation.

Crucial to this process are the indications of "reality," by which the person assures himself or herself that opportunities for instinctual satisfaction are safe and morally and socially acceptable.

In further criticizing this theory I will focus on its contained assumptions about the biological function of consciousness, which well demonstrate its implausibility, its thought-inhibiting effect, and therefore its harmfulness when applied clinically. In Freud's view, reality is, biologically, a necessary impediment to "wish-fulfillment," the ideal aim of which is to achieve "perceptual identity" with the original conditions of satisfaction, which bring the person as close as possible to a state of minimal arousal. In this scheme the ideal situation for a person is to arrange his or her life so that the impediments to such wish-fulfillment coming from reality are at a minimum. In such a life the inevitable obstacles would be as predictable as possible so that the great Oedipal desires would be achievable as effortlessly and automatically as possible, in which case the biological aim of consciousness—to rid oneself of unwanted excitation and to achieve the most efficient detours to satisfaction of primary wishes—should be maximally achieved, consciousness would be at its height, and the person would be happy. There is much, however, to suggest that neither consciousness nor human happiness works that way, but rather the opposite: that *under conditions of maximal predictability con-*

sciousness would not be heightened but extinguished and the only happiness possible a vegetative state.

We might consider first our common-sense reaction to a person leading such an "ideal" life. Is it not a picture of an uninspired, unimaginative, and childish person, a pathological rather than a mature character? Does not neurosis, and psychopathology in general, represent an excessive need for predictability, an excessive intolerance of variability and change? We would be disinclined, I believe, to regard such a person as functioning with a high degree of consciousness.

What is consciousness, after all, when it comes to personality? To help free ourselves from Freudian preconceptions, it is useful to reflect on how consciousness functions at elementary levels, based on everyday observation. For instance, we are typically unconscious of sensory stimuli that are predictable, that routinely and unproblematically fulfill our expectations. The ticking of a familiar clock or the hum of a computer in the study in which we are working fades into the background and does not distract us from reading, writing, and thinking. If the ticking or hum suddenly and unpredictably stops, we become conscious of it, alert to the existence of something unexpected that constitutes a problem to be investigated. This suggests that consciousness is a biological mechanism for attending to unexpected outcomes, which require our attention as indicators of problems to be solved.

At a more cognitive level, the same relation between predictability and level of consciousness would appear to hold. Experiences that routinely and unproblematically fulfill theoretical expectations become uninteresting background perceptions. For example, the theory of planetary motion predicting the daily "appearance" of the sun and succession of seasons is by now so well supported as to be uninteresting and unconscious for most of us. Until human beings possessed this theory the regular appearance of sun and seasons was typically a matter of great interest and concern, motivating behavior that seems now strange or barbaric, such as blood sacrifice. And if one day the sun failed to appear at its predicted place and time, we would be alert to the existence of a major problem. These everyday examples suggest that *the crucial factor in awakening consciousness is not the perception per se of inner or outer stimuli, but the unexpectedness of perceptions compared to anticipations.*[40] In general, when life

[40] I hope it is obvious that this discussion does not suggest that unexpected outcomes are universally good, consciousness-raising things, or conversely that predictability is a bad thing. Without a good measure of predictability it is hard to imagine that life, including the development of the individual, could go on. In discussing primal repression in Chapter 2, pp. 71–73, I addressed the other side of this coin, the mental paralysis that can afflict the person in the face of outcomes that are not only unexpected but remain incomprehensible, thus "traumatic." The point of my discussion of Freud's neurological view of consciousness and cognition is to demonstrate that it is weighted excessively in the direction of predictability and conventionality, and that it does not stand up to critical inquiry.

is predictable, when it satisfies our expectations (our theories of how things are) there is no problem, and the stimuli that confirm our expectations fade into an unconscious background.

A view of the biological function of consciousness that derives from such observations and many similar ones, and that runs directly counter to the Freudian theory, is one proposed by Popper (Popper & Eccles, 1977, 125-126): that consciousness serves the adaptive, evolutionarily selected, biological function of *attending to unanticipated outcomes* and nonroutine problems as a condition of trying to understand them. This theory can be applied to much of mental life and to many of the phenomena of psychoanalysis with much greater plausibility than the Freudian theory. To do so requires the assumption, which ought to be unproblematic but which is disallowed by Freudian theory, of a wealth of innate, unconscious knowledge of the world that people bear in their genes, expressed in expectations of various sorts, dispositions to think and to act, and so forth, of which we must know remarkably little. Such knowledge is of course not to be confused with the narrow appeal made to genetics by many biomedical scientists and social engineers who seek or pretend to find the "causes" of "antisocial" behaviors and troublesome pathologies in specific genes—just as prior generations found them in "instincts" for things they disapproved or sought to control.

It appears to me that much of the activity of a good psychoanalyst is oriented toward helping people reflect on the defeat of innate psychological and moral expectations when they were young. The analyst helps the patient to understand that he or she approaches the current world equipped with expectations and implicit theories based on these defeats, which have become so well entrenched as to be unconscious. Psychoanalysis is largely a matter of understanding the difficulties that people have in this process of alerting and reacting effectively to such failures of innate expectations, because they have overadapted, unconsciously validating the conditions of failure over and over. One of the analyst's main functions is to disrupt this unconscious automaticity of patients with respect to their personal theories.

To briefly recapitulate this argument, the primary wishes, to which an almost mythic significance is attached in Freudian theory, are nothing more than an expression of the original social conditions to which the child adapts, or, more correctly, of the *theory established in the mind of the child that survival is dependent on those original conditions.* There is an element of truth, based on naturalistic observation, in this mythical explanation, and it is this element that represents Freud's truly valuable contribution, corresponding to what I have described as one of the two general theories of psychoanalysis: that we tend, more strongly than previously believed, to experience later life in light of expectations shaped by early life, just as the dogs in Pavlov's experiments come to attribute special significance to otherwise indifferent sensory stimuli like lights and bells, about which they have formed plausible causal theories.

Psychoanalysis offers a systematic way of examining such expectations and theories. We discover that they operate powerfully and unconsciously, as though they had been established beyond refutation for all time, unconsciousness being the fate of theories or expectations that are always validated. But it is also a matter of naturalistic observation—and here is where Freud's preconceptions caused him to turn a blind eye—that people, like dogs, can change their minds in light of subsequent experience that does not conform with their theories. The theories of dogs "conditioned" in a Pavlovian paradigm undergo "extinction" in face of subsequent experiences that refute them—although those explanations put into a curiously passive voice what the dog is actively doing, revising his expectations or theories. In psychoanalysis it is no less a matter of naturalistic observation that people can change their theories about themselves and the world, theories "conditioned" by adaptation to childhood experience, in view of later, improved, experience, of which the psychoanalytic relationship and dialogue ought to be an example. It is also a matter of naturalistic observation that the more adverse the conditions of early life, and the more authoritarian the upbringing, the more rigid will the child's, and later adult's, thinking tend to be, although this is fortunately not an invariant rule. Typically this "waking up" to the inadequacy of existing expectations starts before the analysis begins, and it is to promote the spontaneous process, when it runs into difficulty, that people seek out analysis.

Two aspects of Freudian theory contribute to the reification of what are, in effect, childhood-based and inadequate theories of the self and the world. One is the inaccurate and misleading neurological theory of instinct, which, depriving the infant of any innate knowledge, portrays him as absolutely dependent on caregivers for creating a motivational system. The other is Freud's evolutionary instinct theory, which seeks to explain how the genetic disposition to an Oedipal, or patriarchal, family and social order, was selected out in behavioral evolution. In a formal sense, this evolutionary instinct theory seeks to supply the content of innate genetic knowledge that is missing from the neurological instinct theory. Freud's evolutionary ideas are, however, so embedded in the type of socially conventional state-of-nature psychological theorizing represented by Hume on one hand and the culturalist anthropology school represented by Frazer on the other, that it provides little actual balance to the neurological theory. I suggested in my remarks about linguistics and thinking that, in his attempt to refashion his psychoanalysis, Freud leaned especially heavily for inspiration on Hume, who most influentially articulated the reaction against Lockean rational empiricism. Freud was considerably indebted to Hume as a psychological thinker too. Hume's detailed account of the anthropological, psychological, and developmental processes that lead to a particular type of social and moral self are, in my view, a substantial prototype of Freud's reasoning as it developed in ego psychology.

Freud's Social Psychology: Further Relation to Hume

The stated goal of Hume's lifelong project was to challenge the dogmatic rationalism of his philosophic predecessors, especially in the realm of morals, by putting the study of human nature on a scientific basis, as indicated by the title of his major, three-part work, *A Treatise of Human Nature: Being an Attempt to Introduce the Experimental Method of Reasoning into Moral Subjects* (1739–1740). These goals are best stated in the early parts of Book 3, *Of Morals.* It is the phenomenon of individual conscience as a basis of social cohesion that fascinates Hume, and for which he can accept neither the explanations of the moral rationalists (the Aristotelian philosophers, Christian or otherwise, who believed in some form of innate moral reasoning) for whom "virtue is nothing but a conformity to reason" (456), nor of his antecedent moral philosophers generally, whom he (469, italics in original) challenges as follows:

> In every system of morality, which I have hitherto met with, I have always remark'd, that the author proceeds for some time in the ordinary way of reasoning, and established the being of a God, or makes observations concerning human affairs; when of a sudden I am surpriz'd to find, that instead of the usual copulations of propositions, *is,* and *is not,* I meet with no proposition that is not connected with an *ought,* or *ought not.* This change is imperceptible; but is, however, of the last consequence. For as this *ought,* or *ought not,* expresses some new relation or affirmation, 'tis necessary that it shou'd by observ'd and explain'd; and at the same time that a reason should be given, for what seems altogether inconceivable, how this new relation can be a deduction from others, which are entirely different from it.

It is the existence of the individual, internal "ought," incomprehensible from received wisdom or innate knowledge, that is the problem for Hume.

From his carefully reasoned theory of the mind and of the emotions, given in Books 1 *(Of the Understanding)* and 2 *(Of the Passions)*, Hume approaches the problem of moral character from a developmental-psychological point of view. Moral character cannot be a function of reason, since reason is relatively impotent and passive: "Morals excite passions, and produce or prevent actions. Reason of itself is utterly impotent in this particular. The rules of morality, therefore, are not conclusions of our reason" (457). "Reason is wholly inactive, and can never be the source of so active a principle as conscience, or a sense of morals" (458). In this respect Hume is at the opposite pole from

Locke, for whom man's reasoning, reflective capacity is the hallmark of his existence, and for whom *"Morality is the proper Science, and Business of Mankind in general"* (1689, 646; italics in original).

For Hume, moral distinctions "according to modern philosophy, are not qualities in objects, but perceptions in the mind" (469). Interestingly, for Hume, as it would be later for Frazer and Freud, the incest taboo represents a prime example of a uniquely human moral capacity: "I would fain ask any one, why incest in the human species is criminal, and why the very same action, and the same relations in animals have not the smallest moral turpitude and deformity?" (467).

Hume's method in tackling this problem is to derive conscience from its blank beginnings through psychological development of the individual: "As moral good and evil belong only to the actions of the mind, and are deriv'd from our situation with regard to external objects, the relations, from which these moral distinctions arise, must lie only betwixt internal actions, and external objects" (464-465). In Books 1 and 2 Hume elaborates theories of an emergent self and of its relations to these objects, central to both of which are certain principles of mind and a theory of the emotions that in their essentials are remarkably similar to Freud's theories. One first principle is the empiricist assumption that all ideas derive from "impressions" or simple sense perceptions, which is repeated frequently throughout the Treatise: "All our simple ideas in their first appearance are deriv'd from simple impressions, which are correspondent to them, and which they exactly represent" (4, italics in original). A second is the associationist idea that complex perceptions and ideas arise through the combination of simple ideas, according to certain "universal principles" of association deriving from three "qualities" in the world: "RESEMBLANCE, CONTIGUITY in time or place, and CAUSE and EFFECT" (10-11, capitalization in original). It is this tendency to form associations according to these qualities of objects, "by which the mind is . . . convey'd from one idea to another" (11), that accounts for the close correspondence of various human languages (10).

For Hume, it is the emotions (passions) that are the great intermediaries between the qualities of objects in the world and our conceptions, especially our moral conceptions. In Book 2 he develops a complex theory of the emotions, by which he partially explains this enormous importance. Of the range of human emotions, it is pride and humility that primarily influence the formation of the self, and love and hatred that are most consequential for our relations to others:

> Regard now with attention the nature of these passions, and their situation with respect to each other. 'Tis evident here are four affections,

plac'd, as it were, in a square or regular connexion with, and distance from each other. These passions of pride and humility, as well as those of love and hatred, are connected together by the identity of their object, which to the first set of passions is self, to the second some other person. (333)

As to the cause of self-experience mediated by the emotional complex pride-humility, it is one's attitude toward property that is of supreme importance: "But the relation, which is esteem'd the closest, and which of all others produces most commonly the passion of pride, is that of *property*" (309, italics in original). "Property may be look'd upon as a particular species of *causation;* whether we consider the liberty it gives the proprietor to operate as he pleases upon the object, or the advantages, which he reaps from it" (310, italics in original).

It is not only property as such but the power to acquire and maintain it that has such compelling influence on the human mind:

> If the property of any thing, that gives pleasure either by its utility, beauty or novelty, produces also pride by a double relation of impressions and ideas; we need not be surpriz'd, that the power of acquiring this property, shou'd have the same effect. Now riches are to be consider'd as the power of acquiring the property of what pleases; and 'tis only in this view that they have any influence on the passions. (311)

This, then, is for Hume the ultimate cause of pride and therefore of self-identity: pride in possession and the power to acquire. This is affirmed not as an adaptation to a particular cultural and social milieu and set of values but as a natural and "original" (i.e., instinctual) principle. Human greed is elevated to the position of the basic human instinct:

> I find, that the peculiar object of pride and humility is determin'd by an original and natural instinct, and that 'tis absolutely impossible, from the primary constitution of the mind, that these passions shou'd ever look beyond self, or that individual person, of whose actions and sentiments each of us is intimately conscious. (286)

Here we see a movement in Hume's psychology that is quite equivalent to that which I labeled "instinctivism" in Freud, and that I venture to regard as its prototype. Although private property and its panoply of laws, procedures, and privileges is explained as "artifice" and cultural convention, it is nonetheless, in another context, elevated to the level of an "original cause" or instinct.

The findings of Books 1 and 2 are applied in Book 3 to reach certain momentous conclusions about moral concepts and character as well as about cultural developments. Moral concepts are perceptions, which we tend to confuse with ideas and judgments: "Morality, therefore, is more properly felt than judg'd of; tho' this feeling or sentiment is commonly so soft and gentle, that we are apt to confound it with an idea, according to our common custom of taking all things for the same, which have any near resemblance to each other" (470).

This conclusion is bolstered by evolutionary reasoning, although Hume, of course, lacked the Darwinian theory for so expressing it. Moral concepts are not "natural," in the sense of deriving from innate knowledge, and never were. Rather, they are "artifices" in the sense of social rules invented by primeval men and handed down through countless generations. "Our sense of every kind of virtue is not natural; but . . . there are some virtues, that produce pleasure and approbation by means of an artifice or contrivance, which arises from the circumstances and necessity of mankind" (477).

These cultural conventions center on ownership and exchange of private property. Yet although they are not natural, they are derived from natural principles, being motivated by passions (notably, greed), informed by the understanding that realistic satisfaction of these passions requires both mutual restraint and rules and procedures for retaining what one has and resisting the claims of others: "Whatever restraint they [the artificial laws of property justice] may impose on the passions of men, they are the real offspring of those passions, and are only a more artful and more refin'd way of satisfying them" (526). Subsequently, these conventions are given moral attributes, which are in the nature of linguistic conventions (522) and pretenses (523), in order to facilitate the cultural enforcement and transmission of these rules by education and government. A large part of Book 3 is devoted to an exposition of a historical anthropology (a pre-Darwinian theory of social evolution) by which Hume imagines these "artifices" to have arisen, at a hypothetical moment in primeval time that separates subhuman savages from civilized humans.

Hume imagines a moment in primeval history when the key to civilized existence dawned on pre-humans, transforming their "savage and solitary condition" (562) into a semblance of civilized life. This culture-defining step is the concept of private property and the invention of rules to regulate ownership and transfer of property. For the main impediments to humans living together amicably in social groups are the instability and scarcity of their possessions (488). The remedy is the cultural convention that puts "these goods, as far as possible, on the same footing with the fix'd and constant advantages of the mind and body. This can be done after no other manner, than by a convention enter'd into by all members of the society to bestow stability on the possession of those external goods" (489).

This convention, which has a number of elements, is the common basis for the concepts of property and justice, which in Hume's view are two sides of the same coin:

> After this convention, concerning abstinence from the possessions of others, is enter'd into, and every one has acquir'd a stability in his possessions, there immediately arises the ideas of justice and injustice; as also those of *property, right, and obligation*. The latter are altogether unintelligible without first understanding the former. (490–491, italics in original)

The convention, in other words, brings in its train a mechanism by which a natural passion is inhibited in order to attain its aim under the conditions of social reality: "There is no passion, therefore, capable of controlling the interested affection, but the very affection itself, by an alteration of its direction" (492).

The main internal contradiction in Hume's psychology derives from his effectively importing an "ought" of the sort he had previously foresworn, at a point when he realizes the limited explanatory value of the invention of private property. Clearly, such an invention in primeval times could and did develop and evolve in myriad ways in highly civilized societies, as witness the hugely different attitudes toward individual property as against other goods and values in premodern societies. Hume's theory of cultural invention can only account, at a psychological level, for tendencies and dispositions, not for ineluctable reactions. Hume recognizes the limited explanatory value of the basic invention per se: "However useful, or even necessary, the stability of possession may be to human society, 'tis attended with very considerable inconveniences" because the cognitive principles, and social conventions based on them, that determine which goods qualify as property and who is to possess them "depend very much on chance, [so] they must frequently prove contradictory both to men's wants and desires; and persons and possessions must often be very ill adjusted" (514). He deals with this reservation in a purely conventional way, invoking an arbitrary "ought" corresponding to the theory of capitalism ascendant in the admired, adopted England of Hume's day (Hume was Scottish): "The relation of fitness or suitableness ought never to enter into consideration, in distributing the properties of mankind" (514). By fiat, in other words, individual merit and social justice *ought not* to be considered in distributing the wealth of society, a quite telling exception to Hume's self-imposed task of inquiring rationally into the bases of moral judgment.

The correspondences with Freud's theory are obvious, and easier to understand in light of my analysis of the ego psychology. The idea that the invention of human society is in the nature of an artifice or convention follows from the state-of-nature assumption, which Freud (1927, 6) shared with Hume:

> [C]ivilization has to be defended against the individual, and its regulations, institutions and commands are directed against that task. They aim not only at effecting a certain distribution of wealth but at maintaining that distribution; indeed, they have to protect everything that con-

tributes to the conquest of nature and the production of wealth against men's hostile impulses.

Thus, when Freud wrote, ostensibly in response to Marx, that "aggressiveness was not created by property" (1930, 113), he was actually denying Hume's precedence for a theory that he substantially appropriated, while changing the emphasis from private ownership to the patriarchal authority that enforces such ownership. The idea of the "artificiality" of civilization follows, too, as an extension of the artificiality of moral character and is an implication of the irrational-empiricist doctrine in the cultural sphere. For just as this doctrine, by disallowing innate knowledge, makes the child totally dependent on his or her social environment for all knowledge of self and the world, so must it deny, at the level of evolutionary thinking, any inherent knowledge of society prior to the advent of a certain type of human social organization. Thus, all of animal society and even premodern human societies are regarded as inferior and savage, a problem we recognized in discussing Freud's misconceptions of animal sexuality and will encounter again.

Freud's theory, like Hume's, is pseudo- and cryptointeractionist. In both, the crucial de facto explanations are acceptance by individuals of the prescribed interactions into which they are acculturated; while the de jure explanations involve peculiar conceptions of instinct and detailed mechanisms by which, driven by these instincts, certain patterns of social relations are internalized and made into general rules by the mind of the observer. For Freud (and this must be viewed as an attempt to refine Hume) the culture-defining step is the internalization of Oedipal guilt from the sons' murder of the clan leader, creating the basis of patriarchy as both an enduring cultural institution and a genetic disposition in the human mind.

Freud's Subversion of Meaning

My main conclusion from this review of Freud's 1915 emendation of his psychoanalysis (ego psychology) is that it was a temporizing effort that could not succeed. In overhauling his theory to attempt to deal with the "disagreeable" failure of his earlier mechanistic view of consciousness and unconscious motivation, he turned to linguistics and moral- and social philosophy. But the result of this venture was to become more, not less, reductionistic and socially reactionary, using Hume's ideas and associationist linguistics and psychology for theoretical support. His purpose was to eliminate the moral tension represented by his early self-preservation theory, just as Hume sought to eliminate the moral contradictions of eighteenth-century British capitalism by constructing a complex theory to justify greed as a primary motive, heedless of merit or justice.

In his ego psychology, Freud refined his concepts of consciousness and repression in ways that evaded the central problems and, to make matters worse, did so under the cloak of philosophical and linguistic inquiry whose principal concepts and categories—rationality and justice, for example—he actually subverted. The emendations emphasize the "hypercathexis" of ideas by way of language as the basis for a more complex view of repression. But because Freud's understandings of language and cognition are also outgrowths of his guiding assumption that moral and intellectual development depends strictly on social conditioning and imitation, these emendations actually obscure rather than clarify basic problems. And they obscure important capacities, crucial for intellectual and moral maturity, that Freud represented intuitively in his early theory of self-preservation—those capacities that enable the person, even as a young child, to respond in some "critical" way (i.e., by comparing one thing with another) to the dictates of his upbringing and society. Psychoanalytic understanding of these capacities will remain excessively difficult as long as psychoanalysis remains wedded to Freudian assumptions.

For a number of years ego psychology seemed an adequate way around the difficulties of psychoanalysis. Through ego psychology Freud put off dealing squarely with the seemingly paradoxical phenomenon of repression of self-preservative functions, by noting that they were often *partially* repressed and explaining *how* this might occur in terms of language acquisition and its interference. But in the end all that is rather obvious. Repression is always partial, whether it applies to sex or to moral or intellectual judgment. The questions that most deeply vexed the Dora case still remained. They were to come back in ways that would be harder, and ultimately impossible, to gloss over.

6

THE EMOTIVIST FALLACY

Freud shared with Hume an *emotivist* perspective. This perspective has been little discussed but has great philosophical and clinical significance. For both Hume and Freud, human happiness consists of the emotional experience of pleasure. "What [do] men themselves show by their behavior to be the purpose and intention of their lives. What do they demand of life and wish to achieve in it? They strive after happiness; they want to become happy and to remain so. This endeavor has two sides, a positive and a negative aim. It aims, on one hand, at an absence of pain and unpleasure, and, on the other, at the experiencing of strong feelings of pleasure." (Freud, 1930, 76).[41] And by ruling out innate knowledge and insisting that sense perception and social learning furnish all our ideas, both Hume and Freud are forced to rely on a view of the moral self based purely on the social conventions of their time and class.

Neither Hume nor Freud saw the tautology involved in accounting for the supposedly normal self by conventional emotional reactions to approved modes of social existence—prideful acquisition of property for Hume, pleasure in approved forms of sexual expression for Freud. Thus, both Freud and Hume regard as somehow "primary" typical emotional reactions generated by contact with their respective social worlds, while omitting any critical account either of those worlds or of those emotions. Special significance is attached to

[41] This hedonist assumption is one strongly rejected by Aristotle (ca. 325 B.C., 114-119, 153-163), among many other classical moral philosophers, because of important differences between the pleasure associated with any activity and the choiceworthiness of that activity. It is in general a striking aspect of Freud's intellectual life and development that although classically educated and referring easily to classical authors, he fails regularly to take note of rival classical philosophical *traditions* in his thinking about basic moral concepts like happiness.

particular emotional polarities—pride versus humiliation for Hume, pleasure versus unpleasure for Freud, with the subcategories of the latter being anxiety, depression, guilt, and shame.

But significant emotions always reflect cognitive and moral evaluations and imply moral choices, a fact well represented in the classical tradition that Freud eschewed. In Aristotle's conception of the virtues, both excessive fearfulness and indiscriminate fearlessness constitute moral faults (cowardice and rashness), deviations from the ideal of courage. Such cognitive and moral evaluations are present but obscured (unconscious) in neurosis, and their implications for moral choice unavailable for informed action. The neurotically anxious person feels risk and danger. But without sufficient ability to identify its sources or reasons so as to act courageously, he or she tends to misapprehend the emotion and react to the underlying situation in a cowardly or rash fashion, or to ignore it altogether. This is also true of the neurotically depressed person, who emotionally registers grief, failure, and loss, without understanding their sources. Typically, therefore, problematic conditions are perpetuated, giving rise to what is perhaps the most typical neurotic character trait: endlessly repeating or reexperiencing the same problems. The neurotic has inordinate difficulty answering, unaided, questions like "What I am afraid of?" Is what I am doing safe?" "In what ways is my life up to this point a failure?" "Are the values I am adhering to my own?" Hume and Freud deliberately obscure such evaluative questions.

A key part of Hume's philosophy, as we saw in the last chapter, is a crude effort to rationalize greed by depriving *certain* emotions of evaluative significance, in support of the social status quo. He claimed that moral and cognitive judgments (of "fitness or suitableness") *ought never* to enter into account when it comes to economic interests. Freud follows and extends this method.

His intellectual strategy is similar to Hume's, but its basic elements are probably intrinsic to all hedonist moral philosophies. In his psychoneurological theorizing, Freud treats emotions as epiphenomena of underlying energetic processes, radically differentiated from ideas. "Each instinct expresses itself in terms of affect and in terms of ideas. The affect is the qualitative expression of the quantity of instinctual energy and of its fluctuations" (Laplanche & Pontalis, 1973, 13). While for Hume fluctuations in wealth determine pride and satisfaction, and ought so to do regardless of merit and justice, for Freud fluctuations in the "quantity of instinctual energy" are fundamental. It can hardly be accidental that Freud's theory of mental energetics, one of the three "points of view" (1915c, 181) or "co-ordinates" (1925c, 59) around which his overall theory is built, is called the "economic," while he professes little interest in actual economics. We have seen, however, and will see further, the extent to which Freud actually agrees with Hume's economic views. Given that agreement, his theory in effect provides an extended biological rationale for Hume's effort to strip emotion of evaluative significance with regard to economic behavior.

But when Freud applies his "economics" to developmental psychology and social philosophy, a quite opposite assumption about emotions is invoked. Here emotions have meanings highly determined by their function in maintaining the normative Oedipal personality. His ambitious, and highly influential, developmental theories extend his theory of psycho-sexual development (as expounded in his *Three Essays on the Theory of Sexuality* [1905c] and other works). They involve a normative timetable of interactional crises beginning at birth (birth itself, nursing, weaning, toilet training, sexual awareness, etc.), each of which carries the potential for generating significant anxiety, depression, and, later, shame and guilt (e.g., separation anxiety, castration anxiety). Unresolved castration anxiety from the Oedipal period (ages two through six) is the sine qua non for later neurosis, which is given specific coloring by emotional fixations from earlier points in development.The emotivist fallacy is to take these accounts as explanations rather than illustrations of a particular socialization process.

Another way of putting this problem of emotion is this: Since emotions are taken to arise from simple pleasure-directed discharge processes, they exist in a moral limbo, from which they are rescued by social convention, in the form of Oedipal theory. If one starts with a view of human nature as purely hedonist, one requires an anti-hedonist counterweight, in the form of authority or social convention, to construct something resembling a moral character. But this is a poor, mechanistic, excuse for a moral philosophy.

The knowledge of the self and the world provided by emotions is notoriously untrustworthy, even as is knowledge provided by sensation. Emotivist reasoning would have us believe that, just as the sensation of heat in our skin informs us that we are in proximity to a hot object and provides us directly with the concept of heat, so does the feeling (for example) of subjective fear (anxiety) inform us that our selves are in danger. In some situations both are true. Feelings, like sensations, may generate accurate judgments and predictions. But both may also mislead. In generalized infection, inflammation of the skin, or following extreme cold, sensation gives a false impression of the actual heat of the environment. And the potential for untrue judgments is magnified in the emotional realm, and enormously so in the realm of neurotic experience. People often feel love for those whom they actually hate or fear, and fear those who love them. If a person's concept of self is sufficiently negative, a virtual hallmark of neurosis, he or she will be inclined to experience anxiety or depression in circumstances that are realistically positive and hopeful.

To recall some clinical examples illustrating these almost invariable aspects of neurosis: The engineer (Chapter 1, case 1) typically experienced anxiety in situations that were realistically positive and inviting. The less reason, for example, he had to realistically expect rejection from a woman, the more anxious he was. The married woman (Chapter 3) had become severely neurotic in the context of life changes that realistically and objectively fulfilled some of her most cherished strivings. In the neurotic state, which had persisted for years before she sought help, she routinely misinterpreted symptomatic emotions as confirmations of her perverse nature.

Freud explains these typical paradoxes in terms of a supposed ubiquitous Oedipal danger situation. The Freudian explanation goes as follows: The person develops anxiety in a situation of actual promise or success because the success represents an unconscious wish, unacceptable to his moral system, to vanquish the father and/or possess the mother (or the converse in the case of women), eliciting fear of retaliatory punishment. This explanation preserves the two aspects of the subjective, neurotic explanation that are most problematic: that the life situation is indeed one of danger, but exaggerated; and that the motives at work in the life situation are indeed fundamentally bad, but displaced from childhood and indeed from evolutionary history. To show the entrenchment of this mode of explanation, we might also recall the recent pronouncement of a contemporary leader of psychoanalysis, by no means an orthodox Freudian, that "The analytic setting . . . reproduces the incest taboo, primal oedipal seduction, and the symbolic threat of castration and death related to the violation of this taboo" (Kernberg, 1996, viii).

I conclude that the Freudian scheme for making clinical or philosophical sense of emotions is highly doubtful, not only because of the underlying severe theoretical circularity (a certain circularity is unavoidable in all moral philosophies), but because of the weak and ultimately incoherent hedonist assumption about human happiness that lies at its core. The historically rooted, tradition-embedded, and value-laden emotions that sustain Oedipal morality are used to explain the development of that morality and to justify its imposition on a new generation of patients. The Freudian unconscious-danger paradigm presupposes Oedipal morality, just as for Hume unconscious danger presupposes proper social attitudes toward ownership. Nowhere is there room in either system to question these social arrangements and the histories, philosophies, and attitudes that have brought them about and that sustain them.

The inferred fantasies of patients and of literary and mythical characters that Freudianism uses to bolster arguments for Oedipal morality illustrate the fatelike dangers awaiting the individual who dares to question or disobey. The paradigm here, of course, is the eponymous Oedipus myth itself. Many authors have recognized that Freud interpreted this myth tendentiously to support his argument for Oedipal morality, whereas it contains many other facets and dimensions as a moral tale (for alternate readings of the Oedipus myth, see, for example, Caldwell [1989], Mullahy [1948], Rudnytsky [1987], and Wax [2000]). The outcome of the Dora case is a predictable result of the clinical application of Oedipal-emotivist thinking: where the subject disagrees with Oedipal morality and the rule of the father, Freudianism loses its way and the patient suffers.

Much good post-Freudian thinking has been reoriented with respect to *particular* emotions, but seeing the larger problem of emotivism has proven more difficult. Alternatives are easy enough to envision, however, once we free ourselves from Freudian preconceptions about the moral system.

A crucially important and neglected aspect of the self is the person's theory of self and moral value, which operates with a greater or lesser degree of unconsciousness, depending on the certainty with which it is held. What we call neurosis is a type of mental functioning characterized prominently by strict unconscious adherence to personal theories, typically very negative and determined by adverse conditions of early life. The fact that such theories operate in a highly unconscious way indicates that the person regards them as irrefutable and therefore cannot and does not question them. There is no good reason to believe that negative moral theories of the self, such as the Oedipal theory, are or should be normative or biologically ordained, any more than the negative social utopias of Hobbes or Hume are preordained.

I propose the following as a general way of formulating the problem of anxiety, depression, and other evaluative emotions: they are experiences of mental self-arousal to outcomes unanticipated from and disallowed by our personal theories of self. The crucial difference between the anxiety and the depression reaction is that in anxiety the person deals with the mismatch between theory and reality by unconsciously wishing for a negative outcome; whereas in depression, the negative outcome has already occurred. Neurotic depression is often an aftermath of neurotic anxiety, in the sense that the outcome merely predicted in the anxiety reaction has been fulfilled, subjectively and often objectively, in the depression reaction. But both reactions contain within them the possibility of recognizing the neurotic dogmatism and waking up to new ways of being in the world. An important task of the analyst is to expand consciousness by rendering such emotional reactions comprehensible in terms of operative theories of the self. Seen in this light, emotions become useful signals rather than persecutory pathological phenomena.

7

THE TRAUMA SOLUTION

> In these circumstances [early childhood] instinctual demands from within, no less than excitations from the external world, operate as "traumas" . . . . No human individual is spared such traumatic experiences; none escapes the repressions to which they give rise.
>
> —Sigmund Freud, *An Outline of Psychoanalysis* (1940)

In the middle years of Freud's career the most severe challenge to his view of neurosis came not from the couch but from the war. His attempt to refashion his theory in light of the evidence of the traumatic neuroses represents his second major effort to rescue it from incoherence.

The First World War presented Freud with two main problems as a clinical and social thinker. First, the striking phenomena of the so-called "traumatic neuroses" made it clear that, under the stress of war, psychologically healthy young men routinely become neurotic. This severely challenged his view that neurosis is caused by a childhood failure to resolve the Oedipus complex, but reminded him of earlier ideas that he had set aside, about the relations of trauma to neurosis. Second, there was the sociopathology of the war itself. The war and its aftermath challenged everyone who lived through it, and the generations since, to understand the social, political, and economic conditions responsible for barbarism of a sort that many had thought was a thing of the past but that continued to characterize the twentieth century. In other words, the war compelled critical thinking about modern society.

Traumatic Neurosis

Since his earliest investigations of neurosis Freud had used "psychic trauma" as an etiological concept, undoubtedly borrowed from his mentor

Charcot. But it had always been unsatisfactorily vague and subjective, despite his efforts to give it a precise biological meaning, and it had fallen into disuse as he constructed his Oedipal theory. Transplanted from physical medicine (where its basic meaning was and remains its literal Greek one of "wound" or external injury) to neurology and psychiatry by Charcot and other physicians of the period, it was used to refer to any emotional shock that causes behavioral disturbance. Charcot in particular (1889, 12-14, 335-336) sought to give trauma a neurological significance, precisely describing the symptoms and courses of a variety of "hysterical" conditions and inferring mechanisms in the nervous system. In his early work, Freud carried on this tradition in the form of biological theorizing about mental energetics. His earliest formulations (e.g., Breuer and Freud [1893-1895, 8-11]) employ the trauma concept, described later (1916-1917, 275) as "an experience which within a short period of time presents the mind with an increase of stimulus too powerful to be dealt with or worked off in the normal way, and this must result in permanent disturbances of the manner in which the energy operates."

But whereas the earlier clinical observations had employed theoretical *inferences* about psychic trauma, the epidemic of war neuroses during the First World War presented the opportunity to observe directly cases of young men made neurotic, de novo, by overwhelming events. As I mentioned in my discussion (in Chapter 2) of primal repression, Freud seemed to intuitively recognize that these conditions were of great interest because they could be understood as a direct manifestation of primal repression occurring in later life, thus enabling us to factor out many of the imponderables of early development. This line of thinking led to the formulation, as fascinating as it was threatening to the developmental ideas, that all neuroses are in some sense traumatic, representing responses to overwhelming external events.[42]

Confronting the epidemic of traumatic neurosis—the thousands of shell-shocked soldiers who filled hospital wards and were common sights on the streets of Europe—Freud indeed recognized that the acute traumatic state was real and that it bore striking similarities to the ordinary neuroses he had been working with. These observations posed major challenges to his theory, which he grappled with in the first part of *Beyond the Pleasure Principle* (1920).

To summarize his line of thought: In adult traumatic neuroses the symbolic capacities upon which repression depends have somehow failed. Certain

[42] To continue the parallel I drew in Chapter 2 between problems of economic and psychoanalytic theory, the traumatic neuroses have the same intrinsic interest for psychology as "gangster capitalism" in modern-day Russia has for economics. If, as argued by Holstrom and Smith (2000, 1-15), this phenomenon is not an aberration but supports Marx's inferences about the nature of primitive accumulation, it would appear to refute the theories of the liberal economists upon which the "shock therapy" transition to Western-style markets was based.

types of experience seem to overwhelm the mind's capacity for higher functioning, with the result that the symbolic aspects of memory, thought, affect, action, and dreaming are badly interfered with and the person remains "fixated" on the trauma. Not only libidinal but vegetative processes are disrupted in a profound way, as manifest in disturbances of sleep and dreaming, affect regulation, and severe psychosomatic disease. The fact that severe psychic trauma appears to disrupt, at least temporarily, the mind's symbolizing capacity suggests that something more fundamental than the person's pleasure-driven wish life is being affected, an idea represented by the metaphor of a mental region "beyond" (in the sense of antecedent to or a prerequisite of) the pleasure-unpleasure principle.

In the spontaneous efforts at self-healing following traumatization the person compulsively repeats the trauma, as though to master it retroactively. Experiences that ordinarily serve an unconscious wish-fulfilling purpose, notably dreams, are recruited into the service of repair and, serving a radically different purpose, undergo a change in their very nature. These observations and inferences refute Freud's idea that dreams have an invariably sexual-symbolic content. The clinical paradigm for this process of traumatic psychic injury and attempted repair is the shell-shocked soldier suffering terrifying nightmares, uncontrollable anxiety, outbursts of intense aggression, and overall disorganization of his personality.[43] The acutely traumatized person relies on nonrepressive mechanisms, collectively called "repetition compulsion," until and unless the traumatic state can be mastered. Mastery of trauma enables operation of the pleasure-unpleasure principle, which makes secondary repression, and therefore neurosis, possible. True neurosis following trauma—that is, neurosis employing secondary repression, with all of its symbolic elaborations, as opposed to repetition compulsion—is therefore analogous to scar tissue forming during wound healing.

These observations challenged but did not refute his instinctual theory of neurosis, since the resemblance between neurosis arising in childhood and posttraumatic neurosis could be coincidental. But reflections about life experiences in the ordinary "psychoneuroses" he had been treating suggested to Freud that, while they and traumatic neuroses were distinct enough clinical entities, no clear *etiological* or *conceptual* dividing line could be drawn between the two groups. Life often created traumatic difficulties for children, which were later expressed in symbolic form, as neurosis. From there it was a short step to the idea—formally similar to his earliest ideas on the subject but now

[43] Originally this condition was called "traumatic neurosis," and its classical description and conceptualization by Kardiner (1941) has not been improved upon. The currently fashionable diagnostic term, Post-Traumatic Stress Disorder, actually weakens the concept by being imprecise and overgeneral.

actually quite different—that all neuroses are indeed traumatic in origin. In keeping with his ego psychology, Freud (1920, 14-16) speculated, in the famous observations of the young child inventing the *"fort-da"* game, about the role of symbolic, language-mediated play in mastering adversities that might otherwise prove traumatic.

But if all neuroses are traumatic neuroses in the developmental sense also, then the Oedipal theory of repression would be reduced to a special case of a more general theory—as it should have been earlier, from the variety of other considerations and evidence I have discussed. For then Oedipal repression would have to be seen as a partially successful attempt at self-cure, among a variety of more and less successful attempts—one that depends on accepting the authority of Oedipal morality and the complex of attitudes that accompanies it.

Freud in fact adopted this position, but only as a theoretical possibility. At the same time, he developed arguments that seemed to preserve the integrity of his earlier formulas. He acknowledged the primacy of social trauma as an etiological factor while denying its *generality*.[44] Although recognizing that traumatic experience could override the rule of repression (as he understood it) and act like a "primary" agent, he sought to relate these two factors, trauma and repression, in peculiar ways, including an appeal to the moral and social *superiority* of Oedipal repression. It is the peculiarity of these arguments about trauma that has made it so difficult for psychoanalysts, and even some trained philosophers, to follow the twists and turns of Freud's thinking about "primary" events, primal repression, and so on. But their net effect is to undermine the value of psychic trauma as an example of primal repression.

Trauma Rhetoric: Primary Experience and Gradations of Pathology

Freud modified his theory by conceptualizing how traumatic experience, operating as a "primary" influence, disrupts the usual symbolic matrix upon which repression depends. A nucleus of experience is formed separate from the pleasure-unpleasure principle: "We may argue that the function of dreaming, like so much else, is upset in this condition and diverted from its purposes . . ." (1920, 13). "Overpowering experience," he thought, may give rise to the "impulse to work [it] over in the mind"—a process that "can find expression as a primary event, and independently of the pleasure principle" (16). This is the concept of the "repetition compulsion" (for good discussions

[44] Later, he would also deny its primacy, arguing that the traumatic reaction could be produced, in early childhood at least, by "instinctual demands from within, no less than excitations from the external world" (1940, 185). But that negation of the primacy of social causation could come only after, in the next phase of theorizing, he had rendered his etiological theory *totally* instinctivist, through the death instinct. And, as we will see in discussing that phase, the death instinct theory renders social causation a totally empty category, for there is no way for the individual to judge or legitimately react to it.

of which see Kardiner [1941] and Lipin [1963]). The notion of a "primary event" giving rise to repetition compulsion obviously corresponds to Freud's earlier (1915b, 148) idea of primal repression, and so should have led him to seek to understand the relationship between primary and secondary repression. The logical relationship between the two, as noted, is that Oedipal repression is a special case, less successful than a curative response, more successful than ongoing primal repression. Freud avoided this conclusion by characterizing traumatic reactions as an inferior form of pathology.

According to this idea, nonrepressive or traumatic pathology was to be thought of as "primitive" and exceptional in comparison to neurosis. Just as Dora was displaying exceptional, and unacceptable, aggression in confronting her father about his deceit—which behavior actually showed that the "traumatic" response can in some cases elicit articulate ideas and specific social action to correct it—the traumatized person balancing fear and intense aggression was portrayed as functioning at a primitive level compared to the proper neurotic. Oedipal repression (or "repression proper," Strachey's translation of *eigentliche Verdrängung*), rather than primal repression, was to remain the etiological rule and, in effect, the healthy norm. Correspondingly, the "traumatic" response was particularized and demonized. Phenomena associated with trauma, Freud wrote (1920, 32), "afford us a view of the mental apparatus which, though it does not contradict the pleasure principle, is nevertheless independent of it and seems to be more primitive." Perhaps reflecting his personal difficulty with Dora and other patients, he (18) felt that such phenomena could not be psychoanalyzed through ordinary means because of the *"daemonic force"* of the repetition compulsion (35; my italics). This demonic quality is of course nothing but a metaphor for the *unacceptability* (in Freud's mind, and in his therapy practice) of the person's reactive aggression against the morally incomprehensible circumstances that have been traumatic.

In this scheme of two pathologies, Freud represents nonrepression as a *failure,* leading to nonanalyzable effects. This illustrates, as clearly as anywhere in his writing, the split between an adaptationist and a moral view of psychological health. Traumatic reactions clearly represent a grosser failure of *adaptation* to harmful circumstances than does neurosis, but they are often more open, honest, and direct. They can, and often do, lead to creative understandings and corrective social action. By contrast, neurosis involves compromises with and rationalizations of the damaging influences, and so repression of critical thought and corrective action.

The dual-pathology scheme also illustrates the entrenchment of Oedipal reasoning and Freud's willingness to sacrifice facts and inferences for theory. For in this dualistic scheme, traumatic reactions represent special and unusual cases—a conclusion that runs counter to his intuition that trauma is the root cause of neurosis. This contradictory formulation expresses the bias that repression of sex and aggression in conformity with Oedipal dictates is necessary and realistic, although painful and costly. If a person fails to develop such repression, he or she is assumed to exist in a less-developed state, making analysis problematic. There is even something perverse and wild about this state, as reflected in the image of a "daemonic force." The dual-pathology idea thus provided, and has continued to provide, a justification for limiting treatment in various ways, as he did with Dora. It is the Freudian rationale for the approach, now common in psychiatry, whereby psychotics (and, increasingly, depressed and anxious people) get drugged or medically managed while "proper" neurotics are analyzed.

It should be evident that this hierarchically dualistic scheme of pathology is unconvincing special pleading. One can agree with Freud's thinking about trauma and primary experience, and come to radically opposite conclusions. One can, for example, cogently argue that the traumatic response to incomprehensible, destructive influences reflects a more developed state of consciousness, greater sensitivity to such influences, and less willingness to compromise oneself; that is, strength of character. This view, in fact, informs some interesting debates in post-Freudian psychoanalysis. It is thinkers like R. D. Laing (1967; Laing & Esterson, 1964), Deleuze and Guattari (1983), and Martin-Baro (1994), who have taken it furthest, seeing in some psychotic experience, as in explicit political opposition and much of modern art and literature, an attempt to shake the Oedipal yoke.

Traumatic experience, shattering existing conceptions and expectations, can be daunting if not terrifying to the individual but can also give rise to new conceptions challenging one's theories of self and the existing social order. Revolutionary sensibilities often arise out of such experience. Guattari is one of the rare psychoanalysts to emphasize the creatively transgressive state of mind that the individual and the analyst need to bring to clinical work under such circumstances. Illustrating this point with the life and work of Genet, he (1987, 36) writes:

> A multitude of meaning fragments sweep helter-skelter across the world and the psyche. Anyone . . . whose reflexes have been duly normalized, knows how to discipline or silence these essentially heretical, dissident, and perverse voices. . . . Rather than experiencing these whirlwinds as so many calamities or abysses of anxiety and guilt, Genet opted to accommodate himself to them, to tame and transmute them.

The creative and personal success of such efforts, in Genet's case, did not lead

> through the famous stages of development and adaptation to the real that according to some authors take shape around weaning, toilet training, the

> Oedipus complex and castration, and pre- and post pubescent latency periods. For Genet, everything worked together. . . . His writing resulted not in a dialectical uplifting, but in an exacerbation of his contradictions and upheavals. (35)

To summarize, the extraordinary thing about this phase of Freud's intellectual development is that, while the traumatic neuroses may have refuted key theories of the instinctual origin of neurosis, he steadfastly refused to take this possibility seriously. In fact, he degraded the most creative and constructive responses to trauma and exaggerated his theory's instinctivism. This theoretical move set the stage for the "death instinct," which would make instinctual rather than social causes of repression even more encompassing and inescapable culprits.

To adequately understand and assess that final theoretical shift, however, it is necessary to appreciate his social and political thinking, beginning with the war. For the First World War was as challenging to Freud's assumptions about modern society as the war neuroses were to his assumptions about repression.

The First World War

Freud's Social Thinking

Although sparse, Freud's writing on the First World War makes it clear that it profoundly disturbed a pervasive *belief system* centered on the idea that the capitalist transformation of society would have a progressively civilizing effect on human beings. It is important, for two reasons, that we examine this writing critically for what it reveals about this belief system and its sources, just as we examined the ego psychology and his thinking about trauma. First, the war period coincides with a sharply regressive turn in Freud's thinking. It is difficult to believe that this development was not informed by his reaction to world events, as inclined as he may have been for purely theoretical reasons to make such a regressive move. Second, the writing, like much of his postwar writing that focuses on social philosophy (to be examined in the next two chapters) is highly rhetorical and has been, I believe, widely misunderstood, including by psychoanalysts, who read it narrowly. This section forms a prologue to the next two chapters, which are concerned with the death instinct concept and the social philosophy that informed and was informed by it.

It should come as little surprise that Freud embraced a liberal-capitalist ideology, for he was in his social thinking a fairly typical middle-class intellectual of his time. This partly explains his minimal, and dogmatic, intellectual response to the war. What is surprising, for a thinker of his caliber, is his failure for the rest of his life to consider any other point of view.

In the one short paper (1915d) he devoted to the war, he proposes that human beings have overestimated their capacity for civilization. His emphasis is on the *disillusionment* engendered when "the war in which we had refused to believe broke out" (278). The disillusionment was based on his conviction, along with so many of his era, class, and intellectual bent, that the political and economic order established first in England and then on the European continent and North America over the previous two centuries established a new utilitarian (i.e., interest-based) framework for civic morality that would lead to international peace and cooperation. In the face of the war and the breakdown of this order, Freud never doubts either the rationale of this hoped-for progress or the benefits to the individual of his or her participation in the social order constructed upon it—which he comprehends in terms of instinctual renunciation.

The following statements epitomize the position I am describing: "We had hoped, certainly, that the extensive community of interests established by commerce and production would constitute the germ of such a compulsion [to morality], but it would seem that nations still obey their passions far more than their interests" (288). "We had expected the great world-dominating nations of white race upon whom the leadership of the human species has fallen, who were known to have world-wide interests as their concern . . . to succeed in discovering another way of settling misunderstandings" (276).

Perhaps nowhere in Freud is there a clearer statement of the political-economic morality that parallels his Oedipal view of the individual. Simply put, this is a doctrine that the prevailing order ought to be; and that the power to enforce the status quo equals right. That this is a rhetorical rather than thought-out position is indicated by the fact that he sees no contradiction between *world domination* and worldwide or universal *interests,* any more than he does between the active aggressivity implied in the concept of world domination and the entitled inevitability implied in the ensuing, passively-voiced phrase "has fallen," as though from the sky. The interests "established by commerce and production"—that is, established by whatever means by the ruling business and political elites of the world-dominating nations—are, in his view, right and good and to be regarded as universal, and the individual is well advised to participate in them to achieve the proper deep civilizing transformation.

Given this logic—the equation of world-dominating business interests with morality—it follows that it is only the *pace* at which this great civilizing transformation occurs that is of interest, and the individual's ability to rise to the occasion: "Within each of these nations high norms of moral conduct were laid down for the individual, to which his manner of life was bound to conform if he desired to take part in a civilized community" (276). But "civilized society, which demands good conduct . . . allowed itself to be misled into tightening the moral standard to the greatest possible degree" (284).

Freud's judgment about the causes of the war, following inexorably from this logic, is that the capitalist system has overestimated people's ability to adapt to it, which adaptation is a measure of their "susceptibility to culture" (283). It is unlikely—given his profound acceptance and approval of the underlying philosophy—that he means by this judgment, as many have inferred, to challenge the tenets of classical free-market liberalism. Rather, he is suggesting that *in this instance* it failed because it expected too much instinctual renunciation too quickly.

What are these tenets, and how are they related to the notion of instinctual renunciation? In the social thinking of Freud's day, renunciation was fundamentally a concept of *political economy*. Its central assumption was that massive renunciation of entire ways of life—through forced acceptance of capitalism by domestic laborers, for example, who are bound to receive subsistence or below-subsistence wages, and by peoples colonized by the "world-dominating nations"—are inevitable accompaniments of economic progress. This is part of the nineteenth-century liberal political-economic creed, originally and most influentially articulated by David Ricardo and Thomas Malthus. According to this creed, economic competition under threat of privation, and with actual privation or starvation the fate of the working masses, is a law of nature, obedience to which is therefore a sign of maturity and character. Probably the most famous and oft-quoted example of this view of political economy is Ricardo's (1817, 52) "iron law" of wage immiseration: "Labour, like all other things which are purchased and sold, and which may be increased or diminished in quantity, has its natural and market price. The natural price of labour is that price which is necessary to enable the labourers, one with another, to subsist and perpetuate their race, without either increase or diminution."[45] This "law" persists in many quarters to this day as classical free-market wisdom despite it having long since been demonstrated (Galbraith, 1958) that "the conditions necessary for the rule of the iron law have been in abeyance ever since the nineteenth day of April, 1817, when *On the Principles of Political Economy* was published" (34).

It is an amazing, and amazingly overlooked, fact that Freud nowhere attempts to explain how or why capitalism does or should entail instinctual renunciation. It is simply a part of the assumptive framework of his psychoanalytic view of society, transferred from the then-current economic order. Marxist psychoanalysts like Marcuse, recognizing that Marx also accepted free-market views while seeking to revolt against them, and wishing to see Freud as a social radical rather than reactionary—and thus as covertly congruent with Marx despite his avowals to the contrary—would later attempt

[45] Malthus's correspondingly famous contribution, made somewhat more guardedly than Ricardo's laws, is contained in his *Essay on Population* (1803), in which he posits as an economic principle the inevitability of the mass of working people living on the brink of starvation, based on the consideration that any increase in food supply would result inevitably in population increase, thus maintaining the per capita supply at subsistence levels.

to render this assumption explicit, with dubious success (see my brief discussion of Marcuse on pp. 68–69). In light of the remarkable vagueness and inaccuracy of Freud's instinct theory, I conclude that, not unlike the incest taboo, sexual repression, use of language, and obedience to authority in general, the concept of instinctual renunciation applied to personal and political morality is nothing but a pseudoscientific gloss for the renunciation of Ricardo and Malthus—that is, renunciation of the autonomy of the rest of humanity, for its own good, of course, in the face of subjugation by the ruling powers and business interests.

This interpretation is supported by the fact that liberal economists like Heilbroner, whom I quoted earlier (p. 68), invoke Freudian theory in exactly the opposite way, as a justification for capitalism precisely because of the opportunities it provides for *expression,* not renunciation, of crude instinctual urges. Clearly, in the unrestrained capitalism of Freud's day, which involved massive exploitation, one's greed and aggression, and often ostentation and licentiousness, were either given free rein or had to be massively renounced, depending on which side of the exploitation divide one fell. Formulating this state of affairs in instinctual terms, in the absence of any sound explanation, is nothing more than a psychoanalytic rationalization of what was. Again, an imprecise instinctivist theory does double duty when it comes to justifying the cultural status quo.

In other words, Freud uncritically accepted the psychological rationales of capitalism, adding a new layer of scientific-sounding justification, just as he provided a similar service for Hume's social philosophy. And his thinking, remarkably, underwent little change in his lifetime, despite profound changes in political-economic understandings in the 1920s and 1930s.

It is true that toward the end of his life, on the eve of the Second World War, he began to register some doubt about the reigning ideologies. In a famous public exchange of letters with Einstein on the subject of war, he wrote that only ideas that "give expression to important affinities between members" of a community could be expected to bind them together in idealistic attitudes (1933, 208). "Nor does any idea exist today which could be expected to exert a unifying authority of the sort. Indeed it is all too clear that the national ideals by which nations are at present swayed operate in a contrary direction" (208). This is a step back from his earlier confidence in the civilizing effect of commerce and production. But he does not pursue this doubt, and the bulk of the letter repeats his earlier arguments from 1915, with the newly added idea of the death instinct.

Einstein's contrasting views in this exchange are informative. He (1932, 200-201) questioned the ideologies and the working of the modern nation-state—for example, the undue influence of business in the political process and the corollary problem of control of public opinion through the mass media—questions of immense importance for understanding modern society. He was greatly concerned, therefore, about the subversion of real democracy by powerful business interests parading under the banner of national ideals and economic imperatives. Such ideas completely escaped Freud.

Here is a good example, by the way, of a scientist applying his powers of analysis to important social problems and making sensible inferences about unconscious motives and reasons; while Freud, the ideologically committed psychoanalyst, cannot see them. The contrast demonstrates how dogmatic commitment to *specific* psychoanalytic theories can undermine the general principles of psychoanalysis, a phenomenon familiar enough in the social sciences. Incidentally, Freud's opinion of Einstein's perspicacity in psychological matters was not very high. After a two-hour talk with Einstein in 1927, Freud wrote: "He understands as much about psychology as I do about physics, so we had a very pleasant talk" (Jones, 1957, 131).

To make sense of this blindness in an otherwise outstanding intellectual, we must refer back to the dubious *moral* assumptions underlying Freud's theories, and his willingness or unwillingness to stand corrected by evidence. Libido theory, like the theories of liberal individualism from which it is derived, assumes families and societies that, if not completely benevolent, are at least legitimate authorities, deserving the sacrifices we make to them. Clinical experience showed that this assumption was not tenable on close inspection of family systems like Dora's. I have suggested, as a way of understanding Freud's intellectual history, that it was the clinical challenge that Dora and others posed to his assumptions about families that stimulated the revisionism of ego psychology. Likewise, the First World War raised serious questions about equivalent assumptions regarding national and international social-economic orders, and spurred the revisions made after 1920, of which the death instinct was the central feature. What was thought to be a spreading, democratizing, liberal culture, increasingly able to satisfy material needs and free humankind for a higher existence, not only failed to preserve its citizens but contributed directly to their destruction.

It is at least a highly plausible argument, warranting serious consideration, that this failure was a direct result of the "great transformation" of the Western world into a set of national states organized according to supposedly scientific, but actually improbable, self-regulating market principles (Polanyi, 1944, 30):

> The peculiarity of the civilization the collapse of which we have witnessed was precisely that it rested on economic foundations... . All types of societies are limited by economic factors. Nineteenth century civilization alone was economic in a different and distinctive sense, for it

> chose to base itself on a motive only rarely acknowledged as valid in the history of human societies, and certainly never before raised to the level of a justification of action and behavior in everyday life, gain. The self-regulating market system was uniquely derived from this principle.

Although Polanyi wrote after Freud, he is summarizing the thinking of prior generations of intellectuals who raised warnings about the potentially devastating consequences to a society organized according to the idealized notions of free-market economics, just as many subsequent thinkers continue to warn us of the dangers to political, moral, and intellectual life of social sciences operating in an ethical vacuum.

Political-Economic Historicism

For a profoundly traditional person like Freud, who disdained social analysis and identified with the "great world-dominating nations of white race upon whom the leadership of the human species has fallen," and from which he had expected a gain in the level of civilization, the war of 1914 and the collapse of the nineteenth-century order was incomprehensible. It is interesting to contrast his views with those of other conservative intellectuals who lived through this devastating and sobering period.

Here, for example, is George Steiner (1971, 4-5) discussing the angst and uncertainty to which this destruction gave rise:

> Our experience of the present, the judgments, so often negative, that we make of our place in history, play continually against what I want to call the "myth of the nineteenth century" or the "imagined garden of liberal culture." Our sensibility locates that garden in England and western Europe between ca. the 1820s and 1915. The initial date has a conventional indistinction, but the end of the long summer is apocalyptically exact. [Why Steiner dates the apocalypse 1915 rather than the outbreak of war in 1914 is not clear.]

In judging Freud's reactionary *theoretical* shift, which seems to have been, in large part, a response to this cultural catastrophe, it is useful to compare his approach to that of a thinker like Steiner, also tremendously erudite and steeped in the traditions and values of classical culture. Both men realized that there was something not quite right about the "myth" of nineteenth-century culture, yet both are powerfully drawn to it. Freud's skepticism was based on his concerns, long antedating the war, about psychological and sexual difficulties. On the periphery of his thought was a sense, highly ambivalent and conflicted though it was, of the wider damage that life in modern society can do to social cohesiveness and moral sensibility in general. But his inherent conservatism of thought prevented him from ever looking critically at the social philosophy and political-economic assumptions underlying modern Western society.

By contrast, Steiner, like Einstein, despite the reluctance articulated in the quote above, has this to say about the social-economic destructiveness of the nineteenth-century order:

> If we pause to examine the sources of that knowledge [of the lost golden age], we shall see that they are often purely literary or pictorial . . . the "imagined garden" is, in crucial respects, a mere fiction . . . the crust of high civility covered deep fissures of social exploitation . . . bourgeois sexual ethics were a veneer, masking a great area of turbulent hypocrisy . . . the safety of the *faubourg* and of the park was based squarely on the licensed but quarantined menace of the slum. Anyone who takes the trouble to find out will come to realize what a day's work was like in a Victorian factory, what infant mortality amounted to in the mining country of northern France in the 1870s and 80s. The recognition is inescapable that the intellectual wealth and stability of middle- and upper-middle-class life during the long liberal summer depended, directly, on economic and, ultimately, military, dominion over vast portions of what is now known as the underdeveloped or third world. All this is manifest. We know it in our rational moments. Yet it is a kind of intermittent knowledge, less immediate to our pulse of feeling than is the mythology. (6)

Was Freud blind to this knowledge, or was he fatally drawn to the myth for other reasons? Certainly, when one is so drawn, common sense suffers and it becomes easy to resort to moralistic doctrines and essentialist theories in order to address cultural problems. All traditional value-gradients are seen as catastrophically and senselessly collapsed, which inclines to nihilism and a search for primitive solutions. Steiner (79-80) struggled with this tendency

> to return to an earlier, Pascalian pessimism, to a model of history whose logic derives from a postulate of original sin. We can subscribe today, all too readily, to de Maistre's view that the barbarism of modern politics, the regress of educated, technologically inventive man into slaughter enact a necessary working out of the eschatology of the Fall.

This is precisely the regressive appeal of ideas to which Freud was drawn. The death instinct—the apotheosis of instinctivism in Freud's final, desperate attempt to rescue his theory from incoherence—answers the difficult questions of modern culture by constructing a psychoanalytic eschatology entailing a completely degraded view of human beings, which predictably endorses and calls forth an increase of irrational authority. It has the seduction of a rigorous, universal moralism at a time of upheaval and particularization. But it is a cowardly moralism and only contributes, as Steiner (80) realized, to the problems we face: "There is in our reversion to these earlier, more 'realistic' paradigms an element which is spurious and therefore psychologically corrosive." Again, it is a good, non-Freudian analytic thinker who confronts and corrects the errors of Freudianism.

The tensions that culminated in Freud's proposal of a death instinct are among the most ancient in social philosophy. The overemphasis on change (e.g., "the war in which we had refused to believe") combined with a belief in inexorable and immutable laws of destiny is characteristic of the brand of utopian historicism criticized by Popper (1943, 14)—a concept to be radically differentiated from the fallibilist historicism of MacIntyre (1981, 270), which refers to the rootedness of ethical virtues and frameworks of rationality in particular cultural and intellectual traditions. Popper traces utopian historicism through Plato to the pre-Socratic philosophers, notably Heraclitus's reaction to the democratic social revolutions of sixth- and fifth-century B.C. Greece:

> We can explain this attitude, perhaps, if we interpret the historicist's over-emphasis on change as a symptom of an effort needed to overcome his unconscious resistance to the idea of change. This would also explain the emotional tension which leads so many historicists (even in our day) to stress the novelties of the unheard-of revelations which they have to make. . . . It often seems as if they were trying to comfort themselves for the loss of a stable world by clinging to the view that change is ruled by an unchanging law.

Notice, by the way, Popper's natural use of the concept of unconscious motivation, one that derives from one of the basic psychoanalytic ideas and owes little or nothing to Freud's special theories. For Popper, like Steiner and Einstein, this idea provides a starting point for reflection and speculation about the motives underlying ideology and behavior he judges irrational.

Concluding Thoughts

It is safe to say that, while Freud may have, with extreme reluctance, been leaning in the direction of a more critical attitude toward modern society—that is, a social-psychoanalytic view—he had not come close to it by the end of his life. Throughout his work, his emphasis remains on human beings' failure to live up to a nebulous moral standard, without recognizing that it is actually artificial, authoritarian, and ultimately faith-based, much in the manner of the religious moralism he criticized. What is remarkable is his failure, ever, to recognize the ideological quality of his thought. In his maturest years, during the postwar German devastation and the rise of fascism, which cried out for a considered psychoanalytic response, Freud continued to promote his ideas of conformity and instinctual renunciation, clinging to his death instinct theory.

He never saw the need to think specifically about modern society. In keeping with prevailing ideologies, society was invisible to Freud until it failed, at which point human evil and weakness were blamed. War, political and economic devastation, fascism, imperialism, and colonialism were for him nonentities, in that they had no specific meaning or interest, no discernible antecedents or causes specific to the realm of experience in which they occurred, the realm of social, political, and economic life. He contented himself, rather, with grand theories. Given his blindness to social issues, the Great War and its aftermath could only mean that catastrophes befell society in incomprehensible ways.

This is the decisive, profound lack in Freud's thinking, and the one that dooms the Oedipal view of human beings and society to irrelevance. But in his writing and thinking up to 1920 it was an unsatisfying absence, based on personal prejudices. Freud, the rigorous thinker, needed a theoretical justification for ignoring society. He provided it in the second half of *Beyond the Pleasure Principle.*

8

THE ULTIMATE SOLUTION:
Aggression as Instinct

When Men have found some general Propositions that could not be doubted of, as soon as understood, it was, I know, a short and easy way to conclude them innate. This being once received, it eased the lazy from the pains of search, and stopp'd the enquiry of the doubtful, concerning all that was once stiled innate: And it was of no small advantage to those who affected to be Masters and Teachers, to make this the Principle of Principles, that Principles must not be questioned.

—John Locke, *An Essay Concerning Human Understanding* (1689)

The Second Half of *Beyond the Pleasure Principle*

The second half of *Beyond the Pleasure Principle* is a rhetorical tour de force, reaching a conclusion running directly counter to the evidence presented in the first half. Having acknowledged that social trauma, in the form of overwhelming events, cannot be denied and is a cause of neurosis more fundamental than repressed libido—which implies a need to inquire into such social causes—Freud then took the *theory* in the opposite direction. By arguing that the roots of aggression are to be found in a "death instinct," he rendered inquiry into social causation moot. This is the same strategy we saw in the ego psychology, but more extreme. While the ego psychology solution depended on conventional approaches to language and cognition, and so is predictably regarded as uncontroversial by most analysts, the death-instinct solution depends on a radical and bizarre redefinition of instinct. It is regarded as a bit extreme even by many Freudian analysts, who do not, for the most part, understand its deep connections to the earlier efforts.

Freud had argued in the first half of *Beyond the Pleasure Principle* that the phenomena of the traumatic neuroses reveal a self-preservative function at work in the mind, whose successful operation is a precondition for functioning at the "pleasure principle" level and—since the process was fundamentally the same in posttraumatic and in developmental neuroses—that all neuroses may be conceptualized as traumatic in origin. This implies strongly that the pleasure principle, with its accompanying cognitive principle of "primary process," is not primary at all in the sense of a mental registration of biological urges, but rather depends on a certain expectable organization of the social world, with all that that implies about innate understandings of and responses to social organization. He had recognized that these findings stood to refute libido theory, the ego-psychological emendations notwithstanding, by thrusting social causation back into the forefront—although this is acknowledged in a narrowly understated way: "This would seem to be the place, then, at which to admit *for the first time* an exception to the proposition that dreams are fulfilments of wishes" (32, my italics). The full import of this statement can be appreciated by recalling the fact that dream analysis had long been considered a certain way to understand the repressed wishes underlying neurosis and to demonstrate their unvaryingly libidinal content. Such demonstrations, as in the case of Dora, had been held up as proof of the essential correctness not only of dream theory but of the larger instinct-Oedipal theory. The exception Freud notes with respect to dreams must therefore be regarded as representing an entire set of major exceptions to the larger theory and in fact to the whole structure of Freudianism. In the final three chapters of the book Freud attempts to deal with this challenge, and he takes psychoanalysis in an even more extreme direction than ego psychology.

Freud had differentiated those unconscious repetitions of painful circumstances that can be understood in terms of repressed and symbolized wishes from "a compulsion to repeat which over-rides the pleasure principle" (22). Staying with his predominant biologistic theorizing, he conceptualized this more elementary function as the mind's need to "bind" stimuli (31) so as to avoid traumatization and as a precondition for the operation of the pleasure principle. A crucial element in this theory of trauma is *fright,* to which the person is prone by "lack of preparedness for anxiety, including lack of hypercathexis of the systems that would be the first to receive the stimulus" (31).

Recall that in an attempt to accommodate to the "disagreeable discovery" that what is repressed cannot possibly be accounted for by sexual conflict, Freud had placed great stress on language and meaning as the prime means for hypercathecting *ideas;* but that, given his theories of language and cognition, hypercathexis is little more than a biologistic trope for the double conformity of words and things, that is, conventional thinking. Thus a strong implication of the first half of *Beyond the Pleasure Principle* is that it is the *incom-*

prehensibility of certain experiences, given conventional thinking, that renders the person prone to traumatization. Social reality breaks through in a way that the person is unprepared for and that ordinary understandings cannot render comprehensible. So here is a severe challenge to ego psychology, with its restricted views of cognition and language, and to instinct theory. For when the "economic" explanations of trauma (quantity of excitation, cathexis) are translated into ordinary language, we are left with an explanation in terms of meaning and value. Clearly, a reformulation of the linguistic and cognitive theories is called for.

But Freud is unwilling or unable to either acknowledge the importance of social causation or correct his theories of language and cognition. He therefore turns to the one variable he does allow, given his "principle of principles" (see the Locke epigraph to this chapter)—instinct. Now discarding all vestiges of moral self-preservation, he retreats behind an exaggerated instinctivism.

He does this by proposing a new definition: "*an instinct is an urge inherent in organic life to restore an earlier state of things* which the living entity has been obliged to abandon under the pressure of external disturbing forces" (36, italics in original). And what is more characteristic of this earlier state than nonlife, since life arises from nonlife? With this reasoning Freud takes instinct theory in a radically new direction, which he describes (without, I am sure, intending irony) as "conservative." All instincts are "an expression of the *conservative* nature of living substance . . . we shall be compelled to say that *'the aim of all life is death'*" (36, 38, italics in original). What is the purpose of this new and bizarre definition of instinct?

It provides Freud with the justification he needs to eliminate the troublesome self-preservative instinct entirely and for uniting disparate phenomena under the umbrella of a single overarching conception of instinct, in a radical simplification. It is for this reason that the coherence of Freudianism finally stands or falls on the merits of the death instinct theory.

With this radical simplification Freud takes instinctivist logic to new extremes. Rather disingenuously (for he had all along resisted the notion of developmental instincts) he wrote: "This view of instincts strikes us as strange because we have been used to see in them a factor impelling towards change and development, whereas we are now asked to recognize in them the precise contrary—an expression of the *conservative* nature of living substance" (36, italics in original). He quickly uses his new definition to once and for all rid his theory of the self-preservative instinct, which has all along, troublesomely, begged vital questions of judgment, innate understandings of social life, and so forth:

> The hypothesis of self-preservative instincts, such as we attribute to all living beings, stands in marked opposition to the ideas that instinctual

life as a whole serves to bring about death. *Seen in this light, the theoretical importance of the instincts of self-preservation, of self-assertion and of mastery greatly diminishes.* (39; my italics)

Taking the argument a step further, he now categorically denies any developmental instinct: "There is unquestionably no universal instinct towards higher development observable in the animal or plant world, even though it is undeniable that development does in fact occur in that direction" (41).

This purging of any developmental instinct (the predicate "universal" is pure Freudian rhetoric, without meaning in this context) is extremely problematic because, as we have seen, it is precisely evidence of developmental instincts that have been, all along, incompatible with and threatening to his theory. The self-preservative instinct could not find coherent practical application because it implies innate roots of moral and social understandings incompatible with his theory of instinct as amoral and asocial, just as the anti-incest instinct could find no place because it implies an innate root of exogamy. Such instinctual roots of morality and sociability are vital but can never provide us with more than *inclinations* to react in various ways. They must be developed through ongoing understandings of those social and political conditions under which we actually exist in the world.

The Reactionary Aim of *Beyond the Pleasure Principle*

The reactionary aim of the second half of *Beyond the Pleasure Principle* becomes clearest in its final pages. Here Freud puts forward a radically revised theory of aggression, based on the new death instinct, which serves two purposes simultaneously. It *undermines any social reaction or critical thought* as a motive for aggression, and it *seeks to maintain the hegemony of libido theory* by incorporating aggression into it through the concept of "narcissistic libido." The new theory is introduced in a very roundabout way, in the guise of a speculative effort to find some empirical demonstration of the death instinct, which he thinks he has found in the phenomena of love and hate between people:

> We started out from the great opposition between the life and death instincts. Now object-love itself presents us with a second example of a similar polarity—that between love (or affection) and hate (or aggressiveness). . . . Is it not plausible to suppose that this sadism is in fact a death instinct which, *under the influence of the narcissistic libido,* has been forced away from the ego and has consequently only emerged in relation to the object? It now enters the service of the sexual function. . . . If such an assumption as this is permissible, then we have met the demand that we should produce an example of a death instinct—though, it is true, a displaced one. (53-54, my italics)

If we cut through the complex and barely comprehensible rhetoric about love, hate, and sexuality, and consider this statement in the relevant context of what is being proposed to rescue Freudian theory from challenge, this statement says, in effect, that since there is no longer any legitimate basis for thinking of aggression as reaction to environmental influences (i.e., there is no longer a self-preservative instinct with any substance), we are now to look only to our biology for the source of aggression and are to understand it in a trivialized way as the death instinct turned away from the self under the influence of narcissistic libido.

The advantages as well as the cost to Freudian theory of these new formulations are clear enough, as even stated by Freud, again without intentional irony: "*We have no longer to reckon* with the organism's puzzling determination (so hard to fit into any context) to maintain its own existence in the face of every obstacle. What we are left with is the fact that the organism wishes to die only in its own fashion" (39, my italics). The "puzzling determination" of people to live harmoniously and productively in some reasonable social, political, and economic order is no longer to be reckoned with, *because people fundamentally want to die,* and their interests and passions divert them temporarily from this aim.

Extant critiques of Freudianism fail to note the organic connections between this bizarre theory and the preceding trauma theory and ego psychology, as well as the enormous social and political implications of the new theory and its congruence with other ideologically driven theories in other realms that reach similar conclusions. The death-instinct theory takes instinctivist reasoning to a new low by providing a pseudobiological justification for points of view that are socially and politically extreme, yet which were regarded in Freud's day, as they are commonly today, as conservative. For the supposed inherent weakness and self-destructiveness of people justifies, as it always does, arbitrary authority by superior leaders, a view he explicitly stated later: "One instance of the innate and ineradicable inequality of men is their tendency to fall into the two classes of leaders and followers. The latter constitute the vast majority; they stand in need of an authority which will make decisions for them and to which they for the most part offer an unqualified submission" (1932, 212). Note, ironically, the ease with which Freud employs the concept of innateness—with which he has the greatest difficulty, when it comes to anything positive—to describe a complex feature like inequality between individuals and subjection to arbitrary authority.

Freud's new assumptions about human nature are thus deeply political and social, akin to "theories" of genetic, racial, and cultural inferiority that have recurred throughout the ages and that have in the modern era been developed into refined ideologies for domination. Freud, typically, does not discuss other, mostly philosophical and economic thinkers, who had propounded or were propounding similar ideas in other frameworks. But his ideas are virtually identical to the opinions of other intellectuals who sought to justify the dominion of European culture over the rest of the world. To take one influential example, compare Hegel's opinion on similar subjects, expressed a few generations before Freud. In his famous lectures on the philosophy of history (1830-1831), he explains the grand triumph of European civilization over the rest of the world—when "Spirit" reaches "its perfect maturity and strength" (109)—in terms of the brutishness of other cultures and the need to exterminate them. Native America, for example, was "physically and psychically powerless," its culture so limited that it "must expire as soon as Spirit approached it" (81). This was because the Native American was inferior even to the Negro, "the natural man in his completely wild and untamed state," which is beyond any "thought of reverence and morality—all that we call feeling . . . there is nothing harmonious with humanity to be found in this type of character" (93).

What endows the European with his so-called moral superiority? Contrary to philosophers of the rational-empiricist liberal tradition, like Locke, Mill, Smith, and Humboldt, who regarded a good and just society as one promoting the full development of individual capacities, Hegel viewed the intellectual, moral, and creative development of the individual as dependent on the superordinate religious-military-economic State, an outgrowth of the patriarchal order:

> It is the moral Whole, the *State,* which is that form of reality in which the individual has and enjoys his freedom; but on the condition of his recognizing, believing in and willing that which is common to the Whole. . . . Law, Morality, Government, and they alone [are] the positive reality and completion of Freedom. (38)

The State, "the actually existing realized moral life" (38), is the natural outgrowth of the patriarchal family:

> The basis of the patriarchal condition is the family relation; which develops the *primary* form of conscious morality, succeeded by that of the State as its *second* phase. The patriarchal condition is one of transition, in which the family has already advanced to the position of a race or people; where the union, therefore, has already ceased to be simply a bond of love and confidence, and has become one of plighted service. (41-42, italics in original)

At the same time that Hegel was propounding his version of Manifest Destiny in Germany, across the Channel the architects of British economic liberalism, the true descendants of Hume, were fashioning its "scientific" rationales in the form of free-market economics and the survival of the economic fittest, a blueprint for the free-market state. Malthus (1803), for example, in his widely influential work, introduced the concept of "redundant population" (volume 2, 53) to describe that "part of the society that cannot in general be considered as the most valuable part, [which] diminishes the shares that would otherwise belong to the more industrious and more worthy members" (48). In his famous argument against the Poor Laws of England he writes that social policies to provide for sustenance of these inferior beings "could not be done without the most complete violation of the law of property, from which everything that is valuable to man has hitherto arisen" (52). A half-century later, Herbert Spencer, the precursor of the social Darwinists, began championing similar views. In the late nineteenth century he was an influential voice in English and American philosophy and sociology, and became the darling of the industrial establishment. In an updated version of the "adapt or die" philosophy, he preached a categorical rejection of all state assistance to the poor, as interfering with the laws of nature as applied to society. Poverty was proof of unfitness, and the elimination of the poor a demonstration of nature's iron laws: "If they are sufficiently complete to live, they *do* live, and it is well they should live. If they are not sufficiently complete to live, they die, and it is best they should die" (1864, 414–415).

Freud finally and fervently embraces these extremes of "liberal" thought, without in the slightest recognizing or discussing their implications. His ultimate solution to the problem of the person in modern, conflict-generating society is to exclude from the balance of interests and passions any appeal to considerations of justice and equality, or, for that matter, any quality of the self other than that which renders the individual adaptable to life in modern industrial society, fashioned by the elites of "the great world-dominating nations of white race." Like human brutishness for Hobbes and Hegel, property for Hume, and capital for Malthus and Spencer, the death instinct provides the perfect rationale for adherence to patriarchal rule and its modern "scientific" avatar, the free-market state. As we will see in the next chapter, Freud actually goes *further* in this direction than any of his liberal forebears. In eliminating even the appeal to self-interest, Freud winds up breaking with the liberal tradition.

In the new psychoanalytic thinking it is necessary "to abandon the belief that there is an instinct towards perfection at work in human beings" (1920, 42). The human being is, after all, "a savage beast to whom consideration toward his own kind is something alien" (1930, 112). But not everyone should be so characterized. Freud has his own version of the elite who strive toward perfection and should survive, in contrast to the masses who are little different from animals: it is those who have best adapted to the Oedipal order, either through natural inclination or its inferior substitute, psychoanalysis, by maximally renouncing instinct. And those fortunate few should be under no illusion that their deepest motives are other than bestial and death-oriented, so as to keep them continually prodded toward the ideal: "What appears in a minority of human individuals as an untiring impulsion towards further perfection can easily be understood as a result of the instinctual repression upon which is based all that is most precious in human civilization" (1920, 42). By contrast with his liberal forebears, who could at least point to objective indicators of superiority, however fallacious, Freud's "unceasing instinctual renunciation" is a standard devoid of either coherent meaning or sensible reference to the real world, and therefore infinitely usable in the service of oppression. It is, in fact, the ultimate subversion of meaning.

The change in theory brought about by the death instinct also heralded a sea change in policy for institutional psychoanalysis that decisively insulated it from social reality, for no amount of inquiry into social causes could now affect the Freudian view of human nature as incestuous and destructive. Like an Orwellian government decree that allows journalists to report freely whatever they wish, provided it is approved by a board of national security, there was now no way out of the instinctivist dogma parading as psychoanalytic enlightenment. It became a case of "Freudianism right or wrong," which attitude was reflected in the militantly embattled rhetoric of Freud's inner circle of leading analysts in the 1920s and 1930s. The new theory was greeted with reverential silence from rank-and-file analysts, and overnight became the new touchstone of psychoanalysis. "In the course of time," Freud wrote later (1930, 119), "they [the ideas] have gained such a hold upon me that I can no longer think in any other way." To this day hardly any critics within psychoanalysis, and few without, recognize the theory for what it is, an authoritarian social psychology that attempts to rescue Freudianism from its inevitable incoherence—although many prominent analysts have noted its irrationality and its lack of congruence even with an already stretched notion of instinct (e.g., Barros, 1971; Fenichel, 1953; Fromm, 1973; Simmel, 1944; Szasz, 1952; Waelder, 1956).

Concluding Thoughts

Freud's ultimate death-instinct solution to the problems he encountered very early, beginning with cases like Dora, is the logical outgrowth of his rejection of ideas that might have formed the pillars of a rational psychoanalysis—Westermarck's concept of incest aversion, the self-preservative instinct, a sound linguistic and cognitive theory, not to mention a grasp of evolutionary biology; and it left him with no alternative. It is as much a testament to his consistency as a thinker as a sign of his limited vision that he pursued the solutions most in accord with his instinctivist, essentialist, historicist, and Oedipalist assumptions. As he wrote later (1923, 46): "If it were not for the considerations put forward in *Beyond the Pleasure Principle* . . . we should have difficulty in holding to our fundamental dualistic point of view." This is an enormous understatement. To have not finally embraced the death-instinct theory would have brought his system to an epistemological crisis and to the need to substantially rebuild it. It is his daring, if rather mad, consistency that allows us to assess his work as an integrated whole.

Although Freud wrote other significant works after 1920, it is fair to say that *Beyond the Pleasure Principle* substantially completes the theoretical structure of his psychoanalysis, which is refined in later writing and applied largely to matters of social philosophy.

9

FREUDIANISM POST-1920

I can no longer think in any other way.
—Sigmund Freud, *Civilizations and Its Discontents* (1930)

In his writings after 1920 Freud increasingly turned his attention to social and moral philosophy, notably in *The Future of an Illusion* (1927) and *Civilization and Its Discontents* (1930), while refining and providing summaries of his clinical theory in *The Ego and the Id* (1923), *Inhibitions, Symptoms, and Anxiety* (1926), *Analysis Terminable and Interminable* (1937), *New Introductory Lectures* (1933), and *An Outline of Psychoanalysis* (1940). Of this work, the most significant for an intellectual history are the philosophical writings, commonly identified with his maturest thought, in keeping with his own later assessment (1935, 72):

> My interest, after making a lifelong *détour* through the natural sciences, medicine, and psychotherapy, returned to the cultural problems which had fascinated me long before, when I was a youth scarcely old enough for thinking. At the very climax of my psycho-analytic work, in 1912, I had already attempted in *Totem and Taboo* to make use of the newly discovered findings of analysis in order to investigate the origins of religion and morality. I now carried this work a stage further in two later essays, *The Future of an Illusion* (1927) and *Civilization and Its Discontents* (1930). I perceived ever more clearly that the events of human history, the interactions between human nature, cultural development and the precipitates of primaeval experiences (the most prominent example of which is religion) are no more than a reflection of the dynamic conflicts between the ego, the id and the super-ego, which psycho-analysis studies in the individual—are the very same processes repeated upon a wider stage. In *The Future of an Illusion* I expressed an essentially negative valuation of religion. Later, I found a formula which did better justice to it: while

granting that its power lies in the truth which it contains, I showed that that truth was not a material but a historical truth.

Freudian theory in this final phase is commonly viewed as a modified ego psychology or "structural" psychology (because of its emphasis on the mental structures and substructures of ego and superego) which contains a more sophisticated "Eros" concept of libido. This view is partially correct but misleading because the one idea that is genuinely new, and that exerts a crucial influence on psychoanalysis in this era, is not Eros but the death instinct, which, although an outgrowth of ego psychology, makes a radical departure, as we have seen. Eros and the associated ideas Freud alludes to above as granting a certain "historical truth" to religion are based on the death instinct. That is, he devised them (1920, 50; see my discussion on p. 96) to fill the gap left by his rejection, in 1915, of instinctive self-preservation and his adoption, in 1920, of the death instinct and innate aggression. In fact, Freud's description (1923, 40) of Eros as comprising "not merely the uninhibited sexual instinct proper and the instinctual impulses of an aim-inhibited or sublimated nature derived from it, but also the self-preservative instinct," is incorrect and misleading. It suggests that the concept of instinctive self-preservation was somehow retained, when it, along with its implications of a natural basis for morality, could not have been more forcefully repudiated in all his writing from 1915 on. As though to leave no doubt whatever about this, Freud now explicitly rejects the idea of any natural morality, writing, for example: "We may reject the existence of an original, as it were natural, capacity to distinguish good from bad" (1930, 124). In keeping with his increasingly reactionary position that morality is nothing but internalization of the worldviews of the ruling elites, it is only the trivial (because obvious and nonspecific) affiliative aspects of the original self-preservative instinct that are carried over into the Eros concept.

It is fair to say that after 1920 the death instinct is his key theory; indeed, he could "no longer think in any other way" (1930, 119). The late works are not understandable without taking that fact into account, and these philosophical writings reveal the implications of the death instinct most clearly.

The Future of an Illusion

The Future of an Illusion (1927) is a relatively uninteresting antireligious tract that deserves some notice, however, because it stands chronologically and intellectually between *Totem and Taboo* (1913) and the much more ambitious *Civilization and Its Discontents* (1930). With regard to its title subject, religion, the arguments are the same as those made in *Totem and Taboo,* so I will not review them in any detail. Religious belief is compared to an obsessional neurosis, and Freud makes a plea for its surrender. He uses the new death instinct idea to update the earlier arguments of *Totem and Taboo,* and attempts to put forward his claim for the scientific status of psychoanalysis as against the wish-fulfilling illusions of religious certainty.

The increased energy with which Freud mounts his attack on religion is particularly ironic in that his own thinking, which debases man and idealizes authority, resembles authoritian features of the religions of his society. At the end of *The Future of an Illusion* he (1927, 38) summarizes his contempt for the priestly thinking that has glamourized and enslaved people:

> Thus it was agreed: God alone is strong and good, man is weak and sinful. In every age immorality has found no less support in religion than morality has. If the achievements of religion in respect to man's happiness, susceptibility to culture and moral control are no better than this, the question cannot but arise whether we are not overrating its necessity for mankind, and whether we do wisely in basing our cultural demands upon it.

In fact, this condemnation of priestly thinking could well be applied to late Freudianism, which accords patriarchal authority a transcendent moral value comparable to that given by many traditional religions, and based on a lapsarian eschatology no less mythic and dogmatic than the Christian myth of Adam's fall. One might well ask, in fact, whether there is any essential difference between the qualities Freud attributes to religion and his own maturing view that human beings are "savage beasts" who "stand in need of an authority which will make decisions for them"—except that religion makes no pretense of being "scientific."

Apart from these familiar antireligious sentiments, it is the first chapter of *The Future of an Illusion* that contains the ideas of greatest interest, for it reveals most clearly the death instinct's effect on Freud's philosophy, in an even more regressive view of cultural life than he has previously shown. Although embracing the liberal view that private property, and the social regulations that enforce particular distributions of a society's wealth and wealth-generating capacity, are necessary for the development and maintenance of civilization, he now regards liberalism's interest-based morality as lacking in one respect: It is not coercive enough.

Apart from knowledge and the technology for controlling nature and satisfying human needs, civilization, for Freud, consists of "all the regulations necessary in order to adjust the relations of men to one another and especially the distribution of available wealth" (6). He emphasizes the need for coercion to maintain discipline against individuals who are likely to protest existing arrangements: "Civilization has to be defended against the individual, and its regulations, institutions and commands are directed to that task." Freud does not inquire into the various ways by which cultures have historically approached the matter of wealth distribution or into the theories underlying the modern state with its policies for generating and distributing wealth. He appears to recognize that such study would be useful, for the modern Western culture with which he is familiar leaves something to be desired in happiness and sense of participation. This dissatisfaction is even acknowledged to result from coercion of the many by the few: "civilization is something which was imposed on a resisting majority by a minority which understood how to obtain possession of the means to power and coercion." Thus there is room for criticizing the particular cultural forms that have arisen, because they are largely the result of historical accident:[46] the difficulties of civilization "are not inherent in the nature of civilization itself but are determined by the imperfections of the cultural forms which have so far been developed." Therefore

> one would think that a re-ordering of human relations should be possible, which would remove the sources of dissatisfaction with civilization by renouncing coercion and the suppression of the instincts, so that, undisturbed by internal discord, men might devote themselves to the acquisition of wealth and its enjoyment. (7)

But these possibilities are considered moot because of the death instinct, and it is *at this point that Freud breaks with the liberal tradition altogether.* For "one has . . . to reckon with the fact that there are present in all men destructive, and therefore anti-social and anti-cultural, trends," requiring that "every civilization must be built up on coercion." This makes it seem doubtful to Freud that "if coercion were to cease the majority of human beings would be prepared to undertake to perform the work necessary for acquiring new wealth," so that society would quickly break down. He has decided, in other words, that self-interest, the core of liberal philosophy, is no longer sufficient as a basic motive. Coercion alone explains the apparent but illusory drive for human acquisition and attainment. This conclusion radically simplifies his understanding of culture:

> Whereas we might at first think that [civilization's] essence lies in controlling nature for the purpose of acquiring wealth and that the dangers which threaten it could be eliminated through a suitable distribution of the wealth among men, it now seems that the emphasis has moved over from the material to the mental . . . [i.e., to] the burden of the instinctual sacrifices imposed on men.

---

[46] Note that this is the same problem that Hume came upon in reflecting about the *origins* of private property, and which he sought to resolve by fiat (see pp. 133–135); and the same one, for that matter, that Marx came upon in his reflections about "primitive accumulation," which he addressed historically (see pp. 71–72).

These sacrifices refer, in his theory, to control of our supposed incestuousness and murderousness, the twin pillars of his view of human nature; and in social reality to the sacrifices required of the mass of humanity by conforming to the interests of the world-dominating business elites. These simple psychological formulas mean that we no longer have to study society, observe the effects of our actions and policies, and so on. It is only necessary to conform.

Here we begin to appreciate the full effect of the death instinct on Freud's social philosophy and can better understand what an extreme theory it in fact is. Having rejected the self-preservative instinct in any meaningful sense, now *even in the narrow liberal sense of pursuit of self-interest,* there is only murderousness, laziness, and corruption in "natural man," leaving pure coercion as the only civilizing force and total acceptance of the status quo as the only healthy and legitimate cultural choice. Unsurprisingly, there is correspondingly a heightened contempt for democracy and "the masses": "It is just as impossible to do without control of the mass by a minority as it is to dispense with coercion in the work of civilization. For masses are lazy and unintelligent; . . . and the individuals composing them support one another in giving free rein to their indiscipline" (7-8).

It is this conclusion that provides the context for his discussion of religion, seen as an unsatisfying cultural attempt to appease the inevitable frustration of the masses with an illusion of fatherly beneficence and life hereafter. He is also dismissive of cultural comparisons. Since human beings are innately destructive and require coercion of one sort or another to be civilized, it is irrelevant to compare cultures, systems of wealth distribution, and the principles underlying them. Man's inevitable misery in society is becoming an article of absolute faith.

In his crowning work of social philosophy, *Civilization and Its Discontents* (1930), Freud seeks to explain and justify this inevitable misery (its original title was *Das Unglück in der Kultur,* or *Unhappiness in Civilization*). This work rivals *Beyond the Pleasure Principle* in its complicated rhetoric and theory, and therefore requires detailed scrutiny.

Civilization and Its Discontents

The Message

Civilization and Its Discontents is one of the most celebrated of Freud's works for several reasons. A late work, it is broad in scope and apparently skeptically humanistic in aim, applying his mature theory to great problems of human beings in society. Compared to many of his other works, it is readable without specialized knowledge. And coming as it did in the interwar period, when fascism was on the rise worldwide and the Soviet experience seemed to many to offer a hopeful alternative to capitalism with its severe inequities, the judgments of the now-famous Freud were eagerly sought.

In *Civilization and Its Discontents* Freud expresses a guarded skepticism about the advance of culture through a rational, psychologically grounded ethics, a basis for which, he hopes, is contained in his psychoanalytic theories. This hope, which seems to be in keeping with the ideals of skeptical humanism and Enlightenment rationalism, are most evident in the final section, where he speculates, in the manner of Hobhouse (compare my discussion in Chapter 2), about the cultural equivalents of superego and repression:

> It can be asserted that the community, too, evolves a super-ego under whose influence cultural development proceeds. . . . The super-ego of an epoch of civilization has an origin similar to that of an individual. It is based on the impression left behind by the personalities of great leaders—men of overwhelming force of mind or men in whom one of the human impulsions has found its strongest and purest, and therefore often its most one-sided, expression. (141)

He remains critical of the nostrums of religion, notably the Christian conception of brotherly love, which he attacks sharply as an unrealistic imposition upon man's nature, and therefore, in sum, destructive:

> The commandment, "Love thy neighbor as thyself," is the strongest defence against human aggressiveness and an excellent example of the unpsychological proceedings of the cultural super-ego. The commandment is impossible to fulfil; such an enormous inflation of love can only lower its value; not get rid of the difficulty. (143)

He expresses hope for a more rational, humanistic, ethics based on considerations of "virtue" and "reward" in the practical affairs of daily life: "So long as virtue is not rewarded here on earth, ethics will, I fancy, preach in vain." As in earlier works, he seems to embrace the liberal creed: "a real change in the relations of human beings to possessions would be of more help in this direction [of achieving a rational and practical ethics] than any ethical commands"; while recognizing that actually existing Marxian socialism is hampered by its own "idealistic misconceptions of human nature."

But again, and more decisively than in *Future of an Illusion,* he rejects any such practical solution on theoretical grounds. In *Future of an Illusion* he had criticized economic self-interest as an insufficient civilizing force. In *Civilization and Its Discontents* he makes it explicit that he is unwilling to contemplate any standard for judging ethical goods like "virtue," "justice," and "morality" other than those dictated by those in power. Given his theoretical convictions, in other words, *the rational ethics advertised in the beginning of the book leads to nothing more than a defense of tyranny and a mindless conformity.* And

Civilization and Its Discontents, showing most clearly the social implications of the death instinct, emerges as Freud's most reactionary work.

Freud's conclusions hinge on his treatment of what is the single new idea presented in *Civilization and Its Discontents,* and the real problem it purports to tackle: that it is in the nature of society to *insatiably* suppress the individual. This idea is not introduced until chapter 5. Chapters 1 through 4 function as a prolegomenon, in which Freud recapitulates with minor modifications his familiar ideas about the process of civilization, the nature of individual development in society, and the demand for instinctual renunciation common to the two processes. Let us review these chapters.

Prolegomenon to *Civilization and Its Discontents*

After a digressive opening chapter, a set of reflections about the "oceanic feeling" as a source of religious feeling, Freud turns in chapter 2 to the book's nominal subject, civilized man's dissatisfaction. He first (76) poses the "less ambitious question of what men themselves show by their behavior to be the purpose and intention of their lives. What do they demand of life and wish to achieve in it?" His answer: "They strive after happiness; they want to become happy and to remain so. This endeavor has two sides, a positive and a negative aim. It aims, on one hand, at an absence of pain and unpleasure, and, on the other, at the experiencing of strong feelings of pleasure."

I have noted at several earlier points (p. 84, n28; p. 139, n41) that this definition of happiness, the beginning point of all hedonist moral philosophies, is itself dubious. In fact, much of Freud's theoretical difficulties can be understood as a consequence of this weak assumption, which forces him to counter hedonism with anti-hedonism as a way of constructing a moral character. But even within Freud's framework, his answer begs key questions as to the nature of pleasure, pain, unpleasure, and feeling in general. However, he ignores the fact that these questions remain unanswered *even in his own theory,* as manifest in the need to contemplate what lies beyond the pleasure principle—that is, the conditions making the pleasure principle possible. He therefore categorically equates the human striving for happiness with his "pleasure principle," and thus with the satisfaction of instincts. Contrary to his own earlier conclusions (in the first half of *Beyond the Pleasure Principle*), he writes (76–77; my italics): "This principle dominates the operation of the mental apparatus *from the start.*" The question of human happiness being thus reduced to the satisfaction of appetitive instincts, "our possibilities of happiness are already restricted by our constitution." These formulas are, of course, nothing more than a rehash of his now-familiar definitions and assumptions, untroubled by all the exceptions that *Beyond the Pleasure Principle* left unresolved. It remains to be seen whether anything original can come from them.

Freud (86) goes on to enumerate three sources of unhappiness, now equated with things that interfere with the satisfaction of instincts: "the superior power of nature, the feebleness of our own bodies and the inadequacy of the regulations which adjust the mutual relationships of human beings in the family, the state and society." The first two are the least interesting and important for an understanding of human dissatisfaction. Our judgment

> forces us to acknowledge those sources of suffering and to submit to the inevitable. We shall never completely master nature; and our bodily organism, itself a part of that nature, will always remain a transient structure with a limited capacity for adaptation and achievement. This recognition does not have a paralysing effect. On the contrary, it points the direction for our activity. If we cannot remove all suffering, we can remove some, and we can mitigate some: the experience of many thousands of years has convinced us of that.

It is the third source, the social source of suffering, that is the most relevant for modern individuals, who have already developed so many ways to combat the ravages of nature. Freud might have added that this source—the political systems that determine who receives the culture's honors and prestige and its material, technological, and esthetic benefits— is most relevant because it is in principle the most mutable, the most a function of *human values, decisions, and actions.* These social systems are practically significant, immediately affecting us; intellectually interesting, for their rationales are often far from clear; and, in contrast to the ravages of nature or bodily limitations, *potentially changeable through social action.*

Freud expresses surprise at the "different attitude" that prevails toward suffering from social causes, namely the attitude that "the regulations made by ourselves should . . . be a protection and a benefit for every one of us"—that is, be equitably distributed, or at least decided by some democratic process. Stunningly, he equates such expectations with *an attack on civilization itself,* rather than on its inequities: "This contention holds that what we call our civilization is largely responsible for our misery." He can only think that the solution to this "astonishing" attitude must be "that here, too, a piece of unconquerable nature may lie behind—this time a piece of our own psychical constitution." Although Freud has not yet brought in the death instinct, we begin to suspect which way the argument must go.

Having equated dissatisfaction over inequality with an attack against civilization itself, it becomes sensible for Freud to ask: "How has it happened that so many people have come to take up this strange attitude of hostility to civilization?" (87). He believes it must be accounted for by a "deep and long-standing dissatisfaction with the then existing state of civilization, and that on that basis a condemnation of it was built up, occasioned by certain specific historical events." In other words, criticism of *existing* society, especially the expectation of equity and democracy, is astonishing, incomprehensible, and pathological and must have a psychoanalytic explanation—because, presumably, existing society comes so close to perfection. Of the specific historical events that contribute to this dissatisfaction, the most recent, Freud claims, is his own theory, "when people came to know about the mechanism of the neuroses, which threaten to undermine the modicum of happiness enjoyed by civilized men." The penultimate event, in his view, was the discovery of the New World and contact with "primitive peoples and races":[47]

> In consequence of insufficient observation and a mistaken view of their manners and customs, they appeared to Europeans to be leading a simple, happy life with few wants, a life such as was unattainable by their visitors with their superior civilization. . . . In many cases the observers had wrongly attributed to the absence of complicated cultural demands what was in fact due to the bounty of nature and the ease with which the major human needs were satisfied. (87)

This passage, the only one to my knowledge in Freud's writings to refer directly to the conquest of the New World, is truly astonishing, making one wonder whether it is made out of simple ignorance or willful distortion. Freud (1887-1904, 398) famously professed an identification with the conquistadors, and it would be amazing if he had no familiarity with their detailed firsthand accounts and those of their chroniclers, or the work of later historians like Prescott, all of which had long been available in popular German translations and which attested to the high cultural level and technological sophistication of the New World peoples ultimately slaughtered.

To take but one of many examples, the accounts of Cortés and of his companion and chronicler Díaz del Castillo left no doubt that, in encountering the great cultures of Mexico, the conquistadors were discovering peoples who had solved many of the social and technological problems that made the medieval cities of Europe primitive by comparison. Here, for example, is Díaz's (1632, 271) account of the approach by causeway to Tenochtitlán, a city that had in 1500, by conservative estimates, five times the population of either London or Seville (Stannard, 1992, 4):

[47] Freud confesses ignorance about the exact chain of events, but speculates that "a factor of this kind hostile to civilization must already have been at work in the victory of Christendom over the Luthern religions." His approach here is in keeping with his penchant for historical speculation and for thinking of cultural history in terms of "disillusionment," as in his reaction to the First World War. The fact that he leaps from the development of psychoanalysis to the conquest of the New World, leaving out the Industrial Revolution, the rise of free-market nation-states, colonialism, and so on, is in keeping with his uncritical approval of all those modern developments, as leading unproblematically to a gain in the level of civilization.

> Gazing on such wonderful sights, we did not know what to say, or whether what appeared before us was real, for on one side, on the land, there were great cities, and in the lake ever so many more, and the lake itself was crowded with canoes, and in the Causeway were many bridges at intervals, and in front of us stood the great City of Mexico.

Cortés himself, in his famous "letters" to the Spanish emperor (1522, 101-102), was hard put to describe the splendors he saw:

> Most Powerful Lord, in order to give an account to Your Royal Excellency of the magnificence, the strange and marvelous things of this great city of Temixtitan [Tenochtitlán] and of the dominion and wealth of this Mutezuma, its ruler, and of the rites and customs of the people, and of the order there is in the government of the capital as well as in the other cities of Mutezuma's dominions, I would need much time and many expert narrators. I cannot describe one hundredth part of all the things which could be mentioned, but, as best I can I will describe some of those I have seen which, although badly described, will I well know, be so remarkable as not to be believed, for we who saw them with our own eyes could not grasp them with our understanding.

These marvels included things barely conceivable to a medieval European: heavily populated cities beautifully laid out and landscaped, of extraordinary order and cleanliness, with elaborate systems of water supply and road and water transport, abundant and well-regulated public markets, and a large government bureaucracy enforcing civic laws and regulations. Writing of the great public markets in Tenochtitlán, Cortés (103-104) wrote:

> This city has many squares where trading is done and markets are held continuously. There is also one square twice as big as that of Salamanca, with arcades all around, where more than sixty thousand people come each day to buy and sell, and where every kind of merchandise produced in these lands is found; provisions as well as ornaments of gold and silver, lead, brass, copper, tin, stones, shells, bones, and feathers. They also sell lime, hewn and unhewn stone, adobe bricks, tiles, and cut and uncut wood of various kinds. . . . There are many sorts of spun cotton, in hanks of every color, and it seems like the silk market at Granada, except here there is a much greater quantity.

Accounts such as these have led to the conclusion, now a commonplace among historians of the period, that the conquistadors, like most other colonizing conquerors, rather than being deluded in their assessment of the level of culture and happiness of the people they "visited," rather suppressed their knowledge and their judgment in the service of demonizing the people they were committed to destroying. There is now a large scholarly literature in this area, with abundant bibliographies; the interested reader might consult the works of Coe (1984), Galeano (1982), Stannard (1992), and Todorov (1984).

To return to *Civilization and Its Discontents:* convinced, for no discernible reason, that the European chroniclers of discovery and conquest were under the same wishful delusion as the social malcontents he perceives all around him, Freud forges on. He dismisses as unanswerable the question "whether and in what degree men of an earlier age felt happier and what part their cultural conditions played in the matter" (89). Thereby eliminating any useful perspective that might derive from a comparative study of the non-Western world, Freud feels justified restricting his view to what is around him, "to turn our attention [back] to the nature of this civilization on whose value as a means to happiness doubts have been thrown."

Not wanting to jump to conclusions until he has "learned something by examining" his own civilization, Freud starts (89) by enumerating its leading characteristics. He uses the theoretical formula he proposed in *The Future of an Illusion:* "the word 'civilization' describes the whole sum of the achievements and the regulations which distinguish our lives from those of our animal ancestors and which serve two purposes—namely to protect men against nature and to adjust their mutual relations." The "first stage" of this enumeration "is easy" (90) because it corresponds to the external sources of suffering: science and technology deployed in the service of controlling the ravages of nature and providing for material well-being—agriculture, mining, manufacture, communications. Second, and somewhat paradoxically, civilized human beings value things that seem to have no direct utility value but appeal to esthetic sensibilities—art, architecture, fine craftsmanship, landscaping, and beauty in general. Next, we value cleanliness and order to a high degree: "Beauty, cleanliness and order obviously occupy a special position among the requirements of civilization" (93). But "no feature . . . seems better to characterize civilization than its esteem and encouragement of man's higher mental activities—his intellectual, scientific and artistic achievements—and the leading role that it assigns to *ideas* in human life" (94, my italics). The reader might raise eyebrows a little at this priority Freud accords ideas as the crowning glory of civilized existence, given his rejection of ideas as a basis either of cognition or morality, in favor of *received, conventional associations,* at every point in his theorizing. Undaunted, he specifies religion, speculative philosophy, and human ideals, adding a revealing proviso, however:

> Nor must we allow ourselves to be misled by *judgements of value* concerning any particular religion, or philosophic system, or ideal. Whether we think to find in them the highest achievements of the human spirit, or whether we deplore them as aberrations, we cannot but recognize

> that where they are present, and, in especial, where they are dominant, a high level of civilization is implied. (my italics)

A further raising of eyebrows might be in order here, given the enormous value Freud places on *particular* cultural traditions over others. After all, Freud consistently sides with Hegel and Spencer in regarding the elites of the world-dominating white nations to be entitled by their supposed superiority and "world-wide interests" to enslave and exterminate "inferior" peoples, whatever their level of civilization, in pursuit of economic aims. Typically, these contradictions do not deter him.

Freud comes finally (95) to the function that is hardest to assess, corresponding to the social sources of dissatisfaction he discussed earlier:

> the manner in which the relationships of men to one another, their social relationships, are regulated—relationships which affect a person as a neighbour, as a source of help, as another person's sexual object, as a member of a family and of a State. Here it is especially difficult to keep clear of particular ideal demands and to see what is civilized in general.

It is worth paying close attention to the reasoning here, for Freud's manner of describing this function sets the stage for the whole subsequent argument.

His thinking is remarkable for the degree to which, building on his earlier rhetoric, it cancels out any role whatsoever for ethical judgment. In this chapter it becomes clearest how thoroughly the death instinct in Freud's hands has undermined even the limited rationality and utilitarian morality accorded human beings in the classical liberal tradition, by shifting the emphasis from self-interest as both instinctive and social regulator of behavior to pure coercion. A corresponding irony, little appreciated by critics, is that Freud the reductive materialist is in process of abandoning his faith in materialism by shifting "the emphasis . . . from the material to the mental" (1927, 7)—which means, given his assumptions, coercion pure and simple. That is, coercion now is unhinged from its earlier justification of material domination, and is to be employed in the service of compelling instinctual renunciation for its own sake, an ideal so nebulous that, as we have seen, it can be used to justify any outcome.

Freud now refashions his state-of-nature theory of civilization to keep with his new appreciation of the sole importance of coercion. He (1930, 95) takes the position that the "general" feature of civilization is an artifice by which a group is formed capable of suppressing the wills of individuals:

> [T]he element of civilization enters on the scene with the first attempt to regulate . . . social relationships. If the attempt were not made, the relationships would be subject to the arbitrary will of the individual: that

is to say, the physically stronger man would decide them in the sense of his own interests and instinctual impulses.... Human life in common is only made possible when a majority comes together which is stronger than any separate individual and which remains united against all separate individuals. The power of this community is then set up as "right" in opposition to the power of the individual, which is condemned as "brute force." This replacement of the power of the individual by the power of a community constitutes the decisive step of civilization.

In other words, the concept of "right" is purely a matter of historical accident and power.

The crucial thing to notice about this argument is that, although Freud will shortly define the power of the group over the individual will as "justice," he has deprived the word of any significance derivable from a standard other than the group's power itself; it is now a purely self-referential concept: "The first requisite of civilization, therefore, is that of justice—that is, the assurance that a law once made will not be broken in favour of an individual. *This implies nothing as to the ethical value of such a law*" (95, my italics).

Justice, in particular, has nothing to do with morality, but is simply the rule of the collective, enforced against the individual, who is assumed to be innately antisocial and immoral, and therefore to require such discipline. But before the collective, there is brute force: "The further course of cultural development seems to tend towards making the law no longer an expression of the will of a small community ... which ... behaves like a violent individual towards other, and perhaps more numerous, collections of people," but rather the consensus of the majority. Human beings, innately asocial and violent, are civilized by having violence perpetrated against them, which then takes on the status of moral law and justice when it comes to be widely tolerated. This is a political philosophy of terror and coercion.

This conception of morality and justice leads to predictable confusion. No sooner does Freud define things in this way than the natural moralist in him rises up in protest, siding with the individual who rebels: "It does not seem as though any influence could induce man to change his nature into a termite's. No doubt he will always defend his claim to individual liberty against the will of the group" (96). But, committed to the idea that justice is merely obedience to a collective will, and ultimately to coercion, all ethical claims are without intellectual or moral force.

What makes itself felt in a human community as a desire for freedom *may be* their revolt against some existing injustice, and so *may* prove favourable to a further development of civilization; it *may* remain compatible with civilization. But it may also spring from the remains of their original personality, which is still untamed by civilization and *may* thus become the basis in them of hostility to civilization. (96, my italics)

The conditional verbs are the crucial terms in this statement, emphasizing Freud's confusion. Under what conditions ought "may" to become "does"? That is, on what basis is it possible to decide whether resistance to a dominant cultural form or institution is a valid response to actual error or injustice, and therefore capable, if successful, of advancing civilization, or an expression of pathology, the "remains of their original personality" yet untamed by civilization? The very notion that such a distinction is possible implies a moral standard apart from social consensus or convention.

This is, of course, one of the most ancient problems in moral and political philosophy. But in Freud's system, the problem, while it arises naturally in his mind, cannot be coherently formulated. His logic dictates that "may" will and ought to become "does" only if a given claim prevails by force, establishing itself thereby as a new power to be reckoned with.[48] Claims for social and economic justice, and in fact all political claims based on moral considerations, remain wayward ideas without substance, because no independent way of judging their merit—even, now, recourse to the liberal creed of enlightened self-interest—is available. Freud's failure to grasp the nature of the distinction that he is alluding to with his repeated "mays" leads him back to his earlier, fanciful, assertion that there are large numbers of people interested in doing away with civilization altogether. From this premise, he comes to the conclusion that "the urge for freedom . . . is directed against particular forms and demands of civilization *or* against civilization altogether" (my italics). This idea is at best irrelevant, even allowing some truth to it. For whether political and cultural criticism is narrow or broad, the key question is always its *rightness*. For that question to be meaningful, a standard apart from the conventions being challenged must exist—and the possibility of such a standard is precisely what Freud has finally done away with.

In the remainder of chapter 3 Freud, believing that he has "obtained a clear impression of the general picture of civilization" while claiming that there is nothing in this picture "that is not universally known," proceeds to develop a point of view "which may lead in a different direction." This direction is, of course, the point of view that is by now very familiar, according to which individual and cultural development are two sides of the same coin, rationalized by instinctual renunciation: Individual development is socialization, and socialization is the aggregate of individual development.

[48] The reader may recall at this point Russell's similar comment (see n. 35, p. 115) on Hume's destructive effect on judgment and reason, making the intellectual difference between sanity and insanity strictly a matter of public opinion.

In chapter 4 Freud seeks to enhance this familiar argument with a new explanation of patriarchy as arising simultaneously with the earliest human group-formations. He had earlier asserted that civilization begins with the first artifice by which protohumans, for the sake of being able to live and work in groups, attempted to regulate their social relationships so as to protect themselves against "the arbitrary will of the individual" (95). He now extends this notion to the creation of families:

> After primal man had discovered that it lay in his own hands, literally, to improve his lot on earth by working, it cannot have been a matter of indifference to him whether another man worked with him or against him. The other man acquired the value for him of a fellow-worker. Even earlier, in his ape-like prehistory, man had *adopted the habit of forming families,* and the members of his family were probably his first helpers. (99, my italics)

In other words, the invention of families is added to coercive group-formation as a key "artifice" of civilization. To this supposed invention Freud attributes the relative permanence of human sexual attachments, the loss of sexual periodicity, and most importantly the peculiar significance of *sexual possession* in patriarchal culture:

> One may suppose that the founding of families was connected with the fact that a moment came when the need for genital satisfaction no longer made its appearance like a guest who drops in suddenly, and, after his departure, is heard of no more for a long time, but instead took up its quarters as a permanent lodger. (99; see also n1, 99-100)

The male therefore has reason, by virtue of the continuous proximity of and sexual attraction to the female, to assert a permanent claim on her. The artifice of private possession of *property,* central to Hume's theory, is here transformed into *sexual possession of and dominance over the woman,* in a striking justification of patriarchy. In this construction of the primal family, the "unrestricted" and "arbitrary will of its head, the father" (100) sets the stage for the rebellion of the sons, leaving a permanent residue of conflict and guilt, which, however, binds the children together.

In this final argument of the prolegomenon, Freud is seeking to strengthen his view that the nuclear, patriarchal family is of ancient provenance and simultaneously biologically ordained and an artifice, much as Hume did with respect to attitudes toward property. The weakness of the argument lies in the fact that the aspects of social life that Freud cites to explain patriarchy and the ownership of women—nuclear families, stable and long-lasting male-female relationships, and individual and cooperative work—are not peculiarly human, so human invention cannot account for them. What are peculiarly human are the ratiocinative myths and theories to explain these cultural forms.

Nuclear families and stable male-female relationships, but not, of course, the explicit explanations, are found among animals who possess (as Bischof [1975, 42] said in connection with incest) "the ability to recognize each other *individually,* and the *inclination to affiliate with acquainted conspecifics,*" from insects to primates. And the most rigorous historical account of patriarchy, by Lerner (1986), suggests that stable nuclear families existed for eons before its advent in fourth-millennium B.C. Mesopotamia, making patriarchy a relatively recent development.

So Freud's notion that primal humans "adopted [in the sense of invented] the habit of forming families" is most certainly incorrect. Clearly, humans invented neither family life nor enduring male-female relationships, any more than they invented incest aversion. It would be more correct to say that in the course of evolution these features of social, family, and sexual life "adopted" human beings, which they, by virtue of their expanding capacity to speak, think, and reflect, sought to understand and in many instances modify. The argument for primal patriarchy fails for much the same reasons as Freud's argument for primal incestuousness.

Oblivious to its fatal weaknesses, this argument nonetheless serves Freud as an additional motive for the child's (in this phylogenetic reconstruction) inhibition of instincts, through repression, sublimation, or other mechanisms, which together with guilt serves as a kind of social glue "binding together considerable numbers of people" (102). It also provides a strengthened rationale for the ontogenetic suppression of childhood sexuality. For in light of his new insights into the importance of coercion, "a cultural community is perfectly justified, psychologically, in starting by proscribing manifestations of the sexual life of children, for there would be no prospect of curbing the sexual lusts of adults if the ground had not been prepared for it in childhood" (104). This statement shows how far in a reactionary direction Freud had retreated from the protester against hypocritical sex-moralism of 1908.

With this augmented Oedipal theory, the prolegomenon comes to an end and the stage is set for tackling, in chapter 5, what Freud takes to be the real problem of civilization.

The Insatiability of Society

The real problem of civilization, for Freud, is stated on the first page of chapter 5 (108-109, my italics):

> So far, we can quite well imagine a cultural community consisting of double individuals [i.e., loving couples] like this, who, libidinally satisfied

> in themselves, are connected with one another through the bonds of common work and common interests. If this were so, civilization would not have to withdraw any energy from sexuality. But this desirable state of things does not, and never did, exist. Reality shows us that *civilization is not content with the ties we have so far allowed it.* It aims at binding the members of the community together in a libidinal way as well and employs every means to that end. It favours every path by which strong identifications can be established between the members of the community, and it summons up aim-inhibited libido on the largest scale so as to strengthen the communal bond by relationships of friendship. In order for these aims to be fulfilled, a restriction upon sexual life is unavoidable. But we are *unable to understand what the necessity is which forces civilization along this path and which causes its antagonism to sexuality. There must be some disturbing factor which we have not yet discovered.*

Knowing Freud's intellectual development and rhetorical style as we now do, it takes little imagination to realize that this is another preparation for the death instinct to enter on the scene like a deus ex machina, which happens in due course. But let us first examine the supposed problem and the observations on which it is based.

Freud claims that "civilization" is insatiable. Like a demonic machine, it demands inexorably more instinctual renunciation from individuals in order to supply ever more of the neutralized energy and group identification that holds society together. Is this a valid observation?

Certainly societies, when they function well, create demands and provide opportunities for cooperative experience and action, and those demands and opportunities will change over time, sometimes expanding, sometimes contracting. A nation under threat of war, for example, will have need for ready mobilization of a prepared citizenry to defend its homeland, a need that diminishes in times of stable peace. But it is also true that well-functioning societies, at least democratic societies, will safeguard the rights of individuals to think, express themselves, and act in ways apart from and at odds with dominant social ideologies and trends, including the right to contest what represents a threat to the homeland, or a justifiable war, or the proper conduct of a war. The phenomenon Freud describes as normative—the rigidification of society, the suppression of dissent, in fact any number of outcomes that make social and political life hostile to rather than supportive of individuals— is in reality a risk, not an inevitability, of social life. The supposed phenomenon that Freud perceives to be inherent in "civilization" is a fortunately not inevitable liability of society, from which enlightened cultures strive to free themselves. This is the universal problem bypassed by Freud in allying himself with the heinous tradition that glorifies authority and denies any rational standard of moral judging.

Yet Freud remains oblivious to the possibility that it is his own increasingly dogmatic instinctivist constructions—primal patriarchy on top of primal incestuousness, all underpinned by primal aggression—that are giving rise to the sense of insatiable demand to renounce instinct, in a way that increasingly resembles the neurotic mentality itself.

Freud's reasoning in the balance of this chapter shows how far he has traveled in the direction of absolute conviction about the death instinct and the need for authority, of contempt for democracy, and of disdain for anything approximating natural moral knowledge that might be realized in social arrangements and institutions. He does not introduce the death instinct directly, but after a short attack (109-110) on "one of the ideal demands, as we have called them, of civilized society"—namely, the moral idea of loving one's fellow beings. This idea, embodied both in the classical virtues of friendship and magnanimity and in the religious virtues of faith, hope, and charity (but which Freud identifies exclusively with the Christian tradition) is, according to Freud, irrational, unpsychological, even absurd: "What is the point of a precept enunciated with so much solemnity if its fulfilment cannot be recommended as reasonable?" (110). Now (111) he comes to the "element of truth" behind this absurd and misguided moral idea—which is, as we might expect, the death instinct:

> Men are not gentle creatures who want to be loved, and who at the most can defend themselves if they are attacked; they are, on the contrary, creatures among whose instinctual endowments is to be reckoned a powerful share of aggressiveness. As a result, their neighbour is for them not only a potential helper or sexual object, but also someone who tempts them to satisfy their aggressiveness on him, to exploit his capacity for work without compensation, to use him sexually without his consent, to seize his possessions, to humiliate him, to cause him pain, to torture and kill him.

A person is in fact "a savage beast to whom consideration towards his own kind is something alien" (112).

How does this pertain to the problem of insatiability? It is precisely this factor of "primary mutual hostility" that causes "civilized society [to be] perpetually threatened with disintegration." Therefore "civilization has to use its utmost efforts in order to set limits to man's aggressive instincts and to hold the manifestations of them in check by psychical reaction-formations."

But this solution does not quite satisfy either. For "in spite of every effort, these endeavors in civilization have not so far achieved very much." Here (112-113) Freud makes an aside about socialism and communism, harshly criticizing their attempts to improve human well-being by changing relations to property, and culminating in the aphorism, "Aggressiveness was not created by property." But, as we have seen at numerous points in this analysis, it is really liberalism that he is lamenting, not communism. Earlier, he had placed great stock in the liberal view that it is precisely the balancing of material interests that would guarantee a high level of civilization, but had been badly disappointed. Now, society's severe problems indicate to him that people were rotten all along, and he was a fool to believe otherwise. He embraces the Fall, Freudian style. Now only coercion will do.

But this leaves Freud in an intellectual and moral-philosophical limbo. Having ruled out comparative study of traditional cultures, we cannot learn anything from them. Having excluded as irrelevant the study of how modern economies actually work, we cannot learn anything from that realm. And having decided that moral values are merely conventions that rationalize the successful use of power and propaganda, we cannot consult any moral tradition or standard outside our own social conventions to help us decide what in society is good or bad, what deserves our allegiance and what our opposition. Human beings in this scheme are radically alienated from each other, from traditions, and from their own moral inclinations.

Interestingly, in the midst of this deepening cynicism, Freud repeatedly resorts to his own moral inclinations as a basis of criticism: "When we justly find fault with the present state of our civilization . . . when, with unsparing criticism, we try to uncover the roots of its imperfection, we are undoubtedly exercising a proper right and are not showing ourselves enemies of civilization" (115). But there is no support anywhere in his theory, as it has come to be, for such a right, and no source except power to inform or guide us as to what is unjust or imperfect. Thus, Freud concludes that we should "perhaps . . . familiarize ourselves with the idea that there are difficulties attaching to the nature of civilization which will not yield to any attempt at reform" (115).

Chapter 6 is a reprise of his theories by way of justifying the death instinct in this new context. It contains no new ideas; but in terms of philosophical sources, Freud ends this chapter with a paraphrase of Hobbes, who has now, in light of the death instinct and the notion of "primary mutual hostility," replaced Hume as his intellectual standard: "Man's natural aggressive instinct, the hostility of each against all and of all against each, opposes this programme of civilization" (122). As we have come to expect, Freud neither acknowledges his new affiliation with Hobbes nor refers to the then-current debates over latter-day "scientific" Hobbesianism, such as the arguments that swirled around Spencer and the social Darwinists.

Chapter 7 takes the argument one step further in an admiring reference to colony-forming insects:

> Why do our relatives, the animals, not exhibit any such cultural struggle? We do not know. Very probably some of them—the bees, the ants,

> the termites—strove for thousands of years before they arrived at the State institutions, the distribution of functions and the restrictions on the individual, for which we admire them today. (123)

He decides that after long evolution these societies have reached an equilibrium "between the influences of their environment and the mutually contending instincts within them, and thus a cessation of development has come about." In other words, it is only modern human society ("civilization") that is restlessly continuing to develop—a very unbiological point of view, but one in keeping with his historicist mistrust of change. To address this problem of cultural disequilibrium, that is, to provide a supplementary answer to the problem of society's out-of-control quality, Freud takes up the question of guilt, which he will update in light of the death instinct theory and then portray as the driving force behind this phenomenon.

He reviews his understanding of conscience and superego, as representing an internalization of social anxiety, based, in normal development, on the infant's fear of losing the love and protection of his caretakers. He stresses again his rejection of the idea of any natural morality: "We may reject the existence of an original, as it were natural, capacity to distinguish good from bad" (124). Absent natural moral inclinations and given the bestial nature of human beings, disciplining the mind must be purely a matter of socialization through coercion. But why does the individual superego operate in the same *out-of-control* way that Freud perceives in society; that is, why can neurotic guilt never be satisfied? His Hobbesian answer is that guilt needs to operate like a perpetual-motion machine: "Instinctual renunciation (imposed on us from without) creates conscience, which then demands further instinctual renunciation" (129).

Here the death instinct enters the argument in a way that "rounds off the theory . . . in a welcome fashion" (130). For, assuming that "the renunciation in question is always a renunciation of aggression" (129), *there is an endless supply of it*. The child being endowed with enormous innate aggression but no innate judgment, every imposed demand generates more aggression, which evokes more demands from the environment, thus more aggression, ad infinitum. The vicious cycle can only be broken by internalizing the environment's demands, in the form of a continually tormenting superego. "Every renunciation of instinct now becomes a dynamic source of conscience and every fresh renunciation increases the latter's severity and intolerance" (128). Freud's instinctual theory has now reached a point of perfection and symmetry with his machine-like neurological theory, which, as we saw in chapter 5 (pp. 122–123) involves endless arousal through a positive feedback cycle.

In chapter 8 Freud takes further his idea that the aggressive instinct is the predominant source of guilt by proposing that it is *uniquely* the source of guilt:

"I am convinced that many processes will admit of a simpler and clearer exposition if the findings of psycho-analysis with regard to the derivation of the sense of guilt are restricted to the aggressive instincts" (138). And he modifies his view of repression accordingly: "When an instinctual trend undergoes repression, its libidinal elements are turned into symptoms, and its aggressive component into a sense of guilt" (139). For explaining the supposed infinite magnitude of repression and civilized misery, innate aggression, deprived of reason, and guilt, equally deprived, have supplanted libido and anxiety, which proved unequal to the task.

The Death Instinct and the Demonic Machine

As we have seen in previous chapters, the "rounding off" of Freudian theory was achieved in the decade prior to 1930, through the logical perfection of the unified instinct concept. *Civilization and Its Discontents* is the *application* of this perfected theory to Freud's social philosophy.

The perfected Freudian theory leads Freud in a predictable direction. He perceives a generalized dissatisfaction with, if not urge to destroy, society, and from that concludes that society seeks, and needs, insatiably to suppress the individual. From the well-running machine model of the *Project* ("Everything fell into place, the cogs meshed, the thing really seemed to be a machine which in a moment would run of itself" [1895a, 129]). Freud's theory of mind has evolved into a demonic machine of self-torment, driven by an idea (the death instinct) that is endless and without exception—and that, therefore, no longer functions as an idea at all, but rather as an article of absolute faith: a conviction of the inherent and endless defectiveness of individual human beings, who must therefore be endlessly coerced by authority into some semblance of civilized existence.

Where have we encountered this psychology before? It is, in fact, the mental state of the neurotic! With his now-absolute instinctivism, represented by the death instinct, Freud has fashioned a demonic *intellectual* machine (quite like the trash compactor of my engineer patient), one that will predictably reduce every social problem to an instinctual one, thereby cutting away the basis for all critical social judgment. The ideal form of society is, in this view, a society of termites, in which each member knows its place and the places are unchanging. Freud no longer distinguishes, and is perhaps no longer capable of distinguishing, between his own construction and a social reality. He turns our attention from the real to the ideal, from the actual to the utopian;[49]

[49] I use this term not in the sense of Thomas More, to connote places "enjoying a perfect social, legal, and political system" (*Oxford English Dictionary*, def. 1), but in the sense of "impossibly ideal schemes, especially for social improvement" (def. 2b).

that is, from the demands and problems of life in modern society, with the expectation of discovering to what extent they are understandable and correctable, to a monstrous solution that undermines will and reason: human beings are innately bestial and evil, they require violent suppression in order to be "civilized," and they have no recourse to ethical judgment outside the social conventions into which they are socialized. It is a solution of the type Steiner (1971, 79-80) described aptly as one "whose logic derives from a postulate of original sin." The difference is that Steiner recognized that this type of solution is profoundly magical and dangerous. Freud did not.[50]

And so Freud, the antireligious and materialist rationalist, has come in the end to advocate a magically religious, mentalist, and authoritarian solution to the problems of life in modern society.

[50] This development of Freudianism is quite comparable to the one noted by Galbraith with respect to economics. He (1958, chapter 10) points out that a cardinal principle of economics, the supply-demand or marginal utility theory of prices, which depends on *judgments* by consumers of the utility and value of acquired goods, leads to the reasonable conclusion that with increasing affluence and acquisition the intrinsic value of production diminishes. Food and shelter are intrinsically more important and valuable than one's twentieth pair of luxury shoes or an upgraded home entertainment center. The "economic problem" of providing for the basic needs and wants of all human beings, achieving a certain level of affluence, and turning attention to important nonmaterial needs, is in principle solvable. But conventional wisdom in economics, by eliminating as "unscientific" such evaluative judgments and discounting as irrelevant social and intellectual goods that cannot be commodified, promotes the doctrine that unlimited production is a good, apart from any individual or social benefit. And this wisdom is supported by, and supports, a massive advertising machine that successfully engineers "need" for unnecessary goods. In this way does a potentially rational social enterprise transform itself into an ideology in the service of maintaining and exploiting the cultural status quo, a problem for all the social sciences.

10

A THINKING CURE

> [T]he causation of human affairs is too deeply tangled to be wholly unraveled by the wisest minds. There is always a point where we must trust our values in action, so that the urgent forces of the present world may release themselves in new directions towards new goals.
>
> —R. MacIver, Foreword to *The Great Transformation,* by K. Polanyi (1944)

> I am inclined to suggest that most neuroses may be due to a partially arrested development of the critical attitude.
>
> —K. Popper, *Conjectures and Refutations* (1962)

> There could be no fairer destiny for any . . . theory than that it should point the way to a more comprehensive theory in which it lives on, as a limiting case.
>
> —Albert Einstein, *Relativity: The Special and the General Theory, a Popular Exposition* (1920)

Is Freudianism Correctable?

The obvious, and ironic, point that sums up many of the arguments of this book is that the Freudian version of psychoanalysis, supposedly rooted in biology, actually has no rational biological underpinning and, in particular, no meaningful theory of instinct. It relies instead on an indefensible pure-socialization view of morality and personality. The ideas that comprise this view are Freud's "special" theories, as opposed to the general theories of psychoanalysis, which speak to the importance of early experience and the unconscious in mental life.

Contemporary psychoanalysts commonly think that Freud erred in taking an extremely narrow view of instinct. Less commonly is he faulted for holding an uncritical view of our modes of socialization and for being a reactionary social and moral thinker. And even less is it recognized that in his psychoanalysis the two positions are intimately intertwined, one implying the other. The more he depends on instinct, the more uncritical is his attitude toward social and moral life in general.[51] Conversely, the more reactionary the social and moral philosophy, the more instinctivist the psychoanalysis. But it is precisely this intertwining that creates the greatest possible doubt as to the existence of the supposed instinctual entities upon which Freudianism is based.

Perhaps psychoanalysts, recognizing that the whole structure of Freudianism is vulnerable, fear that a cherished body of thought upon which their profession seems to depend would go down the drain. But the end of Freudianism need not imply the death of psychoanalysis. Psychoanalysis refers to a psychology of the unconscious. If the unconscious is real, a psychoanalysis will be needed to understand it.

My conclusion can be simply stated: it is highly improbable that the supposed instinctual entities (e.g., incestuous sexual desire and innate self-destruction) upon which Freud placed so much emphasis are any more intrinsic to people than the desires for more and more possessions, justifying greater and greater production, that are presumed by classical economists. Just as advertising and other means of creating want are embarrassments for such economists, so is socialization for Freudians, and for similar reasons: Most of the phenomena of neurosis can be explained by socialization, not instinct, just as most of the phenomena of consumer demand for specialized and luxury products can be explained by advertising and emulation, not natural wants.[52] And what is not explained by socialization requires a radically different theory of instinct than Freud's.

For if the prospect of unbridled appetitive instincts were indeed such an obvious and powerful source of anxiety, what need would Freud have had to go to such extreme lengths, culminating in the bizarre death instinct, to convince himself, his followers, and his patients that instincts really are demonic and that heroic efforts must be expended, through renunciation, to contain them?

---

[51] I use the term socialization in a broad sense, to refer to aspects of child rearing, education, and information that have as their aim not the development of an ability to think critically but of acceptance of the ideas of others on the basis of authority—in other words, the use of intellect for persuasion rather than critical thought. This distinction used to be described in terms of a tension between rhetoric and philosophy.

[52] Sometimes the two forms of induced want coincide. A good example of phenomena at the intersection of economic want creation and propagandistic socialization are some recent fashions in psychiatric diagnosis and treatment. The most notable example is the supposed astronomic rise in the past two decades of the incidence of so-called bipolar disorder—the old manic-depressive psychosis, toned down. It requires a remarkable innocence of mind (to which the psychiatric profession is far from immune) to overlook the striking correlation between the availability and saturation marketing of "antimanic" and "mood-stabilizing" drugs and the sudden dramatic increase in the incidence of a condition that historically was a rarity—mediated by the wondrous elasticity of psychiatric diagnosis. An unbiased anthropologist would at least seriously entertain as a leading hypothesis that the demand, from doctors and patients alike, for this diagnosis and the drug treatment that accompanies it, is fundamentally no different than the demand for late-model cars or Nike shoes. What is truly remarkable is the virtual absence of skeptical inquiry within the profession.

The argument is also often heard in psychoanalysis that these criticisms have long since been taken into account in correcting Freud in the new and more sophisticated post-Freudian versions of psychoanalysis. Indeed, it is true that some post-Freudian psychoanalysis reflects (but usually ambivalently) disaffection with Freud's instinct theories, often described as "orthodox" or "classical" or something worse. A common strategy among progressive post-Freudian analysts is to regard the orthodox instinct theory as dated but still having a place in a pluralistic set of theories and approaches. I believe, however, that most such efforts to transform psychoanalysis fall far short of what is needed. I also believe that we can surmise what a rational non-Freudian psychoanalysis might look like. That is the purpose of this chapter.

It will undoubtedly be argued, by friends and foes of psychoanalysis alike, that a psychoanalysis without Freud is not psychoanalysis at all but an altogether different approach to depth psychology. I believe this represents a serious misunderstanding of the issues, and is merely a terminological question without substance. I prefer to retain the term psychoanalysis because it is widely equated in people's minds with a depth psychology of the unconscious. Despite the trend, started by Jung and Adler, to label their separate domains with different terms (analytic psychology and individual psychology, respectively), the popular mind considers all such efforts psychoanalysis—and for good reason, having more to do with Freud's inspiration than his theories. Here Freud has made a lasting impression on the modern psyche, one that I wish to acknowledge, rather than litter the intellectual landscape with more confusing new terms. There are too many already.

There is no reason in principle why an alternate non-Freudian psychoanalysis cannot be built up out of a reasonable sociobiology, linguistics, and social analysis. It will require, however, shedding much of the overgrown superstructure that has developed around Freudianism and its heirs, and a return to some such sensible formulations as the ones I have alluded to throughout this book: that selves are theories and that the personal rigidity of neurosis, as Popper suggests (see the epigraph to this chapter) represents an arrest of the critical function, such that what are in fact theories are subjectively experienced, unconsciously and powerfully, as unchangeable facts, rigid rules of identity and existence.

The task of rectifying psychoanalysis is lent urgency by the fact that, in the current psychiatric climate, Freudianism is not only wrong, but dangerously wrong. By endorsing repressive socialization, it promotes blind conformity to authority and undermines the individual's critical and creative efforts to understand his or her self and the world. Its almost exclusive focus on the emotional aspects of early family life as replicated in the treatment relationship, lacking the leaven of intelligent reflection, promotes solipsistic introspection and unreal clinical interactions. Freudianism also provides a rationale for some of the worst aspects of present-day psychiatric thinking—its superficial diagnostic categorizing, its conformist behaviorism, and its pseudobiological treatment strategies based on the pharmacological alteration of symptoms, justified by a crudely reductionist theory.

If my assessment of Freudianism is right—that its artificial perspectives subvert the general intuitions that underlie psychoanalysis and result in a dogmatic theory that gifted practitioners have to fight to overcome—it stands to reason that it is correctable by ridding its theory of those perspectives and rebuilding it in a rigorous fashion. In other words, the fact that Freudianism fails in the *particular* ways that it does—that is, through its dubious biological, linguistic, and moral- and social-philosophical assumptions—points the directions in which such a rebuilding needs to take place. For these ruinous assumptions are, after all, simply theories unrecognized as such or considered irrefutable, and thus operating as more-or-less unconscious habits of mind.

This severe but guardedly optimistic assessment is shared by a number of well-informed critics of psychoanalysis, some of whom I have quoted in this book. Gellner (1985, 210), for example, writes: "Within psychoanalysis there is a tradition of low philosophical sophistication: hence one must bring out and make explicit the ideas which are pervasive implied [*sic*] in psychoanalysis, but remain in a kind of logical unconscious, and which most analysts would not be capable of formulating themselves." Gellner points to the work of rendering ideas conscious and explicit, of rethinking and testing, that must be undertaken in order to rectify psychoanalysis. Unfortunately, Freudians have seriously erred in not taking these critiques to heart, in becoming more inbred, and thus in failing to equip themselves to correct the problems of their field.

Once implicit assumptions are recognized as theories they can be transformed into explicit propositions, debated, and tested against experience. Contrary to a shibboleth of psychoanalysis, since many of these assumptions apply to everyday human experience, their debate and testing can often be carried out through ordinary observation and discourse, requiring neither the special circumstances of clinical analysis nor its particular language. Psychoanalysis need not be the arcane discipline, accessible only to the initiated, that it has sought to make itself.

In this book I have translated the assumptions of Freudianism into such explicit form, in which they appear much more ordinary than at first glance. And it is largely by virtue of being able to do this that I characterize Freudianism as, rather than completely false, an artificially boundaried form of inquiry, or a special-case theory. Its boundaries were created by Freud to leave out of consideration that which he could not see or comprehend. What lies within the circumscribed domain of Freudian analysis is logical enough, given its assumptions. Its fault lies in not recognizing the strangeness of its assumptions, and therefore in equating its highly boundaried "special-case" domain with the full range of human experience. As we have seen, the strange assumptions underlying the theories of Freudianism are political and philosophical.

When a society has attained a level of philosophical sophistication and openness, cultural change evokes debate about its assumptions. In the twentieth century much of this debate has focused on economic and social theories and the institutions and policies they generate, in response to experiences of economic collapse, of war, of social disintegration, of colonialism and imperialism, of unrestrained capitalism, communism, fascism, and propagandistic manipulation of public opinion in nominally democratic societies. Freud's retreat from these debates leads to a psychoanalysis out of touch with the real world; not a space of refuge and reflection but a defensive insularity. A rational psychoanalysis will, therefore, be obliged to reintroduce the social world into analytic theory and practice as an object of critical reflection, not reverence and obedience. If the two intellectual requirements that I have stressed in this book—social reality and philosophical rigor—can be applied consistently to the general theories of childhood influence and unconscious belief, we will have a groundwork for a rational psychoanalysis.

The clinical approach I follow in pursuit of this goal is not a set technique (I have grave misgivings that psychoanalysis can or ought to be reduced to a technique) but a *strategy* with which to engage patients seeking to understand their unconscious limitations. It proceeds not from an assumption of the evolutionary necessity of the Oedipus complex, but rather from the desire to foster a questioning of blind unconscious belief, as befits a reflecting subject informed by an innate intelligence capable of development. Because it depends to a great extent on critical thinking and on the patient's active engagement as an equal, I call it a "thinking cure"—to differentiate it not from an emotional cure (intense emotional reactions are, generally, very much part of the process) but from Freudianism's "talking cure."

Here are some examples of this approach, which illustrate many of the theoretical issues we have been following.

The Basic Curative Reaction

My approach can best be introduced using a concept complementary to the one I introduced in chapter 1. A "basic curative reaction" takes hold as the neurotic reaction is relinquished. It is the *replacement of a dogmatic by a critical attitude* toward those "personal set patterns" that make a person neurotic, especially convictions of intrinsic defect, and including automatic adherence to puritan morality. Such convictions enter into consciousness and begin to be thought about critically. This breaks the neurotic vicious circle (unconscious ideas generating experiences that prove the ideas, keeping them unconscious) and is the condition for a beneficent circle in which ideas interact with external reality.

A central, but little recognized, feature of cognition in neurosis is that beliefs about the self, typically highly negative, are held *tenaciously, unconsciously, and without exception*—that is, they are considered invariably true. Although in the nature of ideas or theories, they do not function in the mind as ideas but rather as unchangeable (and therefore uninteresting) aspects of the self. Patients typically express this attitude, when questioned, with some such phrase as "that is just who (or how) I am." The psychoanalyst and philosopher Matte Blanco (1975, 1988) represented this property of unconscious and unquestioned belief by the metaphor of mathematical infinity, to signify the neurotic's tendency to endlessly fashion replicas of his or her guiding convictions and thus to interpret the world ad infinitum in light of them. In this metaphor, psychoanalytic change starts with rendering the pathogenic convictions finite, which means bringing them into a form in which they can be closely examined. The need is to, almost literally, "get one's mind around" the operative unconscious convictions. This requires identifying them, usually at first by inference from irrationally repetitive patterns, and promoting an interest in challenging total belief. This crucial step, easy to describe in principle but often difficult to accomplish, begins the process by which the individual disembeds himself or herself from the mass of unquestioned ideas, however acquired, embarking on a path from mythic to reflective thinking. Unsurprisingly—given the fact that in most cases the patient has come to fear unfettered thinking—this can be a long path accompanied by intense intellectual and emotional reservations and struggles. In the process, as Freud discovered, neurotic symptoms change, but not always in a linear way. Starting to get one's mind around what one has always unquestioningly believed may exacerbate anxiety, depression, and regret, but the mind is made tougher and more agile.

In many cases, a curative reaction is spontaneously under way *before* the patient seeks treatment and is, in effect, the reason for seeking treatment. Analysis is sought because the spontaneous process causes or increases anxiety, confusion, dissatisfaction, or depression, as in the following two cases.

Cases 1 and 2: Spontaneous Efforts Leading to Analysis

Because they typically present with symptoms of dysfunction, patients often do not understand that the symptoms often result from their spontaneous efforts at cure. But it is important that analysts do. Such clarifications can often be made early in treatment, without lengthy analysis, and provide a momentum that carries the patient forward.

A divorced ironworker in his early forties came to feel, after the failure of his second marriage, uncertain about his gender. Yielding to a long-standing obscure urge, he began to cross-dress. The small and conservative Western city in which he lived was not the most auspicious place to be parading around in long wig, décolleté dresses, and net stockings, but he pursued his fascination within the limits of safety and discretion and discovered that he felt more like his "true self," more liberated and assertive, than ever in his life. Thus, he began to think of himself living as a woman.

Soon, however, he ran into perplexity. Was he really psychically female, and was that the problem in his life all along? If so, should he pursue hormone treatments and possibly a sex-change operation? Such a course would be riskily permanent. And he was far from sure why he was doing this. He liked women but had never gotten along with them, for reasons he didn't understand. There seemed to be an element of irrational guilt, and a tendency to treat them as demanding authorities who must be placated. Now he was having strong fantasies of sex with men. Altogether, he was very far from understanding what the cross-dressing meant.

In the first session he appeared in his usual workingman's garb; in the second, like a "Colfax Avenue whore." What quickly impressed me was his openness and curiosity, and his ironic and self-deprecating sense of humor. When he got his courage up a bit, he would arrive in an outfit more daring than the last and ask me how he looked, fishing for compliments about his legs. He seemed amused by the fact that his five-o'clock shadow and thick workman's hands gave away the show; he was, he reminded me, new at all this.

Although intelligent and curious, he was perplexed as to what he was doing. All he knew was that cross-dressing was strangely liberating, that it felt right, and that he was determined to pursue it to see where it would lead.

What might be the point and purpose of this extravagant transgression? Freudian thinking would incline an analyst to regard this man's transvestism and associated gender confusion and homosexual fantasies as the *outbreak* of a neurosis or perversion, and to seek to explain it as a failure of repression—that is, as a release into consciousness and action of instinctual impulses that had been safely repressed before. For all the reasons detailed in this book, I consider this an inadequate view. My theoretical skepticism inclined me to respect his intuition that what he was doing was genuinely liberating and positive, although confusing and risky.

Subjective assessments can be and often are unreliable. After all, people may experience a sense of freedom for all the wrong reasons. But, when we started looking at his behavior as a spontaneous effort at liberation, his overall improvement, heightened curiosity, and expanded capacity for thinking encouraged both of us. I was struck by the flexibility of his mind. The concept of neurotic perversion implies great fixity of sexual aim and object. For example, the fetishist must have his special object or have no sexual gratification. By contrast, this man became less fixed in his beliefs and desires the more we talked, developing a healthy "split" in his attitudes. He continued to delight in and be fascinated by his cross-dressing, affirmed in his intuition that there was something important here, while increasingly curious as to what it meant and where it would lead him. The element of drivenness in his behavior reflected an irrepressible revelation, not a narrow compulsion. In fact, the overriding features of his mental state, as I came to know him over the first several months, were expanding curiosity, increasing flexibility of thinking, ability to consider strange possibilities, and openness to unexpected outcomes. Clearly, the more we understood about him, the more transvestism took on symbolic, as opposed to literal, meanings. This was very different, he told me, from his typical dour and rigid personality of recent years. Overall, in other words, his consciousness seemed to be heightened rather than constricted—and my main impression was of a man who was willing to take risks in order to free himself from a neurotically constricted personality.

When we began to explore his sexual interests and fantasies, we discovered that they too were remarkably fluid. For example, in early sessions he was inclined to experience rushes of strong sexual interest in me, as we explored the intense homosexual fantasies that accompanied his transvestism. He imagined seducing or forcing me into making love to him orally or anally and would leave sessions intensely aroused. When he started becoming curious about some of the obvious paradoxes of his sexual situation, this driven intensity diminished. Exploration of these paradoxes made us quickly aware of some of the moral and political dimensions of his transvestism as protest and as theater, and raised interesting questions.

The most compelling paradox was this: It appeared that what attracted him most strongly was the prospect of an intense sexual engagement with a man, leading to a stable, affectionate, and sexual relationship. Thus, his image of happiness was living with a male lover in domestic tranquillity. When he imagined such a future, however, he pictured himself as an ordinary male. This suggested that the transvestism was a means to an end, not an end in itself.

But that immediately raised another question. If what he really sought was a homosexual relationship, why was it necessary to go about it in this way? Realistically, his manner of dress was unlikely to attract the kind of homosexual lover he wanted.

One solution to this paradox lay in the fact that he had been raised to think that homosexuality was a great sin and perversion. Despite his courage in flouting convention he remained, without realizing it, curiously obedient to this dictum, which originated with his parents. Thus, he is playing out a magical and almost humorous double entendre reflecting an unconsciously dual attitude toward parental and social opinion. While outrageously transgressing social expectations, he is slavishly obedient to them, and the contradictory tendencies find expression in his dressing as a woman, while clearly not being one. He is expressing something like the idea, "if I pretend to be female and have sex with men, I will not really be homosexual." When this solution was explained to him, he found it wonderfully funny, while realizing that it reflected tremendous perplexity about sexuality and authority.

This realization led to important work on his lifelong tendency, beginning in childhood, to be unquestioningly obedient to maternal authority. He is the adopted child of a strange couple. The mother is a phobic woman, fervently and hypocritically Christian, who overprotected him and demanded worship of her peculiar ideas, including that she was a femme fatale toward whom men were irresistibly drawn. Her overblown sense of her own attractiveness was used to demean her husband before her family and to maintain an illusion of the grand life to which she was properly entitled. The father is a man of no opinions who let his wife rule. Although recognizing the tremendous inadequacy of his parents, my patient had never been able to distance himself from them psychologically and remained strongly influenced by the mother's attitudes.

Understanding this curious situation, which amounted to having been ruled by a conviction that *he must not think for himself,* helped him begin to rethink what he actually believed and wanted, and to do so more realistically. To explore what life as a transvestite might be like he started attending meetings at a gender identity center, where there were many similar men, whom he found decent people with interesting stories. He realized that if he really wanted to pursue a homosexual relationship, he should probably subdue his extreme way of dressing, which now seemed to be a way of caricaturing and competing with his mother. He also decided to stand up to her directly. At first he felt he needed her to accept him with all his idiosyncrasies, as did his loving nineteen-year-old college student daughter, who affectionately teased him about his need to learn to walk in heels. But, after discussing the problem of his mother for a while, he realized that the work we were doing was actually changing his attitude. He would like her approval, but it mattered less.

In keeping with the fluidity of his state of mind, his ideas and desires kept changing. On a business trip to Miami, where he anticipated indulging his wildest transvestite fantasies, he actually found himself dressing conservatively and being attracted to a pretty and smart young woman at the hotel, with whom he had a good conversation about politics and engineering. This suggested that heterosexual desires—as well as suppressed intellectual interests—were still active, given the proper conditions. In light of this experience, he began to reflect on the extent to which his difficulty with women had reflected a powerfully unconscious tendency to submit and give to them excessively, out of irrational guilt. Typically, in his past life, if he slept with a woman, he would feel obliged to shower her with gifts and have her move in. He had twice in this way married needy women he did not love, much to his regret. Thus, another compelling paradox emerged. He had thought of himself as a "slam-bam-thank-you-ma'am" cowboy. Now he realized he had all along been driven by neurotic guilt, not lust. And although he envisioned his sexual life as a woman as being more affectionate and "giving" than he had been capable of as a man, it was also the case that he was simultaneously exploring the possibility of not having to give away everything to a sexual partner.

In his therapy, the focus shifted increasingly to questions as to why he remained, as an adult, so unsure of his own thinking and reactions. Why had he not gone to college, for example, despite his engineering aptitudes, but settled for a safe job? The more he could reflect, in other words, about the convictions, beliefs, and conflicts that underlay his symptoms, the less compelling they became, the more they became objects of ordinary, interesting thought leading to judgments and decisions.

The more neurotic a person is, the more painful and difficult spontaneous change is likely to be. A great deal of existing psychoanalytic knowledge bears on this point, although it is not usually discussed in those terms. I suggest as a general explanation one that keeps with experience in other fields: It appears to be far more difficult than we have realized to give up anything we think we know for certain, especially when it has been learned under early, adverse circumstances. Such learning involves, presumably, the defeat of natural expectations (e.g., to be helped to develop with a minimum of interference) and becomes the means by which the child survives psychically in a difficult or toxic family environment. Survival knowledge is hard to relinquish. Modification of even the very negative unconscious convictions underlying neurosis is typically fraught with a subjective sense of danger.

Here is another, less flamboyant, case. A man in his late twenties sought help with depression and confusion. A previous psychiatric treatment, with medication, had not been helpful. The conscious focus of his depression was his inability to decide whether to marry or leave his girlfriend of six years, but it was clear that he mistrusted his judgment in this as in many things.

Together since college, he and his girlfriend had been eager for life, art, thinking, and adventure. But both proved to be very inhibited in their ambitions. As their life together settled into humdrum routine and bickering, he became bored. Yet whenever he thought of leaving he was assailed by guilt and a fear that he was being irresponsible.

The oldest of three children of an unhappy and vindictive father whose typical interaction with his children was criticism, he had remained his father's victim, in feeling that he could never do things right or be responsible enough. In college he studied abroad on a prestigious scholarship but lacked the confidence later to pursue his chosen field. In the years after college he came to recognize that he was always choosing a lesser, safer choice in life. Plagued by a conviction of inferiority, he went from one undemanding job to another, neglecting his interests in music, history, and politics.

Then an opportunity came to fill a responsible position in the company he worked for. Encouraged by his boss, he found it amazingly easy to do a superior job and reorganize the department. Rather than be satisfied, however, the success and appreciation made him confused and depressed. Since he could do it, he thought, it must not be demanding. Yet he knew that that was crazy. It began to dawn on him that he was probably much more broadly competent than he had given himself credit for and that he could have been doing much more all along. Thus he became vaguely aware of how attached he was to his marginal way of living.

In the first few sessions we were able to clarify his central problem: If his competence were real, beliefs that had kept him safely marginal and a victim of his father would have to be abandoned. He would have real choice, as he did with his girlfriend, but would have to forge a different identity.

Groucho Marx, the comedian and natural psychoanalyst, spoofed the neurotic dogmatism this man demonstrates in his famous quip, "I would never join a country club that would have me as a member."

Main Features of the Approach

My approach to patients is based on the idea that the unconscious reality that needs to be tackled is the complex of dogmatically accepted ideas and attitudes that constitutes the patient's basic neurotic reaction. Symptoms are a poor guide to this reality. Thus, the focus of interest shifts away from symptoms toward unconscious beliefs and their origins. I do not think that any fixed assumptions relating symptoms to the neurotic state are warranted, as demonstrated by both the cases above. The ironworker's transvestism and homosexuality were important elements in freeing himself from his neurotic condition, one manifestation of which was his conventional, guilty, and joyless sexuality. Similarly, the young man's depression, properly understood, was a complex signal of his persistent adherence to anachronistic convictions of incompetence and badness and his dim but nagging awareness of the anachronism. When he understood that, his depression actually became, increasingly, a stimulus to think and act differently.

The practical advantage of this listening stance is that it enables the analyst to gain at least a rough idea, as rapidly as possible, of the patient's reigning unconscious convictions, so as to begin work on them. While, in complex cases, psychoanalysis may take many years to complete, this approach provides knowledge of the central problems from an early stage.

The strategy uses some of the methods of Freudian analysis for this radically different purpose. For example, although I often discuss the patient's Oedipus complex as a phenomenon, it is never with the assumption that it is a developmental imperative but rather with the aim of helping to achieve a critical perspective: How is it that one adopts such attitudes and reactions, and are they worthy of belief? Similarly, questions are raised about the diagnostic thinking with which many patients nowadays approach psychoanalysis. The main qualities of neurosis are simply not adequately captured in diagnostic schemes that organize thinking by secondary properties such as symptoms, prominent affects, or behaviors. Creating "disorders" out of states of anxiety, depression, compulsion, "attention deficits," or sexual habits is sloppy thinking that confuses effect with cause and confines clinical work to a shallow level.

There are features of this approach that might be regarded as quasitechnical. To function properly as an analyst, using this approach, one must make oneself and one's ideas (especially one's psychoanalytic ideas) accessible for explanation, critical exchange, and testing-out. Since neurotic patients suffer from inhibition of critical thinking, they are easily exploited in this regard, a trap for analysts. And since neurotic convictions typically center on beliefs about the self in relation to others that are enacted in relationships, this process of exchange cannot usually be a purely intellectual process. Principles of reciprocity and equality must be demonstrated in the way treatment is conducted. Thus, the analyst cannot legitimately hold back under the pretext of being a neutral observer, much less occupy a position of authority in any other sense than that his or her ideas are worth listening to because they make sense. A considerable amount of work is often required to dissuade patients from their perceived need for authority figures.

In order to maximize the patient's ability to question the analyst and overcome his or her need for an authority figure, the treatment relationship must be as egalitarian as it is possible to make it. The curative reaction and the aim of analysis is a shift in perspective from a dogmatic, unconscious view of oneself to a consciously self-critical one. Both the patient's tendency to attribute, and the analyst's to assume, privileged knowledge and arbitrary authority, being expressions of a neurotic tendency on both sides, must be rigorously examined and reduced. This does not imply empty gestures of friendliness or assurance, false intimacy, an "I'm OK, you're OK" attitude, or in general any loss of rigor or focus.

Given these crucial differences from traditional analysis, the psychoanalytic session bears more resemblance to a philosophical dialogue than to a traditional encounter between a sick patient and a privileged interpreter. The emphasis shifts from interpretation to shared inquiry.

I can best illustrate the practical need for this approach with an anecdote about an experience of the sort that stimulated my serious concern about Freudianism and its effect on psychoanalytic education. During my training a friend and fellow candidate had reached an impasse in his own analysis. His analyst was interpreting various behaviors as expressions of repressed anger toward him and the psychoanalytic institute, with the clear implication that his tendency to anger was neurotic, a function of unresolved Oedipal problems, which ought in due course to abate. My friend was actually the sort of person inclined to be obliging to a fault, not comfortable experiencing or expressing anger when frustrated or injured. He was at the time caught up in a difficult situation: The institute was barring his advancement in training for reasons that, as was becoming increasingly clear, had more to do with his disagreement with certain high-ranking teachers and their ideas than with any lack of professional skill. Many of the candidates and institute faculty shared this judgment about his and other similar situations, but it was a difficult political problem, involving entrenched authorities, theories, procedures, and so on. These issues were difficult for my friend to tackle, largely because of his inhibition of aggression and uncertainty about his judgments. Early life circumstances had contributed to his tendency to be overaccommodating and intellectually insecure.

It ought to have been a matter of interest and pride for his analyst that, in the context of psychoanalytic training, his patient was thinking more originally and independently than was customary. Here, in other words, was a perfect opportunity to understand the operation of an Oedipus complex in an important social-educational context, with potential benefit to the patient and possibly the institution. Seizing that opportunity would have required the analyst to make complex judgments and to apply the principles of analysis to the real political and intellectual world of the psychoanalytic institute. The analyst, however, refused to enter into discussion of the institute's policies or of his own point of view. My friend's analysis ended, but unsatisfactorily. The institute's serious problems, unsurprisingly, worsened.

To return to clinical cases, I first provide an outline of a rather typical case of severe neurosis, based on looking back over many years' work. I then present several cases demonstrating issues to be decided upon in embarking on psychoanalysis, once a preliminary assessment is made. Finally, I present a detailed example of a case well along toward cure.

Case 3: Cognitive Outline of a Neurosis

Here is a retrospective cognitive outline of a typical severe neurosis, to show the broad connections between unconscious belief systems and clinical change.

With his good intellect and ambition, this middle-aged patient had had a bright future as a young man. By winning a scholarship to his state university, a fellowship abroad, and a place in a prestigious university's political science Ph.D. program, he overcame the disadvantages of a poor farm background. But having become severely neurotic during graduate school, he was unable to complete his doctorate and pursue an academic career. Rather, he became a midlevel administrator in a state agency. His interests and pleasures were profoundly constricted. He never married, had no sexual life apart from compulsive masturbation, smoked addictively, and was frequently sick. Prior to our work he had been through several episodes of psychoanalytic treatment, with minimal improvement.

Observations and Inferences

In the course of our work we developed the following understandings, in the nature of observations combined with low-level inferences:

(1) The beliefs actually governing his personal life were typically grossly at odds with his dominant conscious attitudes, beliefs, and values. For example, although consciously a strong defender of individual freedom and equality and attentive to its many problems (in his younger days he was politically radical, an activist for civil rights, and so forth), in his personal life he was conventional and puritanical in the extreme, inclined to defend even trivial social rules as embodying legitimate authority.

(2) While he had always been strongly interested in sex and eroticism, he considered it shameful, dirty, and illicit. His sexual fantasy life indicated that he was both terrified of women and considered himself a potentially sadistic monster who could not and should not be trusted.

(3) He was irrationally afraid of exercising and developing his body, and led a physically inhibited existence. In his addictive smoking leading to emphysema, and chronic insufficient fluid intake leading to recurrent respiratory infections, he revealed an intolerance of physical well-being and real hatred of his body. When he stopped smoking temporarily he felt much better physically but very anxious, even when using a nicotine patch to address the physical addiction, and quickly returned to smoking.

(4) He had a strong tendency to form new obsessive symptoms and to experience ordinary contingencies of life as irrational demands to be obeyed,

resented, and subtly defied, quite apart from his own interests. This tendency informed his work life to the extent that he had great difficulty deciding on projects based on their interest, significance, and purpose. In his tendency to form symptoms he showed a preference for criteria that he could recognize, when helped to think about them, as arbitrary, irrational, and trivial. In fact, the less significant and rational a perceived demand, the more he was inclined to obey it compulsively. This of course created havoc in his work and intellectual life, for he would spend valuable time making and correcting lists or tracking down completely insignificant details.

(5) All these tendencies informed a major pattern in his "transference" relationship to me. Although he came to value highly the analytic sessions as open and beneficial, he persisted in experiencing me as an authority who could only be dealt with by mindless obedience followed by defiant opposition. This resulted in peculiar patterns, which took a long time to identify and change. For example, no matter how thoughtfully, skeptically, and actively he had participated in discovering something about himself, he would often forget what had happened and lose the understanding. In such situations, a defiant feeling of freedom would be accompanied by urges to hurt himself. In this pattern, therefore, he seemed to seek to preserve himself through a defiance expressed by self-injury and quite disconnected from his judgment. The final phase of his analysis involved reconciling these contradictions.

Speculations about His Theory of Self and Its Origins

Considering the observations and low-level inferences I listed above, we constructed a plausible account of his theory of self and its origins. These higher-level inferences represent understandings developed over a number of years, often with difficulty.

Theory of Self

He appeared to believe with something approaching absolute certainty the following ideas, which operated as unconscious imperatives:

(1) His body was bad and dirty. Ordinary experience seemed to be routinely interpreted to "prove" this theory (as a minor example, he shaved compulsively every day, considering it unclean to do otherwise, and had constructed a complex rationale to explain why it was indecent to appear unshaven in public). Efforts to ruin his health demonstrated adherence to this belief, and thus both his rationality and morality within the belief system.

(2) He was innately physically awkward and could not trust himself to learn physical or mechanical skills or to protect himself against ordinary dangers.

(3) His attitudes toward social authority were highly complex. Consciously, he was skeptical of much arbitrary social authority, as revealed in long-standing

political beliefs and activity. At a less conscious level, he seemed to believe that social authority and tradition were to be followed regardless of their irrationality, primarily because of their longevity and status. This level informed a strong behavior pattern, in which he derived a perverse pleasure from painful obedience to such authority and tradition. Correspondingly, he harbored great confusion about the values and virtues that were important to him.

(4) As an extension of (3), he believed that his capacities to perceive, think, and judge in any area of life that might affect his convictions about himself were so defective that no reliance should be placed on them. Late in the analysis he formulated this idea as the dictum, "thou shalt not think," which explained a chronic inability to decide how to live, what values, meanings, and purposes to pursue.

His symptoms could be understood as complex compromises between efforts to obey these intellectual and moral dictates while superficially defying them in an effort to live. For example, smoking was experienced subjectively as a manly defiance of societal and medical authority, while at a deeper level it was slavish adherence to his moral compulsion to destroy his body. Dithering obsessively with trivial tasks had a similar quality with regard to his mind.

Origins

As to the origins of these bizarre convictions, it appeared that, starting as a very young child, he had interpreted ways of being treated, bodily and mentally, as defining his self and his moral universe, and that these interpretations had become rigid and total beliefs. There were a number of very destructive things about his upbringing. His father was an uneducated, kind, but passive farmer who entrusted the raising of his son to his better-educated schoolteacher wife. My patient, an only child, was "raised by the book" in the 1920s and 1930s, meaning according to strict feeding schedules and bodily routines. This included invasive treatment of his body, like being wiped after bowel movements long after he was capable of doing this himself, or routinely having his foreskin peeled back and cleaned during baths. In general he was overprotected by a phobic mother, who instilled a fear of the outdoors, without interference by the father and without benefit of siblings. It appears that he "internalized" these routines to an extreme degree and took them as the basis of psychological and moral laws.

Consequences for Treatment

Progressive awareness of his theory of self enabled this patient to begin to challenge those aspects that were clearly irrational. This brought about slow but dramatic changes. Although he previously considered himself unable to use analysis, our understanding of his theory of self enabled him to make overall sense of his experience of life, which had seemed chaotic. He could understand where the theories came from and how it was that he had developed them, as well as being chagrined by his unreflectiveness and lack of courage in not having challenged them sooner. At times he was extremely sad at his waste of life but not neurotically depressed, as he had often been in the past. He became able to use our relationship in a way that was quite different from previous treatment relationships, to engineer and test out exceptions to his rules of existence. This beneficial change, which extended to other areas of his life, applied especially to his tendency to regard me as an authority and was promoted by many critical discussions of analytic theory and ideas, about which he knew a good deal.

He changed significantly in his capacity to care for himself. For example, he ate and drank more sensibly, and his health improved. His obsessiveness diminished and his intellectual life became richer. In particular, his capacity to read with real engagement and comprehension improved dramatically. He stopped compulsively masturbating and began paying more attention to the sensual aspects of life, including the prospects of having at least friendly relations with women. Although he came to analysis too late to make major changes in his sex life, he recognized that he was a fundamentally sane human being who could learn from experience rather than persist endlessly in self-destruction.

In the final stage of his analysis, he was able to grapple seriously with his persistent tendency to derive a cynical pleasure from being a moral automaton, and thus to avoid choice and deliberate action, including in his treatment. It was our eventual ability to discuss issues at this level of "good versus bad faith" between us that led to the most significant change.

The next cases concern people in the early stages of assessment and decision-making with regard to psychoanalysis. Since my approach requires active mutual commitment, it typically starts with a trial period of work to get an idea what can be accomplished, what the implications of cure will be, whether we enjoy working together, and so on. As might be expected, developing critical awareness of one's unconscious, and therefore absolutely accepted, views of oneself, is discomfiting, even when dramatically helpful, because many life arrangements and relationships are called into question.

Case 4: The Discomfiture of Analysis

This woman achieved rapid and dramatic benefit from some plausible guesses about her concept of self, which then created a certain turmoil in her life.

She is the middle-aged mother of three adolescent children who came for help primarily because of severe anxiety and kleptomania. Since her marriage twenty-five years earlier, she had compulsively stolen from retail stores unnecessary things, as she was married to a wealthy businessman and had no unsatisfied material needs. She had been through several different therapies, including a period of psychoanalysis and drug treatment. The analysis especially had helped her open her mind to the reality of unconscious tendencies, symbolic thinking, and the effect of a horribly inadequate early background but had not affected her major symptoms.

In her childhood, she was vilified by a mother who, clearly miserable in her marriage and unable to leave, accused her of being "crazy," stupid, and selfish. Her father, a town functionary, was devoutly Catholic, alcoholic, and affectionate to her but completely unwilling to interfere with the mother's insanity. Terribly cowed by the mother, she was always a "good" child, accepting her parents' attributions, trying to please, completely mystified why she was treated so badly. She felt she had a decent mind and could figure things out, but neither sought nor received help. She had aspirations to attend college but gave in to her parents' refusal, attending a secretarial school, instead. In adolescence she found some escape in a love affair with a boy from the rich part of town, also desperately unhappy with a horrible family situation but angrily rebellious, who drank, fought, and sought escape in drugs. Narrowly avoiding prison, he refused the elite college he was destined for, and the two eloped. He became a successful businessman.

It required little leap of imagination to infer from this woman's account that she had been driven by intense self-hatred and remained profoundly confused as to whether she was as horrible as her mother perceived her to be. This, of course, was not a new idea to her. But given that inference, what might be the psychology of her kleptomania? She maintained that she was, like her father, "really" a good and devout person. The kleptomania, however, "seized" her, leaving her frightened, guilty, ashamed, thrilled, and pleased. Attempting to reconcile her conscious view of herself as "really" a good person *except* when she stole, with the reasonable inference of intense (but unconscious) self-loathing, I suggested an extended understanding. I speculated that her basic conviction about herself, regarded as absolutely true, was that she was innately and completely bad and defective. Because total and without exception, this idea was infinite and boundless. It could not really be thought about but operated as a proven and irremediable fact. The kleptomania was a complex effort to forge a connection between infinite badness (i.e., for existing) and real action that she could comprehend. Thus it served simultaneously to express and deny the extent of her badness, and to dilute its force by developing a *conditional and real* badness: *I am bad because I occasionally steal, therefore only partially bad.*[53] I explained that this was a hypothesis about the main psy-

[53] This psychology in relation to people and activity is described by Kleinian analysts, but in other theoretical terms, as demonstrating a "container" function.

chology of her symptom, designed to shed light on her concept of self. Undoubtedly, there were other aspects of her stealing that would be of interest, such as the acquisition of things she didn't need, the thrill associated with getting away with something, and so forth.

Within several months, and somewhat to her surprise, she had stopped stealing. The best explanation she could give, which seemed quite plausible to me, was that *stealing was simply no longer of interest.* She experienced the change as something of a loss. She put herself in situations of temptation to see if the urge would return, but it didn't, although she stole a few things during this period (without thrill or enthusiasm) just to prove she still could.

What had happened? Apparently, I had provided her a framework of thinking about that aspect of herself that had been unthinkable because totally believed—her intrinsic badness. In parallel with the cessation of stealing, a number of other long-standing compulsive habits also dropped away, like severe nail-biting. She was impressed by the fact that things could shift around in her mind even without talking about them directly, an observation that confirmed my sense that she was ruled by powerful and completely unconscious convictions.

This is not to say that her problems were over. Rather, she started paying attention to other aspects of her life that had been thrust into the background by her compulsive symptoms and self-created crises: her marriage, which was in difficulty; her relationships with her children, which were a mess; and her chronically unfulfilled life. She now considered that it might be possible to think clearly and constructively, to learn things, and to make some sort of contribution in life, which had always been a distant dream. At the same time, the implications of the ideas we had started developing were disturbing, anxiety-producing, and depressing.

The focus of her thinking shifted to her father, toward whom she had always maintained an idealizing attitude. Was it conceivable that he was really the good and devout man she had taken him to be, if he permitted the horrific conditions in the family? What would be the consequences of extending her critical thinking to the whole of her upbringing? As she began to grapple with this question, she developed severe abdominal pains, which then abated. Her father had died in great torment from undiagnosed abdominal cancer, and this seemed to be a way of guiltily "identifying" with him. Reviewing her early experience, including her adolescent love affair with her husband, she wondered what had become of the two of them. She was a rich housewife from a working-class background who had badly neglected her education and focused all her efforts on being the model suburban mom. Her husband, having made millions, was a reactionary businessman who seemed to have only contempt for working people.

How was she to think about all this, and how was it related to the circumstances of her life and to her personality? To decide to tackle these larger problems would be to dare think about her self with clarity for the first time. This woman decided that it was better, for her, not to.

Case 5: Businessman

A twenty-eight-year-old businessman consulted me because of a problem in his love life. Confused and guilty over the prospect of breaking off with his girlfriend, despite realizing it was the proper and necessary thing to do, he could not act. It was a relationship of convenience for him, which he had misrepresented to himself and her. He did not love her, and marriage, which she insisted upon, was out of the question. In the course of helping him come to the decision to break off, it was necessary to understand something of his tendency to dishonesty and self-deception in general. He was inclined to explain these problems in terms of being a "nice guy" and not wanting to hurt people. That seemed true enough but superficial, if for no other reason than stringing his girlfriend along was in fact hurting her.

In the course of a few months we were able to clarify some psychological patterns. He was the younger son in a Jewish family that prided itself on solidarity, religious values, and accomplishment. Despite his initial tendency to see his family as nearly ideal, he experienced his participation in close family life as achieved at the cost of "breaking [his] will." Feisty and independent as a young child, he sought to know the reasons for doing things rather than blindly obeying. Although not treated with particular harshness, occasional experiences of physical punishment and verbal dressing-down were enough to convince him that his ideas were wrong and his parents' right, a conviction reinforced in religious and public school. A conformist in high school, he harbored a secret wish to be a great rebel or, alternatively, to earn huge amounts of money so that he could eventually "do what he wanted." This attitude toward maturity and success seemed to govern his education and career choices. Rather than pursue what was of most interest, like art or architecture, he went into business administration, at which he was moderately successful. Nonetheless, he was dogged by the feeling that he was not doing what he wanted and could only do so after amassing a fortune. Nor could he describe, with any conviction or passion, what it was that he really wanted to do.

This man was not very symptomatic in the usual sense of the word but he was profoundly neurotic, having accepted destructive family and social values to such an extent that he could not distinguish what he valued and desired from what someone else desired for him, a pattern that came to a crisis with his girlfriend. In fact, he experienced more anxiety as a result of realizing his self-deluding attitudes toward life, society, and established authority than he had when he first consulted me. Between sessions, he often assuaged this anxiety by returning to the kind of conformist, utilitarian morality he had been socialized into. At those times he was inclined to break off treatment as unnecessary and to feel fine.

Discussing important matters with him in such a frame of mind revealed his belief system, which he experienced as self-evident: that one's personality is purely what one has been taught, that those in power know best or at least one must assume they do, that neither children in families nor citizens of countries have any intrinsic rights, and that in discussing moral and social issues everyone has different opinions that, being purely subjective, cannot really be commented on. When I pointed out that his belief system was a particular and not at all self-evident one, clearly derived from his early experience and informing his difficulties in love and career, he was interested but disturbed. He was not at all sure that he wanted or needed to understand himself to that degree, even though the new perspective had been very useful in solving an important life dilemma. His existing beliefs seemed both too obvious and too necessary to question.

He did in the end decide to pursue analysis. In discussing his decision, he recalled two important, rare, childhood experiences of being "recognized." Both involved valued teachers acknowledging and engaging his good ability to think. We both felt that an important capacity was being awakened and that analysis would be fruitful.

In the foregoing cases the main problems stem from unrecognized unconscious beliefs from childhood. In the following case neurosis was triggered by a political crisis in the patient's current life.

Case 6: Whistleblower

This man is a reluctant whistleblower, who found himself enmeshed in a corrupt bureaucracy. He is a dedicated senior manager in the computer division of a large state agency, a comfortable bachelor, and amateur historian. He had become aware that the division director, having seriously erred on a major project, was misrepresenting facts and figures to state oversight agencies and deceiving and manipulating staff. The result was large cost overruns and demoralization. Attempts to discuss and correct the situation resulted in his being scapegoated, given an unfavorable review, and demoted, effectively halting his career. Reluctantly, he fought back. In the midst of the legal case he consulted me because of tremendous stress, sleep disturbance, migraines, and broken teeth from nocturnal gnashing.

I speculated that he was symptomatic because, to judge from the details of the case, there was a good chance of his prevailing (as he in fact did six months later) and knew intuitively that the inevitable radicalization his situation entailed would be hard to bear. It challenged the aspect of his character that was inflexible: a belief in people's reasonableness and benevolence despite strong evidence to the contrary in specific situations.

He had always been a great altruist and optimist, the sort of person for whom life's problems, including his own troubled upbringing, were simply interesting challenges to overcome. Abandoned by his father and raised by a tough but alcoholic mother, he was always precocious, living by his wits, earning money, taking care of others. He was married and a father at seventeen. Later, in the army, he was recruited for the intelligence service because of his computer aptitudes. After several years of rapid promotion, he quit over refusal to do work that was ethically suspicious. Later, following graduate school and a successful consulting career, he joined state service. Never in his work experience had he been forced to confront corrupt authority and bear the consequences. Now reality and conscience were forcing him into an uncustomary radical position.

Events over the next year enabled us to test out this hypothesis. He was, by virtue of the strength of his case, the only person in memory to win his kind of appeal, putting him in a strong position not only to redress the wrong done him but to negotiate with his agency over major and chronic problems, to assure that similar things did not happen again. Naturally, there was great discomfort and polarization among colleagues, because his victory meant exposure of wrongdoing, likely disgrace of the division director, and a potential end to the electoral ambitions of the agency director. In understanding this situation politically and psychologically it was, of course, important to be clear and forthright in our respective judgments about who in the cast of characters was being truthful and who deceitful. His symptoms abated.

Gradually, however, it became clear that his legal victory would change him forever in unforeseeable ways. He would always be known as a whistleblower, even though his fondest wish was to return to the status quo. He was left with a nagging anxiety that he could never adjust to this radicalized role, even though he believed it was necessary. In this context he had a dream: *He is walking fast or jogging, and turns a corner. Just as he glimpses what is around the corner, he awakens, feeling frustrated that he could not quite see where he was headed.* Here is the essence of his psychological situation. Life is forcing him to confront his unrealistic altruism, which had, presumably, operated as an infinite construct, always believed, always true. Now it is being disproved. He knows intellectually that there is life around this blind corner and, intuiting that it will require difficult adjustments, is not sure he wants to find out what it entails.

Thrust into a political battle, this man had been forced to confront his version of the Oedipal dilemma, his exaggerated deference to authority in the form of overidealized expectations. While it came at a time in life when he had considerable wherewithal to do battle, it was extremely stressful and he became overtly neurotic, as did Dora under similar circumstances.

The following material concerning a woman I presented earlier provides an opportunity to put in perspective issues of sexual transference that are, I believe, given exaggerated importance in Freudian analysis.

Case 7: Personal Theories and Sexual Transference

In its clinical method Freudianism places great emphasis on interpreting sexual "transferences"—overt or covert conflicts over sexual fantasies toward the analyst. Such transferences reflect the sexual immaturity characteristic of neurosis, in which normal sexual desire is experienced as transgressive, reflecting the persistence into adulthood of an incestuous (i.e., childish) sexual attitude. I have discussed at length the problems inherent in attempting to treat sexual immaturity with theories that regard such a state as normative.

To address some of these problems, consider the further progress of the doctor I discussed in Chapter 1 (Case 3). In her early life she was subject to the whims of a depressive psychoanalyst father and a pill-addicted mother. In keeping with her parents' perception, she developed an entrenched view of herself as inferior, bad, and impossibly demanding, "a harsh taskmaster," as her father described her when she sought attention from him—although she was, in reality, quite self-reliant. There was also a great lack of physical affection, especially harmful for this isolated only child (recall Westermarck), which left her with a profound, very irrational sense of sexual unattractiveness and awkwardness. What were in fact theories of self that had reasonably enough accounted for the circumstances of her early life, now operated in her mind as proven facts.

I will pick up the story of her analysis at a point when she had substantially relinquished the central idea that she was defective, that a better child in her place would have handled things with less difficulty, and so on, and was beginning to take seriously the possibility that she was a normal human being entitled to being dealt with reasonably. This began to include having a satisfying sex life rather than the deprivation she imposed on herself.

A difficult thing for her to surrender, and which interfered particularly with using the treatment relationship imaginatively to explore this aspect of life, was her persistent tendency to treat me as a prohibiting authority. Like many patients, although she had developed a good general appreciation of what she came to call her "private religion" of negative convictions, she persisted in reacting to me as something akin to a religious-moral authority. Some of this attitude she had inherited from her father's beliefs about psychoanalytic theories and "rules," of which she was becoming increasingly skeptical.

Two dreams expressed her need to challenge these particular dogmas. In one, *she is in her childhood home. Her parents had died* [her father had actually died some years before, and her mother six months earlier] *and she was there survey-*

ing the house and its contents, with a view toward deciding whether to keep it, occupy it, or get rid of it. There had been a meeting of analysts, who are all leaving. A gray-haired woman remains, hovering nearby, and she cannot tell what she wants or whether her intentions are friendly or hostile. Someone knocks on the side door. An analyst colleague of her father seeks entrance. She tells him the meeting is over and sends him away.

She was at the time still grieving over her mother's death, which included a good deal of irrational guilt, for her mother had never been much of a friend, despite my patient's efforts to befriend her. The mother had died as she had lived, fading away with no discernible cause, possibly a covert suicide. In the dream mother and father are lumped together as co-owners of the family home and tradition—including the father's orthodox psychoanalytic tradition—about which she is having to decide. The gray-haired woman refers to an actual maid from her childhood, who treated her cruelly. Her parents had refused to believe her accounts of this bad treatment until confronted by independent evidence. Thus, she is asking in this dream whether she can learn to rely on her own judgment about whom and what to retain from her past.

In another dream, *she is with a friend* [a medical school classmate who, in reality, had become an analyst and colleague of her father, before his death]. *The friend is reading to her a lecture she plans to deliver, but it is in Greek.* She [my patient] tells her that she doesn't understand Greek. This friend, a classmate who had disappointed her early promise by becoming an uninspired analyst, represented multiple aspects of herself, her father, me, and psychoanalysis. The more she understood that analysis is simply a way of disembedding and thinking critically about unconscious convictions, the more confidence she had in using her good abilities to recognize and react to "Greek" (i.e., unnecessarily obscure ideas) when she encountered it.

With better ability to think, her scope of effective activity increased. She was able to stand up to her husband and insist on his taking responsibility for himself. She took a greater hand in family matters, became more interested in political affairs at work, and was less irrationally guilty and depressed over the sad deaths of her mother and father. Less fearful of the inevitable risks of malpractice suits as a front-line physician, she developed renewed interest in her profession.

She came to recognize a variety of subtle but absurd ways in which she continued to experience me as a prohibiting authority who must be obeyed. For example, it was somehow "against the rules" to get up and move around the office. This tendency was particularly apparent in any discussion of sex, which for some still-obscure reason was difficult to think or talk about. She had retained a sense of the "potency" of sex but for the most part accepted an asexual existence, convinced that she was unappealing and incapable. Her present attitude was an outgrowth of her passive and defensive childhood attitude toward growing up: helpless to do other than wait for time and events to propel her out of her awful surroundings. Thus she experienced her immediate world as enforcing her dogmatic negativism, and the beckoning adult world lay in some vague future that could not be actively sought. Increasingly, I occupied a place intermediate between these two subjective worlds, for the sessions were now unfailingly interesting and challenging like the adult world, yet she continued to experience me automatically as a prohibiting authority. The sessions were also emotionally and at times sexually stirring, for the reality of being liked, taken very seriously, and treated as an equal would rouse her to a kind of passion and bring tears. The more she understood her difficulty responding to these complex but lively reactions, the more dissatisfied she was with herself, realizing that she would not change automatically.

I challenged her to set aside her obeisant follower attitude as a patient, which, neither flattering to me nor constructive, only proved and reproved her anachronistic theories about her incapacities. She needed to decide how important a sexual life was to her. If important enough to pursue, it would be necessary to stop indulging her negativity. Although frightened, she thought it could be useful to imagine us as physically or sexually involved in some way; after all, we had come to know and like each other, she trusted me, and ought to be able to play with possibilities in the safety of the analytic room. For example, it might be interesting to touch, with more than a perfunctory handshake. On a number of occasions, she had taken particular notice of my hands. One involved a gift she had given me: I seemed to unwrap and handle it with tenderness, and she was moved. For a woman whose early experience was so deficient in physical affection and touch, ideas and experiences of being caressed or held were both moving and extremely conflicted. Such imaginings seemed presumptuous and, in some vague way, dangerous. She saw the problem as "jumping a gap," like nerve impulses jump the synapse, suggesting that her problem had partially to do with actual sexual feeling. The terrain on the other side of this gap was now, in light of our ongoing discussions, neither totally unknown nor terribly frightening (like the abysses and black holes of earlier analysis), only daunting in an adult way, posing the challenge of facing life as a grown woman. She knew that she was really a sexual woman. On occasions when she had yielded to affection and desire and made love with men, usually during outdoor adventures away from home, she had been overcome by intense regret: She could have been living a more intense life all along. Returning home, however, she would anesthetize this regret. Thinking about touching or holding made her realize how truly "mad" she was with regard to this whole aspect of life, for she imagined herself disintegrating or, alternatively, being tattooed or branded, as though she would not survive what she recognized rationally to be an ordinary and sane experience. More than anything to date, this demonstrated both the strength and the profound irrationality of her conviction of defectiveness and enforced isolation. Eventually, we did affectionately hug one another at the end of a session. She was neither overwhelmed, destroyed, nor preoccupied by the experience, but it made her aware that continued change would require she overcome her extraordinary and profoundly irrational sexual and intellectual inhibition.

A dream revealed this newly important aspect of change—sexual maturation and aliveness. *She is shopping with her husband and stepdaughter, and they are going separate ways. Outside a department store, she comes upon a display of perfumes, which involves five or six diminutive female mannikins. Before her eyes, several of the mannikins are slowly but definitely moving, as though alive. She motions excitedly for her stepdaughter to witness this amazing thing.*

Clearly, the curative reaction is well established in this woman. Around this point in her treatment she began to feel, for the first time, a deep sense of optimism. She related this to a transformation in the way her mind worked, described in one of the graphic metaphors she was so good at: traveling over a vast network of connections, as opposed to an earlier set of linear rails with abysses on either side.

The last case is another follow-up presentation of a patient introduced in Chapter 1, the engineer, whose treatment is approaching its end.

Case 8: The Rip Van Winkle Effect: The Basic Curative Reaction Established

I pick up this man's story at a point where the curative reaction is well established. Psychoanalysis can come to an end when this reaction is independently maintained and used in the activities of daily life.

Its establishment requires that the patient recognize a difficult truth to which neurotics are remarkably blind: that one in fact knows very little about oneself with any certainty. This man was particularly resistant to that truth. His cynicism and defensive sense of superiority had often led him to excoriate analysis. He considered it unsatisfyingly slow and maddeningly imprecise because, contrary to his scientific approach to life, analysts knew pathetically little about how the brain functions, about emotions, and so on. This attitude concealed a rigid dogmatism that was difficult to demonstrate convincingly. Its demonstration, which finally consolidated the curative reaction, came about in an interesting way, through theoretical discussions and an interpersonal crisis.

He was, without realizing it, a confirmed emotivist, convinced that the solution to his problems lay in unraveling the mysteries of his maddening lapses into carping criticism, apathy, and then depression. This intractable pattern, which resulted in repeated failures in creative interests and personal relationships, seemed to prove that he was somehow "intrinsically flawed" or permanently damaged, for which he sought explanation in various psychological theories. There must be some "prime cause" for this perverse behavior, beyond the obvious fact that he had grown up thinking of himself as flawed and failed and for some reason had clung to this belief. Although he had found a prior analysis ultimately unhelpful because of the analyst's formulaic interpretations, he now found himself using those interpretations against me. Was not depression indeed anger repressed and turned against the self? How could I be an analyst and not believe in repression? Was not there some way to "release" the repressed anger in a useful way?

It appeared to me, however, that he was overestimating what we could learn from his emotional reactions, which, being highly stereotyped, had little more to teach us. Since repression was such a theoretical passion of his, I explained at some length why I did not think much of the concept: It was based on negative assumptions about people that not only made little sense but were identical to the assumptions of innate defect so central to his personal theory of self.

It made no sense to me that his type of neurotic difficulty could be cured using theories that employed the same irrational assumptions. As an alternative, I suggested that unconsciousness is the fate of ideas that he treated as unexceptionable truths and therefore were not experienced as ideas at all, but as dogmas that he compulsively validated. I proposed a different and counterintuitive way of thinking about his anxiety: that it was an indication of his terror of approaching life with expectations that were reasonable but subjectively beyond the known world.

He had in fact provided example after example of a self-confirming process by which new possibilities were reduced to the familiar. Perhaps the most striking was a delusion on the occasion of receiving a gift from a woman. When she seductively reached into a bag to deliver a present she'd hinted he would especially enjoy, he was convinced she was about to grab a revolver and shoot him, and was seized with panic. The relationship ended shortly after. In general, anything strongly positive had been defeated in his life, to his bitter regret.

Out of extreme impatience and irritation, he broke off treatment in the midst of this discussion, contemptuously describing my approach as dwelling misguidedly on "philosophical nuances." He was convinced, as so much psychological literature seemed to affirm, that his problems were primarily emotional. Since I didn't agree, he would have to continue his search elsewhere. I was reasonably sure that I had lost the case.

Some weeks later, however, having given the matter considerable thought, he decided to resume treatment. As frustrating as I was to him, he could not justify rejecting the basic ideas. If analysis meant relearning how to think about oneself, he could not in good conscience turn away from thinking that made sense and was already bringing about a shift in consciousness.

This was perhaps the first time in his life he had acted bravely in an important matter on the basis of reason rather than fear and prejudice. It seemed to put him in a new position, embracing which would mean giving up a cherished personal belief system.

What is this system? Neurotic people typically have great difficulty grasping the central paradox of their condition. Their symptoms connote great doubt and uncertainty in coping with ordinary life, whereas each outbreak of symptoms indicates precisely the opposite at a cognitive level: a lapsing into a position of absolute certainty. This "knowledge," since it knows no exceptions, is experienced not as thought at all but as blind impulsion to enact that which they believe. It is when the person begins to wake up to the fact that such convictions fail to provide relevant knowledge of himself or herself and the world that treatment is sought. And *it is the analyst's task to bring this intuitive understanding to a point of explicit and bearable crisis.* This man's struggle to maintain his system against all odds had peaked in his encounter with me, and he had allowed himself to enter into an epistemic crisis.

From this point on in his life and treatment exceptions to his typical pattern of self-affirming failures began to appear with some regularity, which enabled us to study his reactions to them. They followed a typical pattern, in which initial excitement gave way quickly to loss of interest, leading to a renewed failure of some kind, attempts to justify the failure, then depression at his "stuckness." Several months after resuming treatment he entered into a new relationship with a woman, which provided a good opportunity to study this pattern with regard to, among other things, sex; for, rather suddenly, he found himself at times potent, a dramatic and not altogether welcome change.

His experience of sexual potency with a willing, interested, and interesting partner disproved once and for all his theories that he might be physiologically impaired or that the woman wasn't attractive enough. He also realized that, although it was better to be potent than impotent, it didn't affect his basic reactions: He, and his penis, could lapse into indifference at a moment's notice. Around this time the impotence drug Viagra came on the market, and I recommended it as an aid to confidence. Indeed, it was impressively effective, both to achieve magnificent erections and to clarify that erections alone would not cure his neurotic tendency. Erect or not, he could overrule any interest with indifference; for example, he could discharge his potency with a quick orgasm and lapse back into indifference.

As a result, there came into focus the key problem of tolerating exceptions to the rule of his private belief system, which were accumulating faster than he could erase them. During this time we talked a good deal about a kind of applied epistemology—the difficulties and complexities of fashioning a reasonable theory of self and permitting the world to pass judgment on it by engaging seriously and honestly with it, rather than distorting the outcome as he so typically did. Psychoanalysis, he realized, was like an experiment, not a conversion or an exercise in positive thinking. He could not be whatever he wanted, nor could psychoanalysis provide a conviction of goodness and efficacy comparable to his negative convictions; that would have to come from life, once he was freed from his automatisms. The crucial understanding—what I term the basic curative reaction—is that neither was he fated to infinitely replicate his past just because he had done so for fifty years.

During the period of about a year when these changes were taking place a sense of guarded optimism arose, accompanied by what he called the "Rip Van Winkle effect"—waking from a lifelong slumber to life's real challenges, accompanied by a strong sense of regret over having wasted so much of it.

In his dreams he used familiar symbols and dramatic, heroic scenarios to portray conflicts between safety and danger, moral and intellectual wakefulness and slumber, responsibility and irresponsibility. In one, *he is traveling with work colleagues aboard a large jet. Something happens, and he finds himself at the controls—but falls asleep. Later, he is magically back with the colleagues left behind, who inform him that the plane has crashed*. The possibility of change began to inform his perception of time, experienced now as preciously limited. His dissatisfaction with engineering was translated into specific and realistic plans for an auxiliary career as a technical writer and perhaps translator. He embarked on a course of evening study in writing and editing, and found himself remarkably open to the instruction.

Always having wanted to develop himself as a writer, he began to think it would be a valuable contribution to others to set down and publish an account of his own struggles with therapy as he neared the end of it; he embarked on sketching an "analytical diary." As he engaged in this project, he realized that while he was changing in significant ways, he could not put his finger on any particular dramatic insight that had ever occurred. He thought, as I did, that the personal-epistemic crisis of the year before had liberated him decisively. He found it fascinating that the process of personal change seems to parallel the way knowledge of the world, in general, develops.

Concluding Thoughts

Psychoanalysis can be, and has largely been, based on cultural myths, but it is better to base it on sound reasoning and the accumulated evidence of practice.

That is a statement of value but also an assumption and a hypothesis about how a rational psychoanalysis might be constructed. It predicts that people, however deeply indoctrinated into reigning belief systems, will benefit best from a thoughtful examination of their beliefs, reformulating them if necessary, and having the opportunity to test old and new beliefs against experience. When it comes to thinking and moral life, with which psychoanalysis is largely concerned, hypotheses and value statements are not mutually exclusive. Rational thinking about values is, in fact, in the tradition of the "moral science" approach that was taken for granted from ancient times up to the Enlightenment, that has been an unfortunate but needless casualty of modern intellectual life, and that it is one of the purposes of this book to restore.

Since we know precious little with any reliability about how moral character originates, develops, and changes, hypotheses are very much in order. Of special importance for psychoanalysis is the fact that we tend to take our particular modes of socialization and thinking so for granted, and have grown so used to our modern brand of utilitarian morality, that the plausible and venerable hypothesis of an innate moral system is often dismissed out of hand, as Freud did, as naive. It is nothing of the sort. It is an optimistic but reasonable idea worth pursuing, perhaps now more than ever.

The hallmark of a rational pursuit of knowledge is not pessimism but skepticism about dogmas and an insistence on theories that move closer and closer to reality. Naturally, dogmas about our selves are among the most deeply unconscious of our ideas, and therefore among the hardest to see and think about. They, along with dogmas about the society in which we live, reflect the "cultural unconscious" of our times. It is an interesting reflection of our modern age that so many of our intellectual utopias—classical economics, the classless society, the Freudian superego, and (for the faithful) divine revelation—are so pessimistic about human capacities. Freudianism is a case in point. Its intellectual and clinical weaknesses stem from its embrace of ideal negative assumptions held in common with economic and social theories that assume the intellectual incompetence, not to mention the innate and unbridled savagery, lust, and greed of human beings. Its transformation into a rational psychology lies in the direction of substituting for these caricatures an open-ended approach to biology, society, history, language, education, and their convergence in the development of individuals. I hope I have demonstrated through clinical examples that this can be done without sacrificing Freudianism's important emphasis on detailed understanding of the individual's history, emotional life, and relationships.

I do not propose a new psychoanalytic system to replace Freudianism or any of the numerous post-Freudian systems that have grown up in emulation of or competition with it—but a process of shared inquiry through which the patient is able to initiate, perhaps for the first time, a thoughtful investigation of the self unburdened by dogmatic convictions. Customarily, psychoanalytic systems place undue emphasis on certain typical mental contents (the Oedipus complex, the inferiority complex, the collective unconscious, and so on) and reified entities (such as id, ego, superego, internalized objects), "interpretation" of which is supposed to free mental energies for useful, social, and enjoyable purposes. To the extent that the complexes and entities of the various psychoanalytic schools are based on received beliefs acquired when young, it is not interpretation but critical discussion of them, leading to the formulation and courageous testing, through life experience, of more reasonable concepts of self, that can free creative energies.

Freudianism has had a century to prove itself. It is time to develop a psychoanalysis that, rejecting the allure of negative utopias, enhances that capacity without which human life is degraded beyond measure: reflection and critical judgment about ourselves and our origins, our abilities and limitations, our families, and our societies.

BIBLIOGRAPHY

AARSLEFF, H. 1982. *From Locke to Saussure: Essays on the Study of Language and Intellectual History.* Minneapolis: Univ. of Minnesota Press.

ABERLE, D., et al. 1963. The incest taboo and the mating patterns of animals. *Amer. Anthrop.* 64: 253-266.

ALLEN, E. et al. 1978. Against "sociobiology." In *The Sociobiology Debate: Readings on the Ethical and Scientific Issues Concerning Sociobiology,* ed. A. Caplan. New York: Harper & Row.

ARISTOTLE. ca. 325 B.C. *Nicomachean Ethics,* tr. T. Irwin. Second ed. Indianapolis: Hackett Publishing Co., 1999.

BARROS, C. 1971. Thermodynamic and evolutionary concepts in the formal structure of Freud's metapsychology. In *World Biennial of Psychiatry and Psychotherapy,* ed. S. Arieti. New York: Basic Books.

BENTHAM, J. 1864. *The Theory of Legislation,* second ed. Translated from the French of Etienne Dumont by R. Hildreth. London: Kegan Paul, Trench, Trubner, 1931.

BERNHEIMER, C. & C. KAHANE, eds. 1985. *In Dora's Case: Freud—Hysteria—Feminism,* second ed. New York: Columbia Univ. Press, 1990.

BETTELHEIM, B. 1969. *Children of the Dream.* New York: Macmillan.

__________ 1983. *Freud and Man's Soul.* New York: A. A. Knopf.

BISCHOF, N. 1972. The biological foundations of the incest taboo. *Soc. Sci. Inform.* 11 (6): 7-36.

__________ 1975. Comparative ethology of incest avoidance. In *Biosocial Anthropology, ASA Studies 1,* ed. R. Fox. London: Malaby Press, pp. 37-67.

__________ 1985. *Das rätsel Oedipus: Die biologischen Wurzeln des Urkonflictes von Intimität und Autonomie.* Münich: Piper.

BOCKOVEN, J. 1963. *Moral Treatment in American Psychiatry.* New York: Springer.

BRENNER, C. 1957. The nature and development of the concept of repression in Freud's writings. *Psychoanal. Study Child* 12: 19-46.

BREUER, J. & S. FREUD. 1893-1895. *Studies on hysteria. I. On the psychical mechanism of hysterical phenomena: Preliminary communication.* In *The Standard Edition of the Complete Psychological Works of Sigmund Freud,* vol. 2, ed. J. Strachey, A. Freud, A. Strachey, & A. Tyson and tr. J. Strachey. London: Hogarth, 1955.

CALDWELL, R. 1989. *The Origin of the Gods: A Psychoanalytic Study of Greek Theogonic Myth.* New York: Oxford Univ. Press.

CHARCOT, J. 1889. *Clinical Lectures on Diseases of the Nervous System,* vol. 3, tr. by T. Savill. New York: Classics of Medicine Library, 1994.

CHOMSKY, N. 1957. *Syntactic Structures.* The Hague and Paris: Mouton.

__________ 1965. *Aspects of the Theory of Syntax.* Cambridge: MIT Press.

__________ 1996. *Power and Prospects: Reflections on Human Nature and the Social Order.* Boston: South End Press.

COE, M. 1984. *Mexico,* revised and enlarged ed. London: Thames and Hudson.

COHEN, J. 1980. Structural consequences of psychic trauma: A new look at Beyond the Pleasure Principle. *Int. J. Psychoanal.,* 61: 421-432.

__________ 1985. Trauma and repression. *Psychoanal. Inquiry* 5: 163-189.

__________ 1993. Die zwei Arten der psychoanalytischen Rekonstruktion: Warum Analysen beide benötigen (The two classes of psychoanalytic reconstruction: Why analyses require both). *Jahrbuch der Psychoanal.* 30: 65-100.

__________ 1998. Letter to the Editor. *In These Times,* March 8, 1998.

__________ 1998-99. Review of E Hoffman, *The Drive for Self: Alfred Adler and the Founding of Individual Psychology. Independent Scholar* 12-13: 16-18.

__________ & W. KINSTON. 1984. Repression theory: A new look at the cornerstone, *Int. J. Psychoanal.* 65, 411-422.

COHEN, J. & W. KINSTON. 1984. Repression theory: A new look at the cornerstone. *Int. J. Psychoanal.* 65, 411-432.

CORTÉS, H. 1522. *Second letter to Emperor Charles V.* In *Letters from Mexico,* tr. and ed. A. Pagden. New York: Grossman Publishers, 1971.

CREWS, F., ed. 1995. *The Memory Wars: Freud's Legacy in Dispute.* New York: New York Review Imprints.

__________ 1998. *Unauthorized Freud: Doubters Confront a Legend.* New York: Penguin Books.

DALY, M. & M. WILSON. 1983. Explaining inbreeding avoidance requires more complex models. *Behav. Brain Sciences* 6: 105.

DARWIN, C. 1868. *The Variation of Animals and Plants Under Domestication.* New York: Appleton, 1890.

DELEUZE, G. & F. GUATTARI. 1983. *Anti-Oedipus: Capitalism and Schizophrenia,* tr. R. Hurley, M. Seem, & H. Lane. Minneapolis: Univ. Minnesota Press.

DEMAUSE, L., ed. 1974. *The History of Childhood.* New York: The Psychohistory Press.

DEUTSCH, F. 1957. A footnote to Freud's "Fragment of an analysis of a case of hysteria." *Psychoanal. Q.* 26: 159-167.

DÍAZ DEL CASTILLO, B. 1632. *The Discovery and Conquest of Mexico, 1517-1521.* Tr. A. Maudsley of *The True History of the Conquest of New Spain.* London: George Routledge & Sons, 1928.

DOLLARD, J., MILLER, N., et al. 1939. *Frustration and Aggression.* New Haven: Yale Univ. Press.

ECCLES, J. 1966. Cerebral synaptic mechanisms. In *Brain and Conscious Experience,* ed. J. Eccles. Berlin, Heidelberg, New York: Springer-Verlag.

EHRENFELS, C. VON. 1903. Sexuales ober- und unterbewusstsein. *Politisch-anthrop. Rev.* 2.

____________________ 1907. *Sexualethik. Grenzfr. Nerv-. u. Seelenleb.* 56. Wiesbaden.

EINSTEIN, A. 1932. Letter, reprinted in Freud, Why War?, *The Standard Edition of the Complete Psychological Works of Sigmund Freud,* ed. J. Strachey, A. Freud, A. Strachey, & A. Tyson and tr. J. Strachey, vol. 22: 199-202.

ERIKSON, E. 1950. *Childhood and Society,* second ed. W. W. Norton, New York, 1963.

____________ 1962. Reality and actuality. *J. Amer. Psychoanal. Assn.* 10: 451-474.

ESTERSON, A. 1998. Delusion and dream in Freud's "Dora." In *Unauthorized Freud: Doubters Confront a Legend,* ed. J. Crews. New York: Penguin Books.

FARAH, M. 1984. *Marriage and Sexuality in Islam: A Translation of al-Ghazali's Book on the Etiquette of Marriage from the "Ihya."* Salt Lake City: Univ. of Utah Press.

FEI, HSIAO-TUNG. 1939. *Peasant Life in China.* New York: E. P. Dutton.

FENICHEL, O. 1945. *The Psychoanalytic Theory of Neurosis.* New York: Norton.

______________ 1953. A critique of the death instinct. In *Collected Papers,* first series. New York: Norton.

FERENCZI, S. 1985. *The Clinical Diary of Sándor Ferenczi,* ed. J. Dupont and tr. M. Balint & N. Jackson. Cambridge and London: Harvard Univ. Press, 1988.

FEYERABEND, P. 1981. *Realism, Rationalism, and Scientific Method: Philosophical Papers,* vol. 1. Cambridge: Cambridge Univ. Press.

FINKELHOR, D. 1979. *Sexually Victimized Children.* New York: The Free Press.

FOX, R. 1972 Alliance and constraint: Sexual selection in the evolution of human kinship systems. In *Sexual Selection and the Descent of Man,* ed. B. Campbell. Chicago: Aldine.

_______ 1980. *The Red Lamp of Incest.* New York: E. P. Dutton.

FRANK, A. 1969. The unrememberable and the unforgettable: Passive primal repression. *Psychoanal. Study Child* 24: 48-77.

FRANK, A. & H. MUSLIN. 1967. The development of Freud's concept of primal repression. *Psychoanal. Study Child* 22: 55-76.

FRAZER, J. 1910. *Totemism and Exogamy,* (4 vols.). London: Macmillan.

FREUD, A. 1936 *The Ego and the Mechanisms of Defence,* rev. ed. London: Hogarth, 1968.

_________ 1966. *Normality and Pathology in Childhood.* London: Hogarth.

FREUD, S. 1887-1904. *The Complete Letters of Sigmund Freud to Wilhelm Fliess, 1887-1904,* tr. and ed. J. Masson. Cambridge and London: Harvard Univ. Press, 1985.

_________ 1891. *On Aphasia,* tr. E. Stengel. London: Imago, 1953.

_________ 1895a. *The Origins of Psychoanalysis: Letters to Wilhem Fliess, Drafts and Notes: 1887-1902,* ed. M. Bonaparte, A. Freud, & E. Kris and tr. E. Mosbacher & J. Strachey. London: Imago, 1954.

_________ 1895b. *Project for a scientific psychology, The Standard Edition of the Complete Psychological Works of Sigmund Freud,* vol.1, ed. J. Strachey, A. Freud, A. Strachey, & A. Tyson and tr. J. Strachey. London: Hogarth, 1966.

_________ 1900. *The interpretation of dreams,* std. ed., vol. 4. London: Hogarth, 1953.

_________ 1905a. *Fragment of an analysis of a case of hysteria,* std. ed., vol. 7. London: Hogarth, 1953.

_________ 1905b. *Psychical (or mental) treatment,* std. ed., vol. 7. London: Hogarth, 1953.

_________ 1905c. *Three essays on the theory of sexuality.* std. ed., vol. 7. London: Hogarth, 1953.

_________ 1908. *"Civilized" sexual morality and modern nervous illness,* std. ed., vol. 9. London: Hogarth, 1959.

_________ 1909. *Analysis of a phobia in a five-year-old boy,* std. ed., vol. 10. London: Hogarth, 1955

_________ 1910. *The psycho-analytic view of psychogenic disturbance of vision*, std. ed., Vol. 11. London: Hogarth, 1957.

_________ 1911. *Formulations on the two principles of mental functioning.* std. ed., vol. 12. London: Hogarth, 1958.

_________ 1913. *Totem and taboo*, std. ed., vol. 13. London: Hogarth, 1953.

_________ 1914a. *On the history of the psychoanalytic movement*, std. ed., vol. 14. London: Hogarth, 1957.

_________ 1914b. *On narcissism. An introduction*, std. ed., vol. 14. London: Hogarth, 1957.

_________ 1915a. *Instincts and their vicissitudes.* std. ed., vol. 14. London: Hogarth, 1957.

_________ 1915b. *Repression*, std. ed., vol. 14. London: Hogarth, 1957.

_________ 1915c. *The unconscious*, std. ed., vol. 14. London: Hogarth, 1957.

_________ 1915d. *Thoughts for the times on war and death I. The disillusionment of war*, std. ed., vol. 14. London: Hogarth, 1957.

_________ 1915-1916. *Introductory lectures on psychoanalysis (Parts I and II)*, std. ed., vol. 15. London: Hogarth, 1963.

_________ 1916-1917. *Introductory lectures on psychoanalysis (Part III)*, std. ed., vol. 16. London: Hogarth, 1963.

_________ 1920. *Beyond the pleasure principle*, std. ed., vol. 18. London: Hogarth, 1955.

_________ 1923. *The ego and the id*, std. ed., vol. 19. London: Hogarth, 1961.

_________ 1924. *A General Introduction to Psychoanalysis.* Garden City: Doubleday, 1956.

_________ 1925a. *Some psychical consequences of the anatomical distinction between the sexes*, std. ed., vol. 19. London: Hogarth, 1961.

_________ 1925b. *The resistances to psycho-analysis*, std. ed., vol. 19. London: Hogarth, 1961.

_________ 1925c. *An autobiographical study*, std. ed., vol. 20. London: Hogarth, 1959.

_________ 1926. *Inhibitions, symptoms and anxiety*, std. ed., vol. 20. London: Hogarth, 1959.

_________ 1927. *The Future of an Illusion*, std. ed., vol. 21. London: Hogarth, 1961.

_________ 1930. *Civilization and its discontents*, std. ed., vol. 21. London: Hogarth, 1961.

_________ 1932. *Why war? Open letter to Einstein*, std. ed., vol. 22. London: Hogarth, 1964.

_________ 1933. *New introductory lectures on psycho–analysis*, std. ed., vol. 22. London: Hogarth, 1964.

_________ 1935. *An Autobiographical Study: Postscript*, std. ed., vol. 20. London: Hogarth, 1959.

_________ 1937. *Analysis terminable and interminable.* std. ed., vol. 23. London: Hogarth, 1964.

_________ 1939. *Moses and monotheism*, std. ed., vol. 23. London: Hogarth, 1964.

_________ 1940. *An outline of psycho-analysis*, std. ed., vol. 23. London: Hogarth, 1964.

FROMM, E. 1973. Freud's theory of aggression and destructiveness. In *The Anatomy of Human Destructiveness.* New York, Chicago, San Francisco: Holt, Rinehart and Winston.

GALBRAITH, J. 1958 *The Affluent Society.* New York: New American Library.

_________ 1971. *The New Industrial State*, second edition. Boston: Houghton Mifflin.

GALEANO, E. 1982. *Memory of Fire: I. Genesis*, tr. C. Belfrage. New York: Pantheon, 1985.

GELLNER, E. 1985. *The Psychoanalytic Movement: The Cunning of Unreason*, second edition. Evanston, Ill.: Northwestern Univ. Press, 1996.

GOULD, S. 1978. Biological potential vs. biological determinism. In *The Sociobiology Debate: Readings on the Ethical and Scientific Issues Concerning Sociobiology*, ed. A. Caplan. New York: Harper & Row.

GOULD, S. & R. LEWONTIN. 1979. The spandrels of San Marco and the Panglossian paradigm: A critique of the adaptationist paradigm. *Proceedings of the Royal Society of London*, series B, 205: 581-598.

GRUBRICH-SIMITIS, I. , ed., 1987. *A Phylogenetic Fantasy.* Cambridge: Harvard Univ. Press.

GRUBRICH-SIMITIS, I. 1988. Trauma or drive—drive and trauma: A reading of Sigmund Freud's phylogenetic fantasy of 1915. *Psychoanal. Study Child* 43, 3-32.

GUATTARI, F. 1987. Genet regained, tr. B. Massumi. *Journal: A Contemporary Art Magazine.* Los Angeles: Los Angeles Institute of Contemporary Art.

_____________ 1995. *Chaosophy*, ed. S. Lotringer. New York: Semiotext[e].

HALL, C. 1954. *A Primer of Freudian Psychology.* New York: New American Library.

HARLOW, H. & C. MEARS. 1979. *The Human Model: Primate Perspectives.* Washington: V. H. Winston & Sons.

HAYNAL, A. 1988. *The Technique at Issue: Controversies in Psychoanalysis from Freud and Ferenczi to Michael Balint*, tr. E. Holder. London: Karnac.

HEGEL, G. 1830-1831. Lectures of 1830-1831. In *The Philosophy of History.* New York: Dover (1956).

HEILBRONER, R. 1993. *21st Century Capitalism.* New York: W. W. Norton.

HOBHOUSE, L. 1906. *Morals in Evolution*, fifth ed. New York: Henry Holt & Co., 1932.

HOFFER, A. 1991. The Freud-Ferenczi controversy—a living legacy. *Int. Rev. Psychoanal.* 18: 465-472.

HOLSTROM, N. & R. SMITH. 2000. The necessity of gangster capitalism: Primitive accumulation in Russia and China. *Monthly Review* 51 (no. 9): 1-15.

HOOK, S. 1959. Science and mythology in psychoanalysis. In *Psychoanalysis, Scientific Method, and Philosophy,* ed. S. Hook. New York: New York Univ. Press

HOSE, C. & W. McDOUGALL. 1912. *The Pagan Tribes of Borneo.* London: Macmillan.

HUME, D. 1739-1740. *A Treatise of Human Nature,* ed. L. Selby-Bigge, second edition, ed. P. Nidditch. Oxford: Oxford Univ. Press, 1978.

HUTCHESON, F. 1725. *An Inquiry into the Original of Our Ideas of Beauty and Virtue.* London: J. Darby for Will and John Smith.

IRVINE, E. 1952. Observations of the aims and methods of child-rearing in communal settlements in Israel. *Human Relations* 5: 247-275.

JAFFA, H. 1952. *Thomism and Aristotelianism: A Study of the Commentary by Thomas Aquinas on the Nicomachean Ethics.* Chicago: Univ. of Chicago Press.

JONES, E. 1957. *The Life and Work of Sigmund Freud,* vol. 3. New York: Basic Books.

KAFFMAN, M. 1977. Sexual standards and behavior of the kibbutz adolescent. *Amer. J. Orthopsychiat.* 47: 207-217.

KANT, I. 1784. What is enlightenment? In *Foundations of the Metaphysics of Morals,* tr. L. Beck. Chicago: Univ. of Chicago Press, 1949.

KANZER, M. & J. GLENN, eds. 1980. *Freud and His Patients.* Northvale, N.J., and London: Aronson.

KARDINER, A. 1941. *War Stress and Neurotic Illness.* Rev. ed. of *The Traumatic Neuroses of War.* New York: Hoeber, 1947.

KERNBERG, O. 1996. Foreword. In *Boundaries and Boundary Violations in Psychoanalysis,* G. Gabbard and E. Lester. New York: Basic Books.

KINSEY, A., W. POMEROY & C. MARTIN. 1948. *Sexual Behavior in the Human Male.* Philadelphia and London: W. B. Saunders.

KINSEY, A., W. POMEROY, C. MARTIN & P. GEBHARD. 1953. *Sexual Behavior in the Human Female.* Philadelphia and London: W. B. Saunders.

KINSTON, W. & J. COHEN. 1986. Primal repression: Clinical and theoretical aspects. *Int. J. Psychoanal.* 67, 337-355.

__________ 1988. Primal repression and other states of mind. *Scand. Psychoanal Rev.* 11: 81-105.

KITCHER, P. 1985. *Vaulting Ambition: Sociobiology and the Quest for Human Nature.* Cambridge and London: MIT Press.

__________ 1990. Developmental decomposition and the future of human behavioral ecology. *Philos. of Science* 57: 96-117.

KROPOTKIN, P. 1902. *Mutual Aid: A Factor of Evolution.* London: Freedom Press, 1987.

KUHN, T. 1963. The function of dogma in scientific research. In *Scientific Change,* ed. A. Crombie. New York: Basic Books.

LACAN, J. 1952. Intervention on transference. In *Feminine Sexuality: Jacques Lacan and the Ecole Freudienne,* eds. J. Mitchell & J. Rose and tr. J. Rose. New York & London: Norton, 1985.

LAING, R. 1967. *The Politics of Experience.* New York: Ballantine Books.

LAING, R. & A. ESTERSON. 1964. *Sanity, Madness and the Family.* London: Tavistock.

LAKATOS, I. 1971. History of science and its rational reconstructions. In *Boston Studies in the Philosophy of Science,* vol. 8, eds. R. Buck & R. Cohen. Dordrecht: Reidel.

LAKOFF, R. & J. COYNE. 1993. *Father Knows Best: The Use and Abuse of Power in Freud's Case of Dora.* New York: Teachers College Press.

LA METTRIE, J. de 1747. *Man, a Machine: Including Frederick the Great's "Eulogy" on La Mettrie and extracts from La Mettrie's [1745] "The Natural History of the Soul,"* tr. G. Bussey, rev. M. Calkins. Chicago: Open Court, 1927.

LAPLANCHE, J. & J. B. PONTALIS. 1973. *The Language of Psycho-Analysis,* tr. D. Nicholson-Smith. New York: W. W. Norton.

LEAR, J. 1990. *Love and its Place in Nature: A Philosophical Interpretation of Freudian Psychoanalysis.* New York: Farrar, Straus and Giroux.

LEAVITT, G. 1990. Sociobiological explanations of incest avoidance: A critical review of evidential claims. *Amer. Anthrop.* 2: 971-993.

LERNER, G. 1986. *The Creation of Patriarchy.* New York: Oxford Univ. Press.

LÉVI-STRAUSS, C. 1963. *Structural Anthropology,* tr. C. Jacobson & B. Schoepf. New York & London: Basic Books.

__________________ 1970. *The Elementary Structures of Kinship.* London: Social Science Paperbacks.

LEWONTIN, R., S. ROSE, & L. KAMIN. 1984. *Not in Our Genes: Biology, Ideology, and Human Nature.* New York: Pantheon Books.

LIPIN, T. 1963. The repetition compulsion and "maturational" drive representatives. *Int. J. Psychoanal,* 44: 389-406.

LOCKE, J. 1689. *An Essay Concerning Human Understanding,* ed. P. Nidditch. Oxford: Clarendon Press, 1975.

MACINTYRE, A. 1970. *Herbert Marcuse: An Exposition and a Polemic.* New York: Viking Press.

________________1981. *After Virtue: A Study in Moral Theory,* second ed. Notre Dame: Univ. Notre Dame Press, 1984.

______________ 1988. *Whose Justice? Which Rationality?* Notre Dame: Univ. Notre Dame Press.

MADISON, P. 1956. Freud's repression concept: A survey and attempted classification. *Int. J. Psychoanal.* 37: 75-81.

____________ 1961. *Freud's Concept of Repression and Defense, Its Theoretical and Observational Language.* Minneapolis: Univ. Minnesota Press.

MAHONY, P. 1996. *Freud's Dora.* New Haven: Yale Univ. Press.

MALTHUS, T. 1803. *An Essay on Population,* (2 vols). London: Everyman's Library, J. M. Dent & Sons Ltd., 1914.

MANDEVILLE, B. 1723. *The Fable of the Bees.* Oxford: Clarendon Press, 1924.

MARCUSE, H. 1941. *Reason and Revolution,* second ed. Boston: Beacon Press, 1960.

____________ 1955. *Eros and Civilization.* Boston: Beacon Press.

MARTÍN-BARÓ, I. 1994. *Writings for a Liberation Psychology,* eds. A. Aron & S. Corne. Cambridge & London: Harvard Univ. Press.

MARX, K. 1889. *Capital: A Critical Analysis of Capitalist Production,* translated from the third German edition by S. Moore and E. Aveling; ed. F. Engels. New York: Appleton.

MATTE BLANCO, I. 1975. *The Unconscious as Infinite Sets.* London: Duckworth.

_________________ _ 1988. *Thinking, Feeling, and Being.* London and New York: Routledge.

MELTZOFF, A. & M. MOORE. 1977. Imitation of facial and manual gestures by human neonates. *Science* 198: 75-78.

MENZIES, R. 1985. Genetic ideology: Observations on the biologicization of sociology. *Canad. Rev. Soc. & Anthrop.* 22: 202-235.

MILL, J. 1859. *On Liberty,* ed. E. Rapaport. Indianapolis and Cambridge: Hackett Publ. Co., 1978.

MOORE, G. 1903. *Principia Ethica.* Cambridge: Cambridge Univ. Press.

MULLAHY, P. 1948. *Oedipus: Myth and Complex.* New York: Hermitage Press.

NAGERA, H., ed. 1969-70. *Basic Psychoanalytic Concepts,* vols. I–IV. London: George Allen and Unwin.

NUNBERG, H. 1955. *Principles of Psychoanalysis: Their Application to the Neuroses,* tr. M. Kahr and S. Kahr. New York: Int. Univ. Press.

OKADA, U. 1949. *Kiso Shakai (Elementary Groups of Society).* Tokyo: Kobundo.

OPPENHEIM, P. & H. PUTNAM. 1958. Unity of science as a working hypothesis. In *Concepts, Theories and the Mind-Body Problem, Minnesota Studies in the Philosophy of Science,* vol. 2., eds. H. Feigl et al. Minneapolis: Univ. of Minnesota Press.

PARKER, S. 1976. *The precultural basis of the incest taboo: Towards a biosocial theory. Amer. Anthrop.* 78: 285-305.

PARKER, S. & H. PARKER, 1986. Father-daughter sexual abuse: An emerging perspective. *Amer. J. Orthopsychiat.* 56: 531-549.

PARSONS, T. 1958. Social structure and the development of personality: Freud's contribution to the integration of psychology and sociology. *Psychiatry* 21: 321-340.

PIATTELLI-PALMARINI, M., ed. 1980. *Language and Learning: The Debate between Jean Piaget and Noam Chomsky.* Cambridge: Harvard Univ. Press.

PINKER, S. 1994. *The Language Instinct: How the Mind Creates Language.* New York: Harper Collins, 1995.

POLANYI, K. 1944. *The Great Transformation: The Political and Economic Origins of Our Time.* Boston: Beacon Press, 1957.

POPPER, K. 1935. *The Logic of Scientific Discovery,* second ed., tr. K. Popper. New York: Harper Torchbooks, 1968.

___________ 1943. *The Open Society and its Enemies,* vol. 1: *Plato,* fifth ed., rev. Princeton, N.J.: Princeton Univ. Press, 1966.

___________ 1957. *The Poverty of Historicism,* third ed. New York: Harper Torchbooks, 1964.

___________ 1962. *Conjectures and Refutations: The Growth of Scientific Knowledge,* second ed. New York: Harper Torchbooks, 1968.

__________ 1974. Scientific reduction and the essential incompleteness of all science. In *Studies in the Philosophy of Biology,* Eds. F. Ayala & T. Dobzhansky. London: Macmillan.

POPPER, K. & ECCLES, J. 1977. *The Self and its Brain: An Argument for Interactionism.* Berlin, New York, London: Springer International.

POTTER, R. & S. MILLMAN. 1985. Fecundability and the frequency of marital intercourse: A critique of nine models. *Population Studies* 39: 461

PRIBRAM, K. & M. GILL. 1976. *Freud's 'Project' Re-assessed; Preface to Contemporary Cognitive Theory and Neuropsychology.* New York: Basic Books.

RABIN, A. 1965. *Growing up in a Kibbutz.* New York: Springer.

RAMEY, J. 1979. Dealing with the last taboo. *SIECUS Report* 7(5): 1-7.

RAPAPORT, D. 1958. Behavior research in collective settlements in Israel: 7. The study of kibbutz education and its bearing on the theory of development. *Am. J. Orthopsychiat.* 28: 587-597.

RICARDO, D. 1817. *The Principles of Political Economy and Taxation.* London, Toronto, Paris: J. M. Dent and Sons, 1912.

RICOEUR, P. 1970. *Freud and Philosophy: An Essay on Interpretation,* tr. D. Savage. New Haven and London: Yale Univ. Press.

ROBINSON, P. 1969. *The Freudian Left: Wilhelm Reich, Geza Roheim, Herbert Marcuse.* New York, Evanston and London: Harper and Row.

RUDNYTSKY, P. 1987. *Freud and Oedipus.* New York: Columbia Univ. Press.

RUSE, M. 1981-82. Is human sociobiology a new paradigm? *Philosophical Forum* 13 (2-3): 119-143.

RUSSELL, B. 1945. *A History of Western Philosophy.* New York: Simon & Schuster.

RUSSELL, D. 1984. *Sexual Exploitation: Rape, Child Sexual Abuse, and Workplace Harrassment.* Newbury Park, London, & New Delhi: Sage Publications.

SESARDIC, N. 1998. From biological inhibitions to cultural prohibitions, or how *not* to refute Edward Westermarck. *Biology and Philosophy* 13: 413-426.

SHEPHER, J. 1969. Familism and social structure: The case of the kibbutz. *Journal of Marriage and the Family* 31: 568-573.

__________ 1971. *Self Imposed Incest Avoidance and Exogamy in Second Generation Kibbutz Adolescents.* Ann Arbor, Mich.: University Microfilms.

__________ 1983. *Incest: A Biosocial View.* New York and London: Academic Press.

SHERMAN, N. 1995. The moral perspective and the psychoanalytic quest. *J. Amer. Acad. Psychoanal.* 23: 223-241.

SHERMAN, P. et al., eds. 1991. *Biology of the Naked Mole-Rat.* Princeton, N.J.: Princeton Univ. Press.

SIMMEL, E. 1944. Self-preservation and the death instinct. *Psychoanal. Q.* 13: 160-181.

SPAIN, D. 1987. The Westermarck-Freud incest-theory debate: An evaluation and reformulation. *Current Anthropology* 28: 623-635, 641-645.

__________ 1988. Incest theory: Are there *three* aversions? *Journal of Psychohistory* 15: 235-253, 277-280.

SPENCER, H. 1864. *Social Statics.* New York: D. Appleton & Co.

SPIRO, M. 1954. Is the family universal? *Amer. Anthrop.* 56: 839-846.

__________ 1955. Education in a communal village in Israel. *Am. J. Orthopsychiat.* 25: 283-292.

__________ 1956. *Kibbutz: Venture in Utopia.* Cambridge: Harvard Univ. Press.

__________ 1958. *Children of the Kibbutz.* Cambridge: Harvard Univ. Press.

SPRENGNETHER, M. 1990. *The Spectral Mother: Freud, Feminism, and Psychoanalysis.* Ithaca, N.Y.: Cornell University Press.

STANNARD, D. 1992. *American Holocaust: The Conquest of the New World.* New York and Oxford: Oxford Univ. Press.

STEINER, G. 1971. *In Bluebeard's Castle: Some Notes towards the Redefinition of Culture.* New Haven: Yale Univ. Press.

STRACHEY, J. 1953. Editor's note. In S. Freud, *Totem and taboo,* std. ed., vol. 13. London: Hogarth.

STRAWSON, P. 1959. *Individuals.* London: Methuen.

SUAREZ-OROZCO, M. 1988. Is aversion a form of repression? (Comment in incest theory: A symposium). *Journal of Psychohistory* 15: 266-270.

SZASZ, T. 1952. On the psychoanalytic theory of instincts. *Psychoanal. Q.* 21: 25-48.

TALMON, Y. 1964. Mate selection in collective settlements. *Amer. Sociol. Rev.* 29: 491-508.

TODOROV, T. 1984. *The Conquest of America: The Question of the Other.* New York: Harper & Row.

TWAIN, M. 1923. *The War Prayer.* New York: Harper Colophon Books, 1970.

__________ 1992. *Mark Twain's Weapons of Satire: Anti-Imperialist Writings on the Philippine-American War,* ed J. Zwick. Syracuse: Syracuse Univ. Press.

van den BERGHE, P. 1983. Human inbreeding avoidance: Culture in nature. *Behav. Brain Sciences* 6: 91-123.

VIDA, J. 1994. *Sandor Ferenczi: Amalgamating with the existing body of knowledge. Cahiers Psychiatriques Genevois,* special issue: 257-263.

WAELDER, R. 1956. Critical discussion of the concept of an instinct of destruction. *Bull. Phil. Assoc. Psychoanal.* 6: 97-109.

WALLACE, E. 1983. *Freud and Anthropology: A History and Reappraisal. Psychological Issues,* monograph 55. New York: Int. Univ. Press.

WALLWORK, E. 1991. *Psychoanalysis and Ethics.* New Haven, Conn.: Yale Univ. Press.

WAX, M. 1999. *Western Rationality and the Angel of Dreams: Self, Psyche, and Dreaming.* Boulder: Rowman & Littlefield.

_________ 2000. Oedipus as Normative? Freud's Complex, Hook's Query, Malinowski's Trobrianders, Stoller's Anomalies. *J. Amer. Acad. Psychoanal.* 28: 117-132.

WEBER, M. 1904. *The Protestant Ethic and the Spirit of Capitalism,* tr. Talcott Parsons. New York: Scribner's.

WESTERMARCK, E. 1891. *The History of Human Marriage,* third ed. London and New York: Macmillan, 1901.

_________________1917. *The Origin and Development of the Moral Ideas,* vol. 2., second ed. London and New York: Macmillan.

_________________ 1922. *The History of Human Marriage,* fifth ed., rev., 3 vols. London and New York: Macmillan.

_________________ 1934. Recent theories of exogamy. *Sociol. Rev.* 26: 22-40.

WHITEHEAD, A. 1954). *Dialogues of Alfred North Whitehead: As Recorded by Lucien Price.* Boston: Little, Brown and Company.

WILLIAMS, B. 1983. Evolution, ethics, and the representation problem. In *Evolution from Molecules to Men,* ed. D. Bendall. Cambridge: Cambridge Univ. Press.

WILSON, E. 1975. *Sociobiology: The New Synthesis.* Cambridge: Harvard Univ. Press.

__________ 1998. *Consilience: The Unity of Knowledge.* New York: A. A. Knopf.

WILSON, J. 1993. *The Moral Sense.* New York: The Free Press.

WOLF, A. 1966. Childhood association, sexual attraction, and the incest taboo: A Chinese case. *Amer. Anthrop.* 68: 883-898.

_________ 1968. Adopt a daughter-in-law, marry a sister: A Chinese solution to the problem of the incest taboo. *Amer. Anthrop.* 70: 864-874.

_________ 1970. Childhood association and sexual attraction: A further test of the Westermarck hypothesis. *Amer. Anthrop.* 72: 503-515.

_________ 1995. *Sexual Attraction and Childhood Association: A Chinese Brief for Edward Westermarck.* Stanford, Calif.: Stanford Univ. Press.

WOLF, A. & C. HUANG. 1980. *Marriage and Adoption in China, 1845-1945.* Stanford, Calif. : Stanford Univ. Press.

WU, HSIN-YUNG. 1943. Sim-pua lei (Poor Sim-pua). *Minzoku Taiwan* 3: 36-37.

INDEX

D

E

F

J

K

L

M

R

S

T

U

V

W

Z